FINDING M

Memoirs and short stories

Peter Deadman

Profits from the sale of this book will go to the Chinese Medicine Forestry Trust

peterdeadman.co.uk
ISBN 9798596678437

with thanks to Carey, Jenny and many others for their helpful comments

Dedicated to my dear family, my dear friends, and all the dear friends I've not yet met

CONTENTS

INTRODUCTION

This is a partial story of my life. In the chapters I have written, I don't hold back. However I decided early on not to share intimate details of my closest relationships to avoid embarrassments, though I'm sure my wife, children and grandchildren will find quite enough to embarrass them here.

I am now a stable member of my community with some reasonable achievements to my name. I specialise in teaching and writing about health and wellbeing, but as you will see if you read this memoir, it was not always so. When I was younger, I was often wild, directionless, hedonistic, risk-taking and selfish, though I got most of that over with by my early twenties. I also had a really fantastic time.

Like most of us, I was driven by forces I didn't understand. Some were personal and some were in response to the cultural explosion of the 1960s and 70s that gave birth to so many of the great social movements that resonate today – feminism, black and gay rights, environmentalism, sexual freedom and more. Though that period is part of my story and therefore still seems fresh to me, it is of course a long time ago. For that reason, my account may be of interest as a historical document – a way of understanding how different those times were. I had great opportunities, immense freedom and the feeling that I was part of unstoppable social changes. While there was a lot to protest about and a lot to try and change, many of us had real optimism that the world could be made a better place. I realise that for many young people today, the future seems much darker.

As I relived some of the episodes in this memoir, I thought (not for the first time) that though we think of our life as one continuous flow, it often feels like a series of quite separate lives, linked by the most tenuous of threads. So the answer to the question 'was that really me that did that?' has to be answered yes, no, maybe.

A few years ago I took a two-year creative writing course at Sussex University. Out of that came a number of short stories and I have included these in part two of this book. Many are linked to life experiences I write about in part one and I indicate where this is so.

I don't regret any moment of the adventures recounted here. They weren't always enjoyable and some were hard indeed, but above all they were adventures – and that is what I craved. However, I do regret the times I wasn't kinder, more understanding and less self-centred. Like many people, I think,

I only truly learned to love unconditionally once my children were born, and I only learned to understand myself better as I reached middle age.

One thing I do believe, however, is that through these adventures, I have always been trying to find my own way and become more truly myself.

Peter Deadman, 2020

PART ONE - MEMOIRS

1. CHILDHOOD

My parents met in British-occupied Palestine in 1941. Pnina Eisenstadt - daughter of Russian-Jewish immigrants - was beautiful, spoilt and adored by her parents and brother. She studied piano and dancing and went horse riding on Tel-Aviv beach before breakfast. The house was full of passing Russian musicians, writers, lawyers and suitors.

Pnina with one of her suitors

Ron Deadman[1] was a handsome, clever, charismatic, fond-of-his-alcohol Major in the Education Corps who grew up in a poor, working-class North London family.

It was a fraught and dangerous attraction. The British were hated for

---

[1] I've been teased about my surname since I was a child, and even more often since I wrote a book called *Live Well Live Long*. The dull explanation is that Deadman is a corruption of the place name Debenham. Alan Watkins in *The Long Straight Track*, a book about ley lines, has a much more satisfying idea - that it is a corruption of Dodman, the name given to early surveyors who used two rods to line up sites either side of hills. The mysterious Long Man of Wilmington in Sussex shows just such a figure. That might explain why, scattered widely across Great Britain, are placenames such as Deadman's Hill, Deadman's Hollow and so on. Dodman is also an ancient name for the snail whose two horns resemble surveyor's rods.

turning back Jews fleeing from Nazi persecution and making faithless promises to both Palestinians and Jews about the future of the land they had ruled since the defeat of the Ottoman empire. Jewish women could be shunned or worse for consorting with British soldiers.

My mother's mother Rosa took against my father from the start. Being a British soldier was bad enough, but when he declared himself a Communist like her she knew for sure he was a spy.

As boys, my brother Alan and I always wanted to hear about his wartime adventures. They mostly seemed to consist of riding his motorbike through the desert and getting drunk – often simultaneously. The rest of his time was spent lecturing soldiers on the merits of Socialism, an opinion shared by the majority of Brits who turned their backs on Conservative Winston Churchill after the war and elected a reforming Socialist government. This was before the cold war when the 'spectre of the Red Menace' stalked the land, threatening to corrupt the very warp and weft of British life.

My father did have one story from when he'd worked in British Intelligence. With a colleague he was sent to Turkey, to the Ankaran residence of Hughe Knatchbull-Hugessen – a man so refined he not only had a double barrelled surname but an extra e in his first - to distinguish him from ordinary run-of-the-mill Hughs. And as if the name Knatchbull-Hugessen didn't roll off the tongue sonorously enough, his official role was Ambassador Extraordinary and Plenipotentiary to the Turkish Republic.

Unfortunately for Hughe, the Embassy was leaking military secrets like a sieve, including precise details of the D-Day landings. Fortunately for Hughe, the quantity of information was so profuse the Germans assumed it was fake and ignored it.

My father and his colleague checked the records of all the Embassy employees and decided that Elyesa Bazna, the Ambassador's Kosovan valet was the likely culprit (virtually a butler - you couldn't make it up). Knatchbull-Hugessen, not one of the brightest, huffed and puffed that he trusted his valet implicitly, but under sufferance agreed to have a new safe installed. Then, to my father's despair, he insisted the valet be in the room when the new code was handed over. That evening the spy-catchers tied black cotton to the door of the safe to check whether it was opened during the night. In the morning the cotton was broken, the safe was empty and the valet had disappeared. It wasn't until a few years later that Bazna was unmasked as one of Germany's most famous spies, working under the code name Cicero.

As for Ron and Pnina's ever-so-romantic love affair, the road was rocky. Apart from the danger of being attacked in the street, there was the fact that my father was already engaged to a woman in England and he held his honour in high regard. Since he wouldn't declare his hand, my mother – in despair – turned elsewhere and married a man she liked but did not love. At the wedding party my father, very drunk, insisted on dancing with her all evening to the indignation of everyone present, not least the groom. Then – in a perfect example of shutting the stable door after the horse has bolted – he whispered hotly in her ear that she was a fool and had made a terrible mistake. Not long afterwards, he passed out on the balcony.

But true love will find a way and before long my mother divorced her husband and married my father. It was a bare bones army wedding, but to show his sincerity and his true political affiliations (how could this not have swayed mother-in-law Rosa?) he converted to Judaism, despite being a lifelong atheist. He always liked studying, so learning enough Hebrew and religious law to satisfy the rabbi was relatively painless - unlike the circumcision. He told me about it when I was a teenager, the only time he was ever to mention penises - his, mine or anybody else's. But he must have been in a confiding mood because he also told me about seeing his first naked woman at the Folies Bergère in Paris and how wonderful it was. I have to agree with him.

My parents in Egypt

Rosa neither accepted nor believed Ron, even after the conversion and marriage, even after the first child. But on their first visit to England, my mother took her parents on a mystery outing to Hyde Park one Sunday morning and there, at Speaker's Corner (a traditional site for public speeches and debates since the mid 1800's), was my father in his French peasant beret holding forth on behalf of the British Communist Party. When he got down from his soapbox (a place he metaphorically occupied for much of his life), she threw herself at him and enveloped him into the warm and ample bosom of the family.

My parents' move to England in 1946 meant my mother had to toughen up quick, to survive her fierce mother-in-law and the change from balmy Palestine to the coldest winter of the century. They first lived in my Nan's house in North London – the one with two tiny, unheated bedrooms, no bathroom and an outside toilet.

Blanche was a tough and doughty Scot who, after her mother died and still a child, was thrown into domestic service by her father. She went on to give birth

Grandmother Blanche holding my father

to six children and raise them alone after her husband was killed in a tram accident (the only thing I ever heard her say about him was that he ate raw onions to stave off colds). After his death she supported the family on her wages as a charlady (domestic cleaner). It was the kind of poverty where an orange in a Christmas stocking was a treat and where there was never enough money to pay the doctor when one of the children was ill (what joy spread through the working classes when our free National Health Service was founded in 1948).

Blanche was a committed socialist who refused to burn coal – her only fuel – to show support for the miners during their 1926 strike. She was an anti-racist and anti-colonialist too, and when her eldest son enlisted in the infamously brutal Black and Tans – recruited to subdue the Irish in their 1919 war of independence (he was killed in action) – she never spoke of him again. She was an atheist into the bargain, and on Sundays when the Salvation Army band struck up in their corrugated iron meeting hall across the road she'd tell my brother and me to go and throw stones at their roof.

My father was the youngest child and the brightest in the family. His sister and brothers had all had to leave school at fifteen to start work – something that his elder brother Eric never allowed him to forget – but Ron was allowed to stay on and finish his education. He was offered a place at University College London, then – realising the size of the fee – said he couldn't afford it and walked away. When his mother heard about it, she marched him back and told them that her son was coming to University whatever it took. To pay for it, she took on extra work washing empty flour sacks for a penny a piece, scrubbing them in cold water in the copper in the scullery.

North London family celebrations were splendid. Three of the brothers and one sister lived near their mother, my father having moved away as he rose to become headmaster of a large London comprehensive school. These uncles and aunts had been brought up in poverty and endured the war and the rationing that followed. Now they lived in a land of plenty, and every Christmas gathered at first one, then another, of the houses, where the aunts competed to lay the most dishes on the table (three desserts at least) and the uncles competed to see who could eat and drink the most.

My mother's move to England continued the family tradition. Her own parents had left half their family behind in Moscow when they emigrated to the promised land of Palestine. But my mother's bonds to her parents, and to her father especially, were tight. So tight, that when I was four years old, my mother took me to live in Israel for nearly a year, abandoning my father, and my brother who had already started school.

I basked in a world of sunshine, sea and sand, and the besotted love of my grandparents. My grandmother Rosa fed and looked after me while my gentle grandfather Shmuel would cuddle me on his lap and talk to me in Hebrew, his bristly beard scratching my soft cheek.

Shmuel Eisenstadt was a lifelong Communist, helped lay the foundations of the legal system in the new country (was it to be based on Biblical Law, Napoleonic Law or British Law?), and sat on the Committee for the Protection of the Rights of Arab Minorities (receiving regular attacks from Israeli nationalists for his pains). He also sat on the Hebrew Language Committee.

The new Jewish state needed a language, and, like the legal system, there were choices to be made. Was it to be Yiddish, the German-based language of the diaspora Jews and a reminder of their struggles in the countries they had fled, or Hebrew with its impoverished biblical vocabulary? They chose

Shmuuel and Rosa, with Shmuel's three brothers, Moscow

Hebrew, but while it was well suited to talking about God and goats, pomegranates and an eye for an eye, it didn't have words for telephone, motorbike, brassiere or just about everything else. So the Hebrew language committee sat, discussed, and every week published a batch of new words in the newspapers.

Smuel was the classic absent-minded professor. Walking along the street one day he bumped into a law student of his. They chatted, and on parting grandfather asked which direction he'd been walking when they met. "That way Professor," the student pointed, and Shmuel replied, "Good, then I've had my lunch."

Many years later, I was stuck in therapy, with a deep feeling of loss and sadness, unable to let go and mourning someone I'd lost. Jackie, my therapist

intuited that it was a harking back to an early event in my life, possibly my time in Israel. She asked me to revisit a clear memory I had of standing on a table in my snowy white fifth birthday shorts, surrounded by my Israeli family.

"Who was there?", she asked. "Tell me one by one".

Powerful inchoate feelings welled up in me. I knew they were attached to someone here but I had no idea who. Was it my mother? After all mummy and daddy lie at the heart of most early pains. It wasn't, and I moved just as easily past my grandmother, then with trepidation to my mother's only brother Eli who hanged himself a few years later (not long after their mother Rosa died in agony from stomach cancer), and whom I worried my fate was somehow linked to. But it wasn't him. With relief I turned to my grandfather, and completely unexpectedly something erupted in the depths of me and I began to weep – real, unstoppable, mucus-and-tears blubbing that went on for the rest of the session and which hijacked me at random moments for the next few weeks.

Children are helpless actors in their own lives and must be survivors. When it was decided that we were to return to England, I efficiently sealed off the pain of love and loss for my grandfather and the happiness of my life In Israel. The moment the plane landed in cold, grey England I announced that I was English now and refused to speak a word of Hebrew ever again.

Back in England, on my first day at school, my senses were assailed by primary colours, strange smells, and the roar of children, most bigger than me

(I was an August child and the youngest in every class throughout my school-days). I clung to my teacher's hand and followed her everywhere for weeks, desperately trying to entertain her with a non-stop monologue. I remember her as kind and patient, qualities which transmuted into casual cruelty from other teachers as I moved onwards and upwards through the school system.

The smell of virgin wool fresh from the shop mixes with the scent of fallen leaves. My new maroon blazer, with its Marian Vian junior school badge, is yet to be flung onto the playground, and this cap has not so far been snatched from my head and thrown over a wall. The red double decker bus that I should be catching sweeps by.

Everything is red or brown on this golden morning. I look down, past bare knees and long gartered woollen socks, to my brown shoes, kicking through the tawny leaves. Hidden under these piles, sometimes still held fast in their green spiked chambers, sometimes peeking from white split skin, are the conkers [horse chestnuts] I hunt. At this moment they are perfect, new-born, and I stuff my pockets with their treasure, though I know that in an hour their brilliance will be dulled and their taut chestnut shine begin to darken and wrinkle. Later I will mummify the largest and strongest, soaking them in vinegar and baking them in the oven till they are toughened and scarred like old soldiers, ready to be tested in conker battles (pierce a hole, thread a cord with a knot at one end, take turns trying to hit and destroy your opponent's conker).

But right now I have to run, heavy pockets bumping my hips, to get to the playground before the bell rings for assembly.

"Our father which art in Heaven, Hallowed be thy name".

We sit on low wooden benches, mumbling the Lord's prayer. The school hall smells of gym shoes and the sourness that lingers from careless milk breaks. The teachers stand guard beside and behind us. In my memory they are all women, vastly bosomed and skirted in tweed. We all face the headmistress on the stage.

"Will the children who sang in the Operetta please stand up".

Twenty of us rise uncertainly.

"Well done, children, you worked hard and sang very well".

I am overcome by feelings of pride though I have the least reason of all of us, since in crucial sections I had been told to open my mouth but not to sing. I turn to Hazel Wheatcroft, whom I am in love with, and in that schoolboy gesture - where did it come from? – breathe on my fingernails, polish them on my chest and inspect the shine.

Assembly finished, I am skipping down the corridor.

"STOP RUNNING!" I know immediately whose voice this is. I turn and there they are, Mrs Bailey and Mrs. Ridout.

"Come here boy".

She knows my name perfectly well for I am in her class. I am anchored to the spot as they bear down on me.

"I saw you" Mrs Bailey says, "making that stupid gesture", and turning to Mrs Ridout, "He's a vain little boy".

"I didn't do anything", I say, the first words that come into my head.

Mrs Bailey swells up.

"What a liar. He's a horrible little liar, isn't he Mrs Ridout?" and Mrs Ridout weighs in. "You're a nasty little liar, boy. What are you?".

By now they are towering over me and all light and hope have gone. Through tears I hear myself saying "I'm not a liar, I'm not a liar".

My brother and I used to stay with our grandmother Blanche for long spells when my mother was away working. My Nan and my brother had been close ever since our mother took me to Israel, but Nan didn't seem to like me much. Later I wondered if she blamed me for my mother's disappearance. Some days she treated us the same, then would suddenly turn on me with vinegary and wounding sarcasm. And the house was cold too. We used to bathe in a tin bath in front of the coal range – cooker and stove in one and the only heating in the house - then climb the steep and narrow stairs to an icy bedroom. I used to think about death all the time we stayed with her - because she seemed so old and because she kept saying, "I'll be in my grave soon and then you'll be sorry".

Though it was a tiny two-bedroomed worker's cottage, the downstairs front room was never used, being kept 'for best' and housing her books by Walter Scott, old copies of the People's Friend, an encyclopaedia of Scottish clan tartans and her store of Edinburgh rock – a sweet she doled out on special and rare occasions.

There were other good moments. My favourite was sitting by the range, its door wide open to reveal glowing coals, toasting endless pieces of bread on an extendable fork and smearing them with rich butter and marmalade.

My mother's working absences grew longer as her career blossomed. Turning down offers to work for the KGB, Mossad and MI5 (she spoke Russian, Hebrew and English and travelled widely), she rapidly became the number one interpreter in Britain for Russian artists, performers and gymnasts, touring with them all over the country. Our childhood was marked by visits from the greats of Russian music (Mstislav Rostropovich, David Oistrakh who gave me a violin lesson and a train set, Dmitri Shostakovich and his son, and many more) and there were endless front and backstage visits to the ballet and the Russian circus.

"This is my son," I hear her say, as she reaches out to pluck the arm of a passing dancer. Actually she speaks in Russian; "eta moy sin," almost the only words of the language I recognise. And I step forward again, rictus smile in place.

The narrow corridors back stage flock with ballerinas, all sinews, feathers and tulle, cartoon features painted to seem natural from the stalls. And most un-birdlike, the smell of sweat which mixes with the smoke from papyrossi cigarettes, my own melting Brylcreem and the lingering perfume from where my mother rubbed my cheek with her moistened handkerchief.

I have had to get used to these introductions from an early age. The stranger in the shoe shop, giving my mother the merest glimpse of an opening, is treated both to her life history and a list of my achievements in a thick foreign accent, as I beg the ground to swallow me up.

"He plays the violin and his teacher says he has promise; once he played in front of the whole school".

Deeply English as they usually are, they respond politely and say 'how nice' or 'how interesting', clearly not meaning it. But here, in this Russian milieu, they seem to understand each other better, and my cheek is caressed or sometimes pinched, and if it is the leather belted belly of a Red Army tenor I am staring into, I am likely to be given a badge of the dove of Peace, Lenin, sometimes even Stalin, or a primitive Russian sweet. Peace and sweets are good things, and so, in my family, is Lenin, though the gilt has been coming off uncle Stalin for some time now.

Then I can step back, the smile slowly ebbing from my face and try to keep out of the way, until my mother announces that she absolutely must speak to Mr. Beritsov, and I am swept up in her wake, though she still stops every other person to present me again, as if to say, "please compliment me on this fine egg I laid".

I may have watched the show from deep in the seat of a box in one of the old London theatres, perhaps through the tarnished binoculars that a sixpence had freed from the back of the seat in front. The red velour is patchy where I stroke it. My mother might have sat with me, or else left me with a lemonade.

She would collect me at the end of the show, and we would go out into the night air and round to the stage door, already busy with shiny faces clutching open programmes and pens. At every one of these theatres, whether faded and old, or still bright with 1950s promise like the Festival Hall, the stage door porter is a member of the proletariat and therefore especially dear to my mother.

Though shocked when she first came to England to be called 'duck' and 'darling' by the grocer and the butcher, she now has no compunction about patronising the staff with terms of endearment, telling me what darlings they are as they stand and listen, unreadable smiles on their faces. Though very rare in those days, if by any chance they are 'coloured', or even Turkish or Greek, that induces an extra outpouring of affection from my mother, who suffers from a curious form of reverse racism. Black people are kinder and better than anyone else, even than the Jews whom she knows too well to idolise.

And as we walk back into the undressed world behind the scenes, past the ungainly props of the ballet or the circus, the cheap swords of the Cossack dancers, notched with dents from where they clash and spark, and the hanging ropes and the lights, I hear my mother say "eta moy cin" and I shuffle forwards again.

At Socialist holiday camp. Ron, Pnina, Alan, me

When we were old enough, we no longer went to our Nan's when our mother was away, but stayed at home with our father who would cook potfuls of beef or chicken stew which lasted - lunch and supper – for days. Then my mother would return in a cloud of perfume and cigarette smoke, flushed from the intensity of her fabulous successes ("Everybody loved me and said how wonderful I was") and from her suitcase produce matryoshka dolls, atrocious Russian chocolates, bottles of vodka and jars of heavenly black and red caviar.

I can understood that my parents' generation were relieved to settle into a comfortable and unexciting life after the war. But given their background, their loud and cosmopolitan friends, their Communism and my mother's ever-so-foreign accent, as I grew older I found it hard to forgive them for moving to the heart of suburbia and expecting my brother and me to fit in. [see semi-fictionalised short story: *A Comrade Summer* in part two]

When I was about twelve I turned to fat. Still short, I acquired the hated nickname Tubs at Beckenham and Penge Grammar School for Boys – an old-fashioned place that modelled itself on a minor public school. In that environment, losing status was a fatal invitation to be bullied and the odds were stacked against me. I was the youngest in my year, tubby, Jewish (well Jew'ish since we were all atheists and observed not a single Jewish tradition – except perhaps argumentativeness), with a Communist father and a Russian-Israeli mother. This in a deeply Conservative, Royalty and Church loving bastion of Englishness.

There were a lot of minor cruelties in the school, including an inscrutable, even Kafkaesque, policy on when boys could graduate from shorts to long trousers. I was the youngest and thus the last, and spent a whole winter suffering the humiliation of being the only one in the whole school to bare my knees – blue from the cold. And of course there were the usual crop of sadistic or weird teachers that these institutions foster, teachers who became steadily more eccentric as their tenure lengthened. The gym teacher, for example, who would pick on one of the naked boys in the shower room, advance half-joking half-menacingly, force his head against the tiled wall and then - all semblance of joking gone - grind his fist into his temple.

Throughout my wife's two pregnancies, I dreaded the thought that our child would be a boy, though I never dared admit it (luckily they were both girls). It wasn't until much later that I realised how much I'd hated being a boy, with all its humiliations and embarrassments and I didn't feel able to watch a son go through all that again (I'm happy to say I got that over with by the time my grandson was born).

To maintain status at school, I turned to the only weapons I had – a sharp mind and tongue - and used them to hold my own against those who were bigger and stronger than me. I'd also long ago learnt the benefits of making friends with one of the biggest - in this case handsome, blonde, curly-haired, sporty and honourable John Gribble.

The years from twelve to around sixteen were not easy for me. I was embarrassed by the body I lived in and spent a lot of energy hiding my shame. When my classmates were starting to go out, getting girlfriends, talking dirty, I was still a child - sitting at home with my parents, watching terrible 1950s variety shows and sitcoms on TV.

The sporting options at school were limited to rugby, athletics and cricket. The first two I did everything to avoid. On cold and foggy rugby afternoons I would put on as many clothes as I could get away with and lurk in the Autumn mist in a far corner of the field. I'd drift into a reverie, to be shocked back by shouts of "stop him Deadman – dive for his legs". I'd look up to see some brute galloping towards me, legs like tree trunks, seven league boots throwing up clods of mud, steam pouring from his nostrils, and think, "are you completely mad?"

Actually I'd have loved to play cricket, but nobody ever showed me how. As I stood there, heart sinking in the knowledge that I'd be one of the last chosen for the bottom team, I wondered what initiation these other boys had received into its mysteries.

After a while, I internalised the idea that I was physically incompetent and uncoordinated, and though I'd 'train' in the garden with rocks, pretending I was a champion shot putter, shadow box like my heavyweight heroes, and spend hours playing table tennis (and even winning) in the after school club, it took me years to realise I was perfectly OK at many kinds of physical things – both sports and manual labour and crafts.

When I approached sixteen, though, everything changed. I shot upwards, the fat transmuting into height, and like a long penned-up animal I burst forth and threw myself into a path of girlfriends, rebellion and as much excitement as I could find.

A few years ago I went to an exhibition at London's Victoria and Albert Museum. *You Say You Want A Revolution? Records and Rebels 1966-197* covered the extraordinary outburst of rebellion that swept through much of the world in the late 1960s. Though I lived through it and was sometimes a part of it, I was shocked to be reminded how radical it had been. Feminism, anti-apartheid, black civil rights, the Black Panthers, drugs, Vietnam, the explosion of working class creativity into British cultural life, sexual freedom, environmentalism and much more transformed the conservative world of the 1950s and sowed the seeds of so much that has happened since.

I've always been an early adopter and I caught a whiff of this rebellion early. I was still fifteen when I started refusing to go to religious assembly where six hundred boys dutifully sang hymns and droned out the Lord's Prayer.

"That's acceptable", my ever-so-liberal headmaster said brightly, "Jews can go to a separate room, all we need is a letter from your parents".

I refused.

"It's my life, my choice, nothing to do with my parents, and absolutely nothing to do with being Jewish".

"It's the law," he said, but like Amy Winehouse I said "No, No, No". I ended up in detention time and time again, but I stuck it out and finally got my way.

My brother Alan soon became my partner in crime. We were close in years (he was just 15 months older) and fought as brothers do. I always lost, ending up on my back, furious and helpless, with his knees burning into my biceps.

Then I took up archery. I had a proper bow, a straw-backed target and metal-tipped arrows with feathered flights. I was practising in the garden one day when he started goading me. I had an arrow notched in the string and pointing casually towards the ground. Without conscious thought, I raised the bow, half pulled it and shot him. The arrow hit him in the upper arm and drew blood and we never fought again.

Our age gap grew in his early teens as he adopted a greasy Elvis hairstyle and started going out without saying where, making me intensely jealous. But by the time I began to catch up with him, we'd got the worst of our sibling rivalry out of the way and began to share the same friends – and we were supremely, life-changingly lucky in the friends that we made.

Our first mentor was bearded, ex merchant seaman Jim Radford, local organiser for the Campaign for Nuclear Disarmament (CND). His house was a hive of political activity and discussion, full of young people and folk music and cups of strong tea made by his earth mother wife who hovered in the background with the children (it never occurred to me to wonder whether she liked that role). It was in Jim's living room that I heard Bob Dylan's very first album and was smitten for life.

It was Jim who organised a tiny CND demonstration in Beckenham High Street. The young policeman who arrested me for obstructing the pavement slipped me a tentative kidney punch as he dragged me away, no doubt rehearsing for more robust days ahead. The case made the local paper on and off for months as the four of us who were arrested kept appealing against the conviction (we won in the end) and resulted in my being summoned to the headmaster's office for heavy discussions about the reputation of the school versus the individual's right to protest.

Alan wasn't there that time but earned his spurs when the police caught him painting the word Ruislip (an air force base destined to receive nuclear weapons and the site of a planned demonstration) on a long brick wall. Unfortunately, he was arrested before he'd finished and for years we'd pass the wall proudly bearing the word RUISLI as we rode the 227 bus to Bromley. Our shared criminal history meant that we often got stopped by the local police when we were out at night.

It was Jim who told me that Nelson Mandela was on trial for his life for fighting apartheid. I took round a petition at school, despite a religious education teacher claiming it was a waste of time. When Mandela survived to suffer the 'lesser' punishment of 27 years in jail, much of it in solitary confinement, I learned not to listen to naysayers.

It was also in Jim's living room that I picked up a leaflet about the Vietnam War and read how American planes were dropping napalm on villages in the North, incinerating men, women and children. I felt such outrage I couldn't sleep.

It was Jim again who planned our part in an early anti-Vietnam war demonstration in 1965 outside the US Embassy in Grosvenor Square, London. We fitted loudspeakers to the top of his VW van, drove as close to the embassy as we could, locked all the doors and took turns shouting slogans through the mic as police hammered on the windows. A bit later, Grosvenor Square was the venue for my second arrest in another Vietnam war demonstration, this time for sitting down in the road and refusing to move. Demonstrating is a habit I've kept up ever since and I must have been on dozens – anti-war, anti-nuclear, anti-Nazi, anti-austerity, anti-Brexit, and most recently Black Lives Matter.

Back at school, my brother and I befriended John Birtwhistle. A couple of years older, he was academically brilliant and austere, like a character from Herman Hesse's *Glass Bead Game*. Birtwhistle was a radical who taught us about revolutionaries such as Pierre-Joseph Proudhon ("property is theft"). Soon we were standing in Bromley High Street on Saturday mornings selling Freedom, the anarchist newspaper. I wouldn't say we were politically sophisticated, or even well informed about anarchism, but we weren't stupid and we didn't much like rules. And we did it as much for the fun of meeting with friends, arguing with passers by and ending up in a cafe for hours, smoking and talking, nursing the one coffee we'd been able to afford.

Birtwhistle, my brother and I – all staunch Republicans - hatched a plot for Speech Day, the most supremely formal occasion in the school year when the headmaster, local dignitaries and the Mayor - weighed down with gold chains and solemnity - took to the stage. We knew the National Anthem would be played (as it still was every night at the cinema once the last film finished) and the whole school would stand to attention.

We rose with the others, then deliberately, and much more noisily than we expected (the wooden fold-down seats clattered like gunshots), sat down and defiantly folded our arms. Within seconds a short red-faced little man – another religious education teacher – threw himself at us, dragged me and my brother out of the hall by the ears (Birtwhistle was untouchable and was allowed to follow sedately) and locked us in an empty classroom. This reinforced my observation that the Church of England, the Conservative party and the Royal Family were one and the same.

Our next mentors were a couple of older anarchists who lived in a rented flat in Beckenham. Roger and Lorraine, in their early twenties but seeming a lot older to me, were the house father and mother, while an ever-changing group of friends came and went. Flat 4 became our second home. It was bare and cold with uncarpeted floors - the kind of place where you'd never find any food apart from a bottle of congealing milk, but it was rich in music (Roger, later an academic specialising in the San people, played blues guitar and sang from a vast songbook), red wine, political debate, books, laughter and precious friendships. Lorraine was wise beyond her years, supportive, caring, passionate for justice and a specialist in the art of friendship.

I must admit that I resisted at first. My schoolboy armour was still in place and I specialised in a kind of defensive cynicism. Lorraine took me aside one day and pretended I was my brother.

"Alan," she asked. "Why is Peter so sharp-tongued?". I blushed and tried to stammer something in my defence but it broke through and from that point I began to change.

Bob Dylan's Dream is a beautiful and melancholic song that captures the sense of loss I feel about those days.

With half-damp eyes I stared to the room
Where my friends and I spent many an afternoon
Where we together weathered many a storm
Laughin' and singin' till the early hours of the morn
I wish, I wish, I wish in vain
That we could sit simply in that room again
Ten thousand dollars at the drop of a hat
I'd give it all gladly if our lives could be like that

Late at night – if we weren't sleeping on the sofas and cushions at Flat 4 – my brother and I would walk home through empty streets. We'd barely get in the door before our mother would appear at the top of the stairs in her nightgown. She'd launch into a half-stern routine of 'what time do you call this?' – our cue to mumble a few apologies - before the magic words we knew would always come.

"Are you hungry?".

"Maybe a bit," we'd say casually, then attack plates of eggs and bacon and beans and toast and cup after cup of tea. Anarchism is all very well, but sometimes a warm, carpeted suburban house and a (non-kosher) Jewish mother really hit the spot.

Though I bridled at the restraints of our deeply conservative Grammar School, I loved reading and studying – especially English. At home, I ploughed my way through fat Russian novels and short stories – Dostoevsky, Turgenev, Chekhov, Tolstoy. At school, I adored Coleridge's *Rime of the Ancient Mariner* and his opium-fuelled *Kubla Khan*, Keats' sensual and erotically delirious poems, and developed a passion for William Blake – mystic, revolutionary, iconoclast. I delved deeply into Shakespeare's *Hamlet*, reading every commentary and interpretation I could get my hands on. I even enjoyed exams – at least in English - and would write at great speed in the purple ink I mixed myself, pouring out all the quotations and facts I'd memorised. I was close to the top of the class in the subjects I liked and my reports were full of praise and the word 'promising'. Then, at age of sixteen – having hovered in the wings for far too long - life just scooped me up with the excitements of Flat 4, the joy of teen friendships and my first girlfriends. I started missing school and ignoring assignments, and the words 'disappointing', and 'failing to live up to his promise' started to appear in my school reports.

By the time I entered the second year of sixth form I'd had enough. My school had planned to get as many pupils as possible into Oxford or Cambridge Universities (Oxbridge) to enhance its prestige and its funding. They'd creamed off 25 of us at the end of the first year (aged eleven or twelve) and accelerated us through the system. We would take our final exams (A levels) one year earlier than anyone else and have a whole extra year to prepare for Oxbridge entrance.

But now I'd lost interest in the treadmill. I stopped going to school regularly a few months before my exams, declaring that I could study better at home – to my father's frustration and disgust.

While my mother was given to volcanic eruptions, my father never lost his temper. He had a quietly commanding presence and a trick of getting people to do what he wanted by giving or withholding approval. This had worked in the army, for my brother and me, for his pupils, for his teachers when he became a headmaster, and for the members of the local Communist party (only Global Capitalism and the right wing of the Labour party seemed immune to his charms). So dependent had he become on this obeisance that he was totally unequipped to cope when I stopped playing his game.

I stuck it out though. I took the exams, and the moment the summer holidays arrived I set off on the first of my travels. As I left, my father refused to say goodbye to me.

2. OVERLAND TO GREECE

"And this was really the way that my whole road experience began, and the things that were to come are too fantastic not to tell."
On the Road, Jack Kerouac

When we were old enough to take trains on our own, my brother and I used to head for London and wander up and down Charing Cross Road, browsing book, record and musical instrument shops. Just off the main road in an alley called Cecil Court, Watkins Books had been selling esoterica since 1897. John Watkins was a friend of Madame Blavatsky, founder of the Theosophical Society and variously lauded as either a purveyor of deep and ancient wisdom or a fraud. The first biography of ritualistic magician and heroin addict Aleister Crowley claimed that he made all the books in Watkins disappear then reappear again.

It's hard to know why we found books on yoga, meditation and mysticism so compelling. It could have been something in the air – the zeitgeist – and our hope that there was something more exciting out there than the early 1960s suburbia we were enduring. I was especially drawn to accounts of travelling through India and Tibet, meeting monks and fakirs and secret masters, taking everything I read for absolute truth.

Then we discovered the Beats. My brother (damn him, I missed out) found himself at the Albert Hall in London on June 11th 1965. This famous event – Britain's first Happening – is said to have launched the UK's counter-culture revolution.

Michael Horovitz, Allen Ginsberg and Adrian Mitchell declaimed poems of rebellion while the audience were handed flowers, and the smell of cannabis filled the air. I still remember the excitement vibrating off my brother when he got back late that night saying "everything's changed".

I started reading the Beats and most of all Jack Kerouac - *On The Road, Dharma Bums* and the rest of them. The romantic vision of 'the road' was imprinted on me at that early age and now, aged sixteen, I was ready to make it a reality.

Four of us set off. Mick and I agreed to meet Bim and Sue in Athens. Mick wore round John Lennon glasses and carried a guitar. We hitched from London down to Dover, sailed the ferry to Calais and started hitching again.

We made good progress - small rides mostly, no long waits, and one of a couple of hundred miles in an open-top car, the lovely driver's long blonde hair whipping my eyes as I sat in the back. We got through France and Germany smoothly enough but somewhere outside of Innsbruck our luck changed. Car after car swept by, heading for the city, each one rubbing the edges off our confidence. And in-between, farmers and their wives crawled by in tractors and ancient cars, faces turned towards us with blank expressions.

Nobody stopped - all that day, all that night, and most of the next day. We got hungry, bored, resentful and finally desperate. We ran out of things to say. I fixated on Mick's long hair as the reason nobody would pick us up and we argued about it for hours. In the end I made him sit on his rucksack while I chopped at it with a pair of nail scissors. It took him at least two years to regrow it and longer than that to forgive me.

It seemed to work though, when at last a lorry stopped. We were so desperate that though the cab reeked of alcohol we climbed up. I sat next to the driver and rammed my elbow into his ribs whenever he nodded off. We were begging him pull up and let us out when we realised he'd got onto the wrong side of the autobahn. Cars were screaming towards us at terrifying speeds, headlights blazing, horns blaring. When the police finally stopped the lorry and we got out, we were shaking. They were kind, though, and took us out of their way to a youth hostel on the either side of Innsbruck, on the road to Greece.

In Yugoslavia, close to the Romanian border, we drank plum brandy with the performers from a bedraggled circus, down on its luck. I lost my heart to a beautiful trapeze artist, and her face and perfume stayed with me all through the night as I lay in my sleeping bag on the cold, hard ground, listening to the sound of howling dogs. [see short story *Emile in the Circus* in part two]

In Athens I also fell in love – this time with ancient streets and sun-warmed marble, smoothed and worn down by the centuries.

I learned a habit there that stood me in good stead in later travels. Every morning I'd buy bread fresh from the oven and eat a whole loaf, eased down with a litre of milk. It meant I didn't need to eat again till evening, when we would walk for an hour to a tiny restaurant on the outskirts, renowned as the cheapest in town.

Mick and I had had enough of each other by the time Bim and Sue arrived and we swapped partners. I hadn't known Sue that well before. She was quiet, very shy, and faded into the background of a crowd. But she was smart, good fun to be with and female, and though she was three years older than me, we started kissing and cuddling pretty much from the off.

We developed a fantasy of living on a deserted beach and hitched East along the coast towards Corinth to find one. One evening we sat on a hillside drinking cheap retsina, looking down on the bobbing lights of anchored boats. The smells of thyme, oregano and pine resin filled the warm night air and I was restless and full of desire. The wine was foul but I was hoping it might make Sue lose her inhibitions. We found a dry cave to sleep in and for the first time got naked together but Sue, still a virgin like me, wasn't ready, and in the end we just lay together, talking through the night.

I bought a cheap spear gun and we rented a heavy wooden rowing boat from a village fisherman. We planned to catch and roast fish over a fire like castaways. With a kilo of oranges and a couple of loaves of bread, we set off, keeping close to the coast, looking for the perfect beach. But suddenly the wind got up and the waves rose higher and higher. We had to get in to shore quick but were surrounded by submerged rocks, the boat scraping and smashing against them. Though we were close to the beach we couldn't find a way through so we dropped anchor and abandoned ship, swimming ashore, dragging our rucksacks.

And there, close to where we landed, was another welcoming cave, smelling of dank stone and cold dry sand. It was set into an ancient Mycenaean wall that fringed the beach. We laid out our clothes to dry in the late sun, though the sodden loaves were beyond rescue. We ate the oranges and wondered what we'd do for food and drink, but in the morning we found a cloth-wrapped parcel at the mouth of the cave. Inside was fresh bread, salty white cheese, ripe figs and a bottle of water. Our guardian angel, the wrinkled and toothless caretaker of the wall, appeared later in the day wreathed in smiles, with a basket of grapes and more figs, and though we couldn't talk to each other we kept up the smiling and nodding and thanking for ages.

I only took the spear gun out once. I snorkelled up and down without seeing a single fish in the barren sea, until I spotted a solitary squat little thing, smaller than my hand. I followed it patiently as it tried to hide in a crevice in the rocks and pointed the spear right at its head. But it gave me such a pathetic, pleading look that I couldn't bring myself to pull the trigger. I swam back to the beach, through deep water where the ocean floor shelved away, and the untied spear slipped out of the gun and disappeared into the darkness.

A couple of days later we swam out to the boat and rowed it back to its worried owner. We paid him a few more drachmas then headed for Athens to start the long journey home, arriving in the middle of a cacophonous anti-government demonstration. We stood watching for a few minutes then were pulled into the mass of marchers by a group of young smiling Greeks. I felt at home. I'd been on demos myself and had been brought up on my father's tales of banned May Day celebrations in the 1950s, when mounted police battered the heads of leftist men and women in Trafalgar Square - until the year the demonstrators scattered thousands of marbles and brought the horses down.

Now, as the crowd packed into Omonia square, tighter and tighter, the shout went round that the police had closed all but one of the exits. Then the tear gas started. The bangs sounded like gunshots and suddenly people were screaming. The crush grew worse as marchers were still trying to get into the square and were blocking the only way out. The moment there was a bit of space Sue and I began to run, desperately clinging on to each others' hands. We heard the thud of canisters hitting people or clattering against walls as we ran in and out of clouds of gas. Weeping, blinded and choking we stumbled on till a friendly hand grabbed us, pulled us through a doorway and slammed it shut on the wildness.

The morning after, Omonia Square was quiet, but there was an edgy feeling in the air. Maybe that was why, as I stepped forward, the suited man in front of me stepped back and his hard-shod heel slammed into my left foot, naked in its open-toed Greek sandal. There was a moment of shocking pain and I looked down to see my fourth toe sticking straight up in the air. I hopped along for a bit, hanging on to Sue's arm, then suddenly felt faint and collapsed onto a chair outside a pharmacy. A curious crowd gathered. The pharmacist came out with a glass of water, took one look and said 'dislocated' in perfect English, then 'come with me'. He led us down to a cool basement, away from the crowd, and invited me to hold on to an iron pipe sticking out of the wall, 'because this will hurt'. He grabbed my toe and with an elegant flourish twisted it hard. I shouted and yanked the pipe half out of the wall. When the mist cleared I looked down to see my toe still standing proudly like a flagpole. 'Again', he said, but I pushed him away and we got out as fast as possible.

The next day we took the ferry to Brindisi, sleeping on the deck in the warm night beneath a blaze of stars. There was a ship's doctor on board but every time I asked to see him he was mysteriously engaged.

When we landed in Italy, Sue headed for the youth hostel and I went to hospital. The doctor who told me I had a broken toe was stern. He clearly thought I was a wastrel and deserved everything I got when I told him I was unable to pay for the x-ray and the treatment he was about to arrange for me. As penance, he parked me in a wheelchair in Accident & Emergency for a couple of hours telling me I should watch the sick and injured patients coming in and learn what real life was all about.

I told him we would be hitching back to England. Maybe because of that, or else to punish me further, instead of the bandage I was expecting, I was encased in a plaster cast from my toes all the way up to my knee. It hurt like hell when he forced the toe down but the pain was eased by a lovely nurse who cradled my head into her warm breasts.

We hitched from the heel of Italy, right up the country to Genoa and then turned left towards Marseille. This was our easiest travelling so far. I'd ripped half of one leg off my jeans, and as we stood by the roadside waving two thumbs and a plastered limb, cars skidded to a halt as if magnetised. People were extraordinarily kind, going far out of their way to get us to the best spot for our next ride, and twice taking us home for a meal, a bed and much-needed baths.

A couple of years before this, my parents had arranged a house swap with a French professor of American literature in Marseille. Le Prof, as my brother and I called him, moved his family into our suburban house on the edge of London and we had his apartment on the 7th floor of La Tour, a mini tower block in a housing estate on the outskirts of the city. We were there for six of the best weeks of my life.

There was a magic to driving down through France. When you're young and fresh, everything new takes on a special intensity and in France everything was new – the coffee, the Gitane and Gauloise cigarettes, almonds roasting in pans of sugar on the street, crisp baguettes and soft croissants in the boulangerie, the Metro, the Monsieur and Madame'ing. I was thrilled to recognise the names of the towns we drove through from my father's wine bottles, from French lessons and from childhood songs – Macon, Avignon, St. Etienne, Dijon, Montelimar. Then, entering Provence in the early morning as the hot sun rose, and sighting the impossibly blue sea, I was transported back to my childhood days in Israel. What a flood of joy after cold grey seaside holidays in England, bundled up in coats, blue from too long in the sea, and everywhere the smell of chips and vinegar.

Most days we'd walk the hot streets of Marseille to the town beach. My brother and I would swim out to the tethered raft where older boys and girls lazed and somersaulted into the warm sea. Then, salt drying on tanning skin, it was back to the sofa in the apartment, and the bookshelf-filled walls. I read for hours every day – William Golding, James T. Farrell, James Baldwin, Sinclair Lewis.

So Sue and I decided to head for Marseille because it was familiar and because we'd completely run out of cash. I reckoned that though they might be surprised, Le Prof and his family would put us up for a few nights until my father could send some money from England. It turned out Le Prof was away for the summer but the neighbours in the opposite apartment remembered me and reluctantly gave us the spare key.

The next morning I rang my father. We'd parted on bad terms but he was almost warm and perhaps a little embarrassed as he read out my so-much-better-than-he'd-predicted exam results.

The first day was OK. We used up all the food we found in the cupboards except for a bag of oat flakes, walked for hours through the city and lingered outside the fish restaurants at the Vieux Port, trying to decide where we'd eat our celebratory bouillabaisse when the money arrived. In youthful optimism we reckoned something would turn up long before that – probably an invitation from the neighbours to join them for meals.

But nothing did. We lived on oat and water porridge with sugar and black tea and grew weaker by the day. The long morning walk into town to the Post Office became tougher and the 'Non, rien' harder to bear. On the fifth day the money finally arrived and we felt rich. Walking out of a Poste Restante in a foreign city with a letter always felt like finding treasure but when it held money, the joy was unconfined.

We rushed back to La Tour via the supermarché where we bought everything we'd been fantasising about for days – eggs and juice and tomatoes and cheeses and olives and croissants and marmalade and cigarettes – and ate till we were stuffed, which was when the neighbours chose to knock on the door for the first time and invite us to an early lunch – a typically French affair with several courses and wine. In the evening – adhering to our plan – we waddled to the Vieux Port and ordered a great tureen of bouillabaisse.

Then we hitched home. There was that familiar donning of socks and sweaters as we travelled North, the brief excitement of seeing family and friends again, and for me at least the determination to get away again – further and longer - as soon as I possibly could.

3. OVERLAND TO ISRAEL

"There was nowhere to go but everywhere, so just keep on rolling under the stars."
Jack Kerouac

My home study plot had worked. I'd done well in my exams and got a place at Balliol College, Oxford to study PPE (Politics, Philosophy and Economics) – the most reliable route to British establishment success – subject to my passing my Latin O level (I'd got an F).

I turned it down for two reasons. First, I loathed Latin with a passion. I've never experienced boredom like I did in Latin class. I spent most of the time seeing how long I could hold my breath – the ticking second hand of the classroom clock moving at glacial pace. It was Yossarian's friend Dunbar in *Catch-22* who deliberately did the most boring things to make his life seem longer, and one Latin class encompassed whole lifetimes.

Secondly, I just didn't want to go to Oxford. I told my school and parents that it 'wasn't me', which was true, but what it took me longer to realise was that I didn't want to go to University at all. I had dutifully trodden the path of others' expectations, but the siren call of the sixties was in full song now and the world was changing around my ears. American cities were on fire, the National Guard were shooting students for protesting against the Vietnam war, Jack Kerouac was on the road, Bob Dylan was firing me up politically then tangling up my heart with stories of love and yearning, Timothy Leary was preaching 'turn on, tune in and drop out' and I was inspired - with only vague ideas of what I wanted to do but clear visions of what I didn't.

Yet one last shred of me wanted to please my parents and anyway I didn't know what else to do, so I got myself a place to study English at Sussex – a newish redbrick University on the outskirts of Brighton on the South Coast, with a reputation for modernity and radicalism.

That was still months away so I took a job in the local library, saved up some travelling money, and set off again, aged 17, this time on my own - soon discovering that travelling solo offered much greater opportunity for unpredictable adventures. My aim, in part to mollify my mother and give a spurious purpose to the journey, was to visit my grandfather in Tel-Aviv.

When my children were teenagers and started going off for even a few days at a time, I demanded regular phone calls. That made me think back to my mother who watched me walk down the road with a rucksack, knowing she'd be lucky to hear from me for weeks on end.

There had been a late snowfall and the bitter, dry wind cut through me as I hung my thumb out on the road to Dover. The first night I slept in a field in Normandy and woke with a face swollen with mosquito bites. The second night I slept under a bridge by the River Seine with random travellers and homeless Parisians. I ate a baguette stuffed with chocolate, shared a bottle of sour red wine and turned down an offer to go to a certain rich guy's house for money.

There was an ease to travelling in those days, with a simple way of identifying friends and allies. All it took was a 'hey man, what's up' to someone with long hair or the right kind of clothes, and I'd be welcomed into the fold and helped to find a place to sleep, to eat cheap, and to acquire mind-altering substances. In Barcelona I found a shared room within an hour and had my first taste of Romilar – an opioid cough medicine on sale in every pharmacy throughout Spain and North Africa. I was cautious this first time and only got a hint of its hallucinogenic powers.

I had a fantasy of 'working my way' through Spain and managed to get work on a building site. When we started at seven it was already hot. The first break was lunch, and that was just half an hour to eat a sandwich and shoot streams of red wine from leather bota bags straight into our mouths, or in my case all over my shirt. My job was to hoist buckets of mortar up to the bricklayers above my head on the scaffolding. Halfway through the morning, to my mortification, my trembling arms just couldn't lift the bucket any more and I was moved on to hod carrying – dragging myself up ladders, step by weary step, laden with bricks.

When I woke the next morning, every muscle and sinew was in torment and it took me half an hour just to get moving. I tried my best back at the site but at lunchtime the foreman paid me off with a friendly-enough handshake and a painful clap on the back. Though there was traveller talk of selling blood, teaching English, or being a film extra on an Orson Welles *Don Quixote* movie being shot in Seville, that was the last day's work I did till I reached the banana plantation on an Israeli kibbutz many weeks later.

In the Youth Hostel in Madrid I fell in with North Bleech, an older charismatic American who quickly became a hero of mine and one I was happy to follow anywhere. He was a friend of Neil Cassady – the inspiration for Jack Kerouac's Dean Moriarty in *On the Road* - and was quite like him. He was tall, Italianate, with black curly hair and long fingers that were always snaking and shaping the air as he talked. He had a way of speaking that laid down the definitive truth on any and every subject and nobody argued with him.

Where he led me first was to a chemist for bottles of Romilar and this time I didn't hold back and took a hefty dose. All that night North, his friend Scottie, South African Dirk and I roamed the night streets of Madrid in the strange altered reality that Romilar induced. I remember North saying, "I know I'm tripping when trails come out of my fingers" and I could see them when he showed me. Dirk was obsessed by his non-existent hat. "Tek my het off" he'd beg every few minutes and we had to yank hard on his hair to shut him up.

The next day, still on Planet Romilar, I wandered through the Goyas and Picassos in the Prado Museum and stumbled on Hieronymus Bosch's *Garden of Earthly Delights*. I'd never seen anything like it before and a great stillness fell over me as I stood for hours, every particle of the painting etching itself into my brain.

When North and his friend Scottie hired a couple of VW Beetles for a jaunt down to Algeciras from where the ferry sails to Tangier, I was first in line. These Americans were crazy, exciting and terrifying in equal measure, like when they raced the cars on narrow winding roads over the Sierra Nevada, mooning and swapping wine bottles though the open windows. It was one of those times – and they added up – when if things had turned out differently I wouldn't be writing this.

Porpoises scudded alongside the Tangier ferry, ushering us over a narrow strait into a different continent, a different world and what felt like a different century. We arrived in the early evening and were led down narrow streets full of noise and donkeys and smells of curing leather, olives, cumin and roasting lamb. Everywhere I turned were men in jellabas, their shadowy hoods drawn low over their heads.

The six of us took a dormitory room with a line of narrow beds. I picked one, lay down and fell straight asleep. I woke in the morning to hear what I'd missed – their journey to buy kif (marijuana), the smoking they'd done, the adventures they'd had. When they realised I'd never smoked before they got excited and rolled me a joint on the spot. I felt nothing at all.

We went out to find breakfast and sat in a little café, drinking milky coffee and orange juice while Egyptian music poured out of the radio. I was watching the café owner make toast when something happened to my brain.

There was a kind of surge, then another, then a third. Each felt like it hoisted me to a new level, a different place where the world was brighter, more crystalline, more intense. It was like I'd never seen properly before, or heard music, or smelled or tasted. Was every human so magically precise and acutely themselves as this wonderful man who was buttering our toast? I felt a wave of love and gratitude towards the world.

Thus I was introduced to a herb that became my great friend, then my dark enemy, and eventually my friend again in the decades that followed, a herb that has significantly changed my life.

We spent a few days in Tangier, much of it in our dormitory room, smoking, laughing, dreaming, listening to the music drifting in through the open window, and eating and drinking the delights of the souk - dates and oranges, salted nuts, cakes dripping in syrup, endless trays of sweet mint tea. Occasionally we'd venture out into a world already strange and made stranger still by our altered state.

Although my plan was to cross North Africa I couldn't tear myself away from these people so I stayed with them as we drove back up through the spine of Spain to Barcelona, arriving as dawn was breaking. I couldn't sleep and walked alone through the empty streets. Turning a corner I came across the most extraordinary building I'd ever seen – a cathedral that looked like it had descended from space, like it was made by dribbling wet sand into fantastic spires and turrets. It was the Basilica de la Sagrada Familia by Antoni Gaudi and was still unfinished thirty years after his death. [see short story *Reading Tolstoy in Barcelona* in part two]

North Bleech left us in Barcelona, and Scottie and I travelled to the coast-with two Canadian girls we'd met at the Youth Hostel. Now overpowered by tourist hotels, Arenys de Mar was sleepy enough then for us to build fires and camp on the beach, Connie and me in one double-zipped sleeping bag and Scottie and Sandy in another. We still had some kif we'd brought from Morocco and would smoke and drink wine as night fell, make love, and lie for hours staring into the fire, watching faces, animals and landscapes appear and disappear in the glowing embers. Months later, Connie and I met up again in London and were a couple for a while.

When the time came for us to part ways, on my own again and feeling lonely and bereft, I hitched down the Spanish coast and ended up in Torremolinos.

"Leave it man. You don't mess with the Guardia".

Tom, built like a wrestler, tattooed, shaven head, turns back to the room where everyone is rolling and smoking, American style – single paper grass joints sucked down till the fingers burn. Tom, reputed friend of Jack Kerouac, owns a place in the centre of town called El Gato Viudo, a small bar down one of the whitewashed streets, but his apartment is in a quiet tree-fringed district at its edge. Laura, his daughter, works at the bar and she's the reason I sit there often, drinking the cocktails that she dreams up, too poor to buy my own drinks.

That afternoon we'd lain in the pine woods on a blanket. Flies buzzing, hot smells of resin and herbs and a whiff of something rotten. I'm hot too, with my hand on her breast over her clothes, my knee pressed against her uncertain thighs.

"No", she says and I back off. I know she likes me but she's only just seventeen and her father keeps a strict eye on her. She says she wants to come with me when I move on, and will I wait for her a bit while she finds the right moment to ask her daddy. But I know she won't really come and anyway I'm not sure I want her to. I like this moment of romance, but my greater passion is to be in my own story, on the road, alone, Dylan's "Don't Think Twice It's Alright' playing in my head. I would have liked to make love with her though before I go - and to break her heart a bit.

When I'm not with Laura, I'm spending a lot of time with a couple of American guys, Wilbur and Daniel. They've got a bag of grass and we sit on the beach at sunset, smoking and drinking cheap wine, and watch the stars come out and talk and laugh a lot. We're all three just so excited by our youth, and our adventures, and still at that stage of smoking when everything's funny, and wonderful thoughts and visions keep rolling in. There can be something worldly and uninhibited about these two, though, and I experience a shock of discomfort when Wilbur asks if I've ever had a girl hold my penis when I urinated. I've never done anything close to that and for a moment feel shame, though whether at my own innocence or their casual physicality I'm not sure. But then again we all three made a play for Laura and I'm the one she went for and that thought redresses the balance.

Daytimes we cruise around the small town, like arrogant princes. Torremolinos, yet to be discovered by mass tourism, is something of an artists' colony and we've developed a relationship with a German painter. Spare, white haired, bronzed - like a war criminal in hiding - he invites us one by one to his place on consecutive nights. When it's my turn he cooks an elegant meal and we sit drinking wine, surrounded by his paintings. He asks me about myself and what books I read and what my plans are. I feel safe with him. He seems too refined to make a move, as though he satisfies his needs with this cultivated tutoring.

Tom invites us one evening to his apartment, at the edge of town. We take an empty bus along the night streets. As we get off and start following the map he's drawn us, a woman appears. She's wearing a glittery trouser suit and high heels. Her face is bleary, lipstick smeared and hair damaged, and she's very frightened.

"You haf to help me, please, my husband, my husband, the tears are coming out of his head, please, please".

Swedish, German maybe, but her voice is unclear. Is she drunk, drugged? We stand uncertainly but she pulls us with her voice and her hands and we slowly follow. Through some open iron gates and along a dark avenue with small detached villas, each embraced by the shadows of tall cypress trees. I'm scared and I pick up a rock.

As we approach the fifth or sixth villa, a terrible cry comes from her gaping mouth as she points towards the open front door. A man falls out of the door and collapses on the ground and she screams and screams and screams.

We ran. Just like that we ran for our lives, ran like the kids we were, and didn't stop till we were inside Tom's flat. This guy was big, experienced, adult, and he spoke Spanish too. We turned to him.

"You've got to call the police, some really bad shit has happened, maybe a murder".

But he's implacable.

"This is Spain, man; you don't have anything to do with the Guardia" and everyone nods.

I can't believe it and try once more. But he makes it all too clear that it's an honour for us to be invited to his place - to sit and smoke with the grown-up writers and artists - and it's time for us to be quiet now. There's a minute or two when I struggle, then Laura comes over and smiles and gives me a glass of wine, and someone passes me a joint, and the moment passes.

I know people of every race have passed through Morocco. The Carthaginians, Romans, Arabs, Spanish and French all came to conquer and many stayed, especially the Arabs, but running like a rich, unchanging seam is the ancient Berber race. It took me several visits to the country to understand this and to realise it was why I was so entranced by the place.

I was intrigued by the signs of Berber magic in market stalls full of dried animal parts, love potions and mysterious seeds. I attended Gnawa healing ceremonies where Berber and African traditions came together in long nights of chanting and trance dancing driven by drumming, the clashing of metal castanets and the thud of the guimbri one-string bass. And I met a string of young Berbers - street-smart, ducking and weaving through the city, buying and selling, knowing everything and everybody, speaking enough of several languages to hook in tourists - who confided to me, sadly, in quiet moments, how they yearned to be back in their home village, often in the remote mountains or desert. That only made sense when I realised that the Berbers are an ancient aboriginal people who lived in North Africa for over four thousand years before the Arabs arrived and are tied to place in ways I could never truly understand.

I took a bus down to Fez and lost myself in the souks of the world's last medieval city, with its guild alleys of tanners, metal workers, leather engravers, weavers, tailors and tile makers, then moved on towards Algeria. I felt like I was the first foreigner ever to pass this way and I met no others on the road. Hour after hour I sat on bumpy buses or wandered through small towns and villages and watched the Moroccan world roll by – much of it incomprehensible. But I was contented in myself and not lonely. I was grateful too for my moderate French - too slow for France but perfect here where it was also the second – and for Berbers third - language. French and Arabic lend themselves to elaborate politeness, and that seemed to be the secret that unlocked the doors of friendship with the people I met. I've never been anywhere with so many glorious and unpredictable encounters as Morocco.

As soon as I got off at a noisy and frenetic bus station I'd point myself away from the newer, mostly French-built streets and buildings and seek the older part of town where the souk provided cheap rooms, kif, street food and endless entertainment. For years afterwards, I'd have a repeating dream. I'd be in some bland modern town, searching for its centre, its heart, the place where life and colour thrive, becoming ever more desperate as I failed to find it.

I crossed the border into Algeria at Oujda and took the bus to Oran, a town

I knew of from reading Camus' *La Peste*. I'd had the gall to present a lecture on the Existentialists to my school's French Society. It was wearyingly long and mostly consisted of me reading out passages I'd copied from books. But what made up for it all (for me at least, if not for my audience) was that girls were invited and both Mary Newland and Mary Lovett came in their school uniforms and sat in the front row.

Outside the Post Office in Oran a funny-looking English guy stopped me in the street. John had a van and was driving to Egypt. He needed people to share the costs and I took the last place. We were a mixed crew. John's squat and hairless legs stuck out of too short trousers and his *Boys Own* pockets bulged with odd bits of metal, wire and batteries. He was 24 going on 57. Francois was an austere and refined looking Frenchman in his forties who told me he was a painter. I treated him with exaggerated respect until his constant moaning got the better of me and it came out that he painted houses not pictures. His friend Aadan was French Algerian. He was younger than Francois, sunny where Francois was gloomy, and full of bounce and enthusiasm. They said they were going to Alexandria on business. When we camped, they took their sleeping bags far away from the rest of us. Regine was a couple of years older than me. She was beautiful with short cropped hair, an always clean white dress, and a long Roman nose. Like me, she was on her way to Israel, and was the inspiration for a story I wrote many years later. [see short story *In Rahani* in part two] Together, our caravan crossed Algeria, Tunisia, Libya and into Egypt as far as Alexandria.

The radio was always on, Aadan singing along. He told me about Umm Kulthum the most famous singer in the Arab world and I realised I'd been hearing her voice ever since I set foot in North Africa, pouring out of radios on buses and in the souks.

We bought a big aluminium pot and a clay brazier in the market and cooked vegetable stews every night over a charcoal or wood fire. Francois and Aadan spiced the stews with cumin, cinnamon, ginger, raisins and paprika though they always argued about quantities, timing and everything else.

In Tunisia, Regine had to sort out a visa problem that involved daily treks into Tunis city so we camped in the ruins of Carthage, leaving scorch marks on the ancient marble flagstones.

We crossed into Libya through a crumbling customs post and were made to haul everything out of the van by suspicious rifle-toting guards. A wooden box we'd been sitting on in the back of the van turned out to hold a croquet set and once we'd opened it and got out the hoops and mallets and balls and John slowly and painstakingly started explaining the rules, the guards swiftly told us to pack up and move on.

"Be careful", they said. "Stick to the middle of the road. There are mines."

We crossed the top of the Libyan desert in searing summer heat that turned to chill in the night. I had an ex US Army sleeping bag thick enough to keep out the cold as we slept on the desert sand, staring up at the stars, but by six in the morning the sun was burning again and the flies relentless.

I barely wrote to my parents but sent long letters to Mary, who had been my girlfriend until I set off. I told her about night skies so clear and bright I could make out the individual stars of the Milky Way; blinding white salt lakes with man-made pyramids of salt looking like Lot's wife; camels who rolled their 'long rubbery lips around thistles with the haphazard motion of gumless old men'; whirlwinds of sand and palm trees reflected in shimmering mirages.

The narrow road across the scrub desert seemed endless, with great distances between tiny settlements. Rusting tanks and jeeps lay swallowed up by sand. We broke down more and more often and John pored over the engine for wearisome hours, fixing things I didn't have names for with bits of wire and silver paper and screws from his pockets, while Regine and I sat in the dust, talked and threw stones at old tin cans. Meanwhile Francois complained about the heat, the flies, the van, Libya and American imperialism.

When we did come across villages there'd just be a few shacks and shops strung out along a single flyblown main street. There were no vegetables to be had in the shops, just dusty cans of tinned fish and rock hard bread. If we ordered food in one of the sluggish restaurants we could never manage to eat the fiery stews floating with grease, chilli and nameless meat. Nameless until we reached a village whose main business was slaughtering camels. Lines of them were tethered in the scrubby sand. Camel heads with lolling tongues, covered with flies, hung on vicious hooks above butchers' stalls. That was when I turned vegetarian and stayed that way for the next few years.

Keeping up our taste for archaeological accommodation, we slept one night, surrounded by pillars and colonnades, in the ruined amphitheatre of the vast ruin of Leptis Magna – first a 7th century BC Phoenician and later a great Roman city. One sleepy guard looked after the acres and acres of tumbling marble and we roamed at will. Delving into a tunnel I removed a piece of Phoenician clay central heating pipe and carried it in my rucksack all the way back to England.

One afternoon a hot wind started to blow and we saw the threatening cloud of a sandstorm on the horizon. We'd passed a US Army weather station a few miles before and turned the van and raced back to it. Isolated in the desert, they were thrilled to see us, welcomed us into their air-conditioned paradise and gave us showers, chilled full-cream milk, Coca-Cola and unlimited food. When I showered I saw that none of the bathrooms or toilets had doors.

With breakdowns we made slow progress and day rolled into identical day. I told them the plot of *Ice Cold in Alex* – a British war film about a trip across the same road we were taking. The 'ice cold' was the beer they thirsted for on their arrival in Alexandria and the breakdowns they suffered in the film mirrored our own, though we weren't being shot at all the time by Germans.

In Benghazi we split up for a couple of days. Inspired by our stay with the Americans I introduced myself to a British Army base on the edge of town but soon regretted it. This bunch of bored and angry squaddies hated everything about their lives and I was fresh meat for them to moan at, bully, threaten and mock. They forced cheap whiskey on me until I was vomiting helplessly into the sand. They told me how the base had two barbed wire fences, the gap in-between guarded by Alsatian war dogs. If any Libyan 'scum' got over the first fence, they said, the dogs would rip them apart. I didn't know how much of this was designed to impress or terrify me but I scuttled away as soon as possible the next morning - though not before a full English breakfast. Two things stayed with me - disgust for whiskey that lasted for years until I got a taste for smoky single malts, and the knowledge (but were they making it up?) that the only thing you can do if attacked by a war dog trained to leap for the throat is to drop on one knee, grab their front paws and pull them apart hard – breaking their chest and their heart.

Regine and I had become close. We parted a couple of days later but agreed to meet up in Israel. She was flying to Tel-Aviv and I was taking the cheaper option of a boat to Haifa via Cyprus.

I had just enough money for the ticket and food, but for reasons nobody understood, the Egyptians had decided not to let anyone out of the country unless they had 50 US dollars in cash. The Alexandria Youth Hostel was full of travellers who - like me - didn't. Many of them were desperate, roaming the streets of the city in case something turned up, endlessly visiting the bank for money that didn't arrive, or giving up and just taking to their beds.

The hostel was comfortable enough. It was run by Amr, a fat and despondent man in a dirty robe and turban, who would deliver sweet tea and fried eggs to the dormitory at any time of the day or night. The hostel also had the advantage of being right over a Romilar-selling pharmacy.

One day Francois and I were walking through a side street when a boy threw a stone at us. Francois immediately threw it back – not hard, but it was enough to conjure up a crowd of men and boys who pelted us with rocks as we ran.

I was too embarrassed to turn to my parents for help and in the end I thought of Regine. She was in Israel already but I had a phone number. I felt like a worm when I rang and asked to borrow $50 but she did it willingly enough and I managed to escape Alexandria. I repaid her when I got back to England, but somehow our paths in Israel didn't cross and I never saw her again.

Cyprus was a cool and pleasant land after the dust and heat of Libya and Egypt, with gardens, flowing water, lemons and flowering trees, but I didn't stay long. I was headed to Tel-Aviv for a reunion with Shmuel my beloved grandfather.

Now that I am older, I realise that not all teenagers are as self-centred as I was. My kind and serious grandfather who had devoted his life to study, teaching, writing and political activism was faced with a dirty, long-haired grandson with no money and in need of medical attention. During my stay in Torremolinos I'd been bitten badly by mosquitos and the bites on my legs had swelled up into boils that had then become infected. They got worse by the day as I crossed North Africa and became acutely painful whenever I stood up and the blood rushed to my legs. My grandfather had to take me to hospital to have them cleaned and bandaged and I felt a terrible pang as I saw him pay for the treatment and the antibiotics from his thin purse. What made it worse was that we could barely speak to each other. His English was minimal and I had forgotten all the Hebrew I spoke when I lived with him as a child (my brother fared better on a subsequent visit when they discovered they could talk in Latin).

He had remarried after the long and painful death of my grandmother from stomach cancer and this new wife made it clear that I was in her house under sufferance. By the time I set off to work on the kibbutz he'd arranged for me, I was keen to get away.

They put me on bananas. We started at five in the morning, riding the open-topped truck out to the plantation. Abram, vast like a bear, ran our team, striding ahead of us, chopping down bunches of green bananas with his machete. Our job was to pick them up and run to drop them onto the slow-moving flatbed, then run back again to keep up with Abram. The heat and humidity slowly mounted and we drank litres of cold water throughout the morning. Then the work changed. Now, equipped with sharp knives we had to cut through the succulent, purple banana flowers that hung fat and vaguely obscene from the trees. There was something disturbing about this job, turning into shock when a giant green chameleon leaped onto my chest, clutching at me with its three legs, the fourth just a stump.

We finished work at noon, took long cold showers and went to the dining hall for fresh salads and a dozen varieties of dairy food. The long afternoons and evenings we sat in the shade, a small gang of Israeli and foreign youngsters, drinking beer and wine and smoking.

It was a healthy life – hard work, good food and lots of time to rest - and I'd had enough after a few days. I slipped away without telling my grandfather (a cause of mildly expressed but deep disappointment on his part) and headed down to Eilat on the Red Sea coast where I knew the travellers hung out. It wasn't a great place to be. Eilat in midsummer is an oven – so hot that finding shade and something cold to drink became almost my sole preoccupations. I shared a tent on the beach – or rather a construction made of hessian sacks draped over branches - with a Puerto Rican guy. The last night I was there, he must have taken something strong. All night long he cried out, "I'm dying" and my reassurances that he wasn't got angrier as the hours passed until I didn't care whether he lived or died. He was over it all in the morning when I left.

It took me around eight weeks to travel overland to Israel and just five comfortable, soft-seated hours to fly home and prepare for University.

4. UNIVERSITY – SHORT, SHARP AND NOT SO SWEET

By the time I turned up for the start of term, I'd just got back from my trip to Israel and it took me many weeks, and quite a few mismatches and periods of loneliness, before I found anyone I could really connect with. There's nothing unusual in that, though, as most students face the same challenge.

Going to University felt like being back at school. This hip, radical place I'd heard about, in reality was still steeped in the 1950s. As a first year I had to board in a guest house – the kind that hung a VACANCIES sign in its net-curtained windows every summer for the thousands who trekked down to Brighton with their buckets and spades. And I struggled to believe that I had to get permission to stay away for even a single night.

I couldn't demean myself to do that, which meant that I would be fined each time – fines I refused to pay. That led to a summons to the student disciplinary committee who imposed an ever bigger fine which I also decided not to pay.

Meanwhile, I found myself in airless tutorials, sweating my way through the sixteenth century Silver Poets as the sun poured through the picture window and I felt like a tortured insect beneath a magnifying glass. Nowadays, I'd love to study English literature but I was too young, it was 1966, and the siren call of the counter culture was too strong.

I made one close friend, Steve. He'd just come back from an overland trip to Nepal via Lebanon and since the kind of travelling we'd both been doing was still rare, we shared a bond. One afternoon, a couple of weeks after we met, he made a big decision.

"Come with me," he said abruptly and led me to a patch of woodland not far from the University library. He scrabbled at the bole of a tree, like a dog with a bone, and pulled out a plastic-wrapped slab of hashish – as big as a dinner plate and as thick as a paperback book, and an almost equally large piece of sticky black opium, both of which he'd smuggled back from Lebanon's Bekka Valley. We smoked a lot of joints that year and swallowed lumps of opium wrapped in cigarette papers to disguise its intense bitterness.

Opium is dangerous precisely because it's so delightful. Your body melts into warm flowing liquid as your mind drifts in slow reveries. Nothing else matters - you could be in the gutter, rats eating your toes, and you'd feel no pain. When I realised that's how people get addicted to opiates, I stopped taking it and that decision inoculated me against falling into the heroin pit.

I'd made friends with a group of second year students. I visited them often – to hang out and listen to music. Two albums got played over and over, The Velvet Underground & Nico and Vanilla Fudge. I loved the Velvets and the driving power of their song Heroin with its echoes of the drug books I'd read as a young teenager – William Burroughs, Alexander Trocchi and others. It was seductive, edgy and compelling, but though my friends – bright, funny, hip friends – got sucked into the habit, I stood on the sidelines, watching as they slipped into addiction, slowly losing their dignity in the face of their increasingly desperate need. As the years passed, some died, some kicked the habit and some went on to have stellar careers.

At the same time, I was reading books about transcendental and psychedelic experiences – Aldous Huxley's *Doors of Perception*, the Harvard research of Tomothy Leary and Richard Alpert (Ram Dass), and *The Tibetan Book of the Dead* – and was keen to get a taste.

I decided to take my first LSD trip in the guest house of all places. I'd heard that I should get a friend to be with me, and my sometime Canadian girlfriend Connie was visiting so I asked her. That was fine until half an hour after I took the acid, when her face turned two-dimensional and I could see right through it.

For those interested in such things, the LSD we took in those times was ferociously strong and this trip took me to the edge. Soon it wasn't just Connie's face that went two-dimensional – it was everything. The entire material universe became insubstantial and I could see into the emptiness that lay beneath. But this wasn't some kind of Daoist enlightenment – it was existential terror. I was so far gone from any human help that I was ready to do anything to stop it, even suicide, but I 'knew' that even if I threw myself out of the window it wouldn't change a thing. At some point – probably when I was curled up, moaning halfway up the guest house stairs, Connie abandoned me in fear and embarrassment.

But all things pass, and after an eon I found myself lying on my bed in the room I shared with Steve. The walls expanded and contracted to the rhythm of my breathing and a warm and gentle breeze blew in through the open window, rippling the curtains. I had an overwhelming sense of the beauty and interconnectedness of all things.

The whole experience could have been enough to put me off for life but I had a real appetite for altered states, it was the summer of 1967, and soon I was tripping every few weeks.

There was one weird coda to that first time. As a child I loathed both cauliflower and Brussel sprouts. Even the smell made me gag. One lunchtime at school I was made to sit at the dinner table until I'd eaten my sprouts and I was there, weeping, for over an hour till they let me go. The day after my LSD adventure I was walking through the University and – from nowhere – I experienced an overwhelming desire for cauliflower. Maybe I'd caught a whiff, for when I hotfooted it to the refectory, it was on the menu and I ate two large platefuls. From that day those two vegetables have been among my favourites, indeed I have an obsession with sprouts. Even as I'm mourning the transition from autumn to winter, with the thought of the cold, grey, wet months ahead, my heart lifts when I remember it's Brussel sprout season.

I soon stopped any pretence of studying, stopped going to lectures and seminars, and it seemed to me that my friends were doing the same. But when I was the only one who failed all my year-end exams I realised that they'd been cheating on me and secretly studying all the time.

On top of that, when the authorities got to hear I'd been taking drugs, I was thrown out. Vice-Chancellor Asa Briggs, later Lord Briggs, summoned me to his office and solemnly told me I was the worst student ever to have attended the University. It wasn't till ten years later that I took up formal studying again when I enrolled in acupuncture school.

5. HUNGER ON THE STREETS OF SPAIN

Some months after I got thrown out of Sussex University, now eighteen, I hitched to Barcelona. I was there for a few days on my own then met my girlfriend G. as she staggered off the 32-hour bus ride from London. We were headed for Formantera – a place that I'd heard a lot about on my last trip, and we were both excited.

We took the ferry to Ibiza and then the smaller boat to Formantera, the tiniest of the Balearic islands. It was desperately poor and the men mostly lived away, working on the mainland. But it was blessed with miles of beautiful beaches and the bluest sea I'd ever seen, so blue it looked like it had been dyed. The island had been discovered by hippie travellers who could hire houses for peanuts, cavort on the beach, smoke dope, and play and listen to music – all of which sounded perfect to our ears. These were the days before mass tourism and before the realisation that sun, sand and sea were riches almost as valuable as oil.

We stayed in a shared house where I met my first 'I've travelled all over India and wear droopy cotton clothes and chant Om Shanti when I smoke a chillum' hippies.

I must admit I was impressed. When I met people who overawed me for whatever reason I found two possible ways to respond. I could either feel cowed and diminished or I could try and rise to the challenge and grow in the process. From my early teens I'd found myself among people who were older, smarter, or more experienced than me and I found it easier to raise myself up than suffer the humiliation of feeling inadequate. But this time it was a tough task as G. took to lying around topless in tight little shorts, stretching seductively whenever these older guys were around. I could see how hungry they were for her. I strained to act cool as fear and jealousy wrestled with self-confidence, neither quite winning.

One afternoon there was a rare storm, with thunder and lightning and a short burst of heavy rain. We emerged from the house when the rain stopped to find the sea, sand and dripping trees lit by a rich low and warming sun. The slanting light made everything glow, the rain drops on the leaves were like jewels and there was that sweet, fragrant smell of long dry earth wetted by rain. Most of all, the faces of these beautiful young people were lit by

In Formantera

what looked like an inner light and we stood still and silent, marvelling at the moment.

G. and I parted back in Barcelona, she for the weary bus journey back to her job in London and me free-as-a-bird, heading for Morocco, with an outstretched thumb and only a serious lack of money to hinder me. I had a Voigtlander camera with me that I'd saved and saved for when I was twelve years old. I'd read every camera magazine I could find and homed in on this one, but I faced a long and frustrating wait before I'd have enough to pay for it. Then one Saturday morning my father decided he'd seen me strive and pine for long enough and announced we were going to go out, right then, to buy it. I could pay him back over time.

I not only bought the camera but also the basics for setting up my own darkroom – enlarger, trays, chemicals and so on. From then on I was mad about taking and printing photos. My father cut a wooden sheet to lay over the bath and I'd disappear into the (only) bathroom for hours, though they seemed like minutes. One evening I was swirling photo paper in the chemical bath when my brother hammered on the door to tell me President Kennedy had just been assassinated.

Now this long-loved camera was just a piece of merchandise to turn into travelling money. I decided to wait till I got to Tangier to sell it and I reckoned that with luck I had enough cash to get me there. But I didn't and by the time I got to Valencia on Spain's Eastern coast I had no money left. I thought of begging on the street but couldn't bring myself to do it. I hung stubbornly to the idea of getting to Tangier before I sold my camera but I was hungry - hungry enough to lose clear judgement. I slept in a park and as the sun came up I felt weak and desperate. All the easy flow of travelling seemed to have vanished. I was invisible, nobody spoke to me and I felt very alone.

The next day I realised I needed help and made a collect call to the British Consulate in Alicante. Yes they would help me but all they were allowed to offer was repatriation to England – not a loan to tide me over. I felt beaten but I had no choice. They gave me the address of a travel agent where I could pick up a bus ticket to Alicante and a hotel to check into when I got there.

I had to wait a couple of hours at the bus station. All I'd had for over 48 hours was water and my stomach hurt. On the bus I sat amidst a large (in all senses) Spanish family who brought out boxes and boxes of food, passing them back and forth to each other, even asking me to hand them on, without once offering me a bite. I laughed bitterly inside since I knew this was the only family in Spain that would treat a stranger like this and it just proved the world had turned against me.

I had the address of a boarding house in Alicante and I dragged myself there. It was still hours before supper and I lay on my bed unable to think about anything but food. Then, when I'd finally eaten and topped that up with breakfast the next day, my energy and my will to get to Morocco returned but I had to 'eat bitter', as the Chinese say, and accept a bus ticket and food money from the Consulate and make my dismal way back to England, my tail between my legs.

6. EARNING A LIVING

After leaving school, in-between my various travels and before I found my vocation in life, I tried my hand at a variety of jobs.

Library assistant

Age 17, I got my first job at Beckenham Public Library and I loved it. First of all, I was getting a regular pay packet and I felt rich. Second, I was surrounded by books. I can still remember the moment, aged four, when I learned to read. I was sitting with my mother looking at a book about fire engines when the words suddenly came into focus and made sense and before long I'd read all the books in infants' school. By the time I started at the library, I was deep into European classics, especially Russian. I've tried to go back to the ones that I loved the most – Tolstoy's *War and Peace*, Dostoevsky's *The Idiot* - but I don't seem to have the patience and stamina that I did then. The only exceptions are the extraordinary, nightmarish *Crime and Punishment*, and *Anna Karenina* which I've read over and over.

Working in a library is a worthy and important job, I was told, and we were there to serve our community. Not that they were especially discerning when it came to reading. The most common requests were for 'a good thriller', or 'a cracking biography - you know film stars or musicians', and above all - and only if they were women - 'a lovely romance'. I enjoyed sitting at the counter crisply stamping books with their return date, as well as mastering the arcane Dewey Decimal classification system ("I think you'll find that in 632: Plant Injuries, Diseases and Pests"). Nowadays I go into bookshops at my peril since I rarely come out without buying at least one, like a wine lover who hoards more bottles than they'll ever be able to drink in their lifetime. But working in the library, I never needed to buy a book and like the *Hungry Caterpillar* I read my way through the shelves. I fell in love with young adult literature, something that has stayed with me. Though I was old for them, I read all of the Narnia books (somehow without realising their Christian message) and of course *The Lord of the Rings*. Many years later I wrote my own young adult novel (*Juice*) though it never reached the publication stage. I heard some YA authors discussing their work on the radio and they all agreed they'd never lost their inner teenager – that acutely special, confusing, hopeful, fresh, alive time of life.

The factory

After I was thrown out of university I went back to my parents' home. They thought I must be mentally ill – such a good student at school and now to suffer the indignity of being one of the few students ever to be kicked out of Sussex University. My mother dragged me to see our GP – a family doctor of the old type who had looked after my brother and me through measles and chicken pox and everything else. He diagnosed depression and though I didn't believe him at the time, I took the amitriptyline he prescribed and went to sleep for ten days, just waking long enough to eat.

When I stopped sleeping I felt different. I wanted to do something and I started taking apart an old motorbike. I cleaned and greased every part, however small, put it all back together and painted the frame fire engine red. Funnily enough I only ever rode it once, though when I later applied for a film extra union card I included motor bike skills as one of my qualifications.

I started looking for a job so I could earn enough to go travelling and, with my fingernails still black with machine oil, applied to a small engineering factory. The boss knew I wasn't going to be there for life but chose to believe me, out of a mix of amusement and curiosity, when I told him I was willing to dedicate a few years to him. It was noisy and smelled of hot steel and grease but the work was easy enough and my fellow workers tolerated me. The factory was barely automated and I spent most of my days placing small thin disks of steel into a slot and drilling out their centres to make washers. My workmates sang along to Radio One belting out Tom Jones ("My, my, my, Delilah, Why, why, why, Delilah) as I swept the swarf and filth from around their lathes and drills and presses. I wasn't there long – just until I had saved enough money to get by on.

Painting a church

G. and I were living in a one room flat above a bakery on the Fulham Road in London. She was the first girl I'd ever lived with. Seeing her make-up on the shelf, her dresses and hats in the wardrobe and her underwear drying in the bathroom, along with regular sex, felt like Christmas. I had one brother and went to an all-boys' school so I didn't really know any girls till I was sixteen. I'd had a few girlfriends before G. but this was what I wanted – a real, steady, settling-in kind of relationship.

We'd got together one night at UFO, the underground club in Tottenham Court Road. I'd gone there with Connie, whom I'd met in Spain on my overland trip to Israel. We'd met up again in London but we'd now got to the point where neither of us really wanted to be with each other and she disappeared with someone else early in the evening.

G. was the girlfriend of one of my best friends, but after we took a little speed, that didn't seem to matter any more. We danced and flirted all night and ended up in her room as the morning sun struck the crystals swaying in the open window, playing kaleidoscopic rainbows over the bed. When we made love, it was like it had been ordained, better than anything I'd ever experienced before. They say the dynamics of a relationship are laid down in the first twenty-four hours. My friend was badly hurt by our betrayal and I went on to be repaid in kind, suffering the intense pain of jealousy when I discovered that G. had cheated on me.

But this was our early days. We got high, dressed up and went to underground clubs at weekends, jigging around to Soft Machine, Pink Floyd and Arthur Brown amid the strobes and liquid swirling lights. She wore her tiny dresses, a floppy hat and a boa while I was draped in beads and finery. Sunday mornings we bought croissants and lay in bed amidst the crumbs. Weekday evenings we cooked and I felt like a married man.

G. worked in Biba's first shop in Kensington and I used to sit there, waiting for her to finish her shift, surrounded by girls trying on dresses, hats and scarves. She had a regular pay packet and I badly needed a job to pay my share of rent, tobacco and food - the smells rising from bakery making me hungry all the time. Every day I went through the jobs vacant pages in the London *Evening Standard*, wondering if I had what it took to be an estate agent's assistant or office temp.

Then one day I saw this ad: YOUNG PEOPLE WANTED TO PAINT CHURCH

I'd done a bit of decorating for my Dad and liked the idea of painting around the stained glass windows and marble statues inside a cool building smelling of old stone and wilting flowers.

There were five of us waiting outside the locked door of a massive church close to Regent's Park when Mr (or was it Major?), Hudson appeared – tweed jacket, short, clipped and no nonsense. We were young and long-haired and he talked to us like we were fresh cadets. If I wasn't an anarchist I'd have saluted. He said he'd persuaded the Parish Board to let him get the outside of the church painted faster and cheaper than any professional decorating company.

A cold wind whipped around our feet as we craned our necks up to the unpainted parapet where pigeons roosted high above London, and then even higher to the bell tower. He told us he'd hired sixty foot (18 metre) ladders and how quick and easy the job would be. But in reality we were his young, expendable troops and it was pretty clear he wasn't going to lead the way into enemy fire.

The ladders were made of wood and so heavy it took three of us to raise each one. Climbing nervously to the top, we left the streets of London, the cafes, buses and taxis, the noise, far below and entered a new world where the wind blew fierce, the ladders shifted and creaked in tune with our trembling, the disturbed pigeons squawked and flapped in our faces, and we hoped we'd live long enough to slap cream paint on the dirty stone and encrusted pigeon droppings and get down as fast as humanly possible. In the face of our shared fear, we bonded rapidly, and it was only the trench-happy camaraderie that brought us back the next morning.

Mr (or was it Major?) Hudson bustled up to us on our second day as we were on our tea break (fried egg sandwich, sugared tea and a couple of roll up cigarettes for me) for a serious word. People had been finding splashes of cream paint on the tops of their cars and they weren't happy. The Parish Board wasn't happy either. You need to take more care, he said. He'd been in Marks & Spencer's that morning and watched some painters working there. They hadn't spilled a drop. We didn't say anything, just looked at him, wondering if he couldn't see the difference between carefully stroking paint onto flat walls in the comfort of a warm shop and climbing to the crow's nest in a howling gale as the ship rocked beneath us.

On the way back to the Fulham Road, sitting on the tube, hair and face caked in paint, I felt glad to be alive yet already dreading the next day.

It must have been around day five that the ladder came down. We were on our tea break again, joking about something, when we heard a scraping sound, quiet at first, then louder and louder, a long breath-holding, silence and then an enormous crash.

We rushed outside to see that one of the ladders had fallen and crushed a car (the vicar's it turned out) like it was made of tinfoil. As we stood there, a couple of guys in hard hats ran over from the building site across the road.

"We've been waiting for that to happen. We've had bets on it. How could you not know about tying ladders"

"Tying?"

"Up top, whenever you go that high in the wind and all, you've got to tie the ladder onto something every time. We thought you were crazy".

Like with Mr (or was it Major?) Hudson we didn't say anything, but if we had it would have been along the lines of "why didn't you bloody come over and warn us days ago?"

British museum

After the church, and still in need of money, I applied for a safer job at the British Museum. The interview went well. Either the modest and elderly interviewer liked me or he just had a kind nature. He didn't ask much (my A levels and previous library work satisfied him from the off) but waxed lyrical aboutthe pension plan as I nodded enthusiastically. I supposed at his age it loomed large. Almost in passing, just as I was leaving, he asked if I liked maps. I said no.

A couple of weeks later I opened a letter telling me to report to the map department the following Monday.

I felt a thrill climbing the stone steps and walking beneath the Greek pediment into the museum, and an even greater one when I was given a key that unlocked the secret doors disguised as book cases, confirming my status as one of the elite who worked in the bowels of the place. The walk to the canteen for my precious tea and lunch breaks took me past the Assyrian winged lions and, if I had time, I'd slip into the British Library (this was before its move to King's Cross) to thrill myself with a peek at Shakespeare first folios and the scrawl of Milton's *Paradise Lost* and Keats' *Ode to Autumn*.

This special feeling lasted until the third day. By then the tedium of the map department had begun to seep into my pores. Like Theodore Roethke, I saw "dust from the walls of institutions, finer than flour, alive, more dangerous than silica, sift, almost invisible, through long afternoons of tedium"[2].

My task, fastidiously explained to me, was to revise the card file system that listed every map in the collection. I had to mark the cards with occult signs - three squiggly red lines if it was on display, two straight blue ones if in store, different coloured asterisks according to which continent the map pictured and so on, endlessly. On the fourth day I found it hard to get up and was late. Then again two days later. The third time, I was summoned to the office. My boss, seemed genuinely puzzled, even hurt, and asked with immense politeness if I was having any problems.

I always dressed more carefully than usual for the job. I especially favoured a multi-coloured striped shirt I'd recently bought and which I thought I looked pretty good in. I wasn't surprised when, after a week and a half, I was called back to the office and fired. She seemed bitter when she told me that I'd been late five times – what could I say - but I was seriously offended when she started on about my shirt, spitting out, "and you even come to work in your pyjamas".

Road sweeper

I was only a road sweeper for a couple of weeks but I liked it. I was assigned to the quiet leafy avenues on the outer fringes of suburban Beckenham and introduced to my team – a half a dozen gentle men who'd been doing the job for years. Slow and easy, they kept telling me, and I soon slipped into their pattern of effortlessly sweeping the wide broom along the pavement and road as one of us followed with the dust cart. Despite my youth, within a few days I was appointed gang leader, presumably because of my greater educational attainments, but none of them seemed to mind. The best moments were when we fanned out across a quiet road like the Magnificent Seven, sweeping the dirt out of town. They seemed genuinely sad when I told them I wouldn't see them again as I was off to Morocco – or somewhere.

Plongeur

After one of my travels, I ended up in Brighton and needed to find work. I'd read George Orwell's Down and Out in Paris and London and though it wasn't his intention, was inspired by the proletarian honesty of being a plongeur (washer up). So I took on washing up the teas and suppers in a hotel. I

Dolor by Theodor Roethke

I have known the inexorable sadness of pencils,
Neat in their boxes, dolor of pad and paper weight,
All the misery of manilla folders and mucilage,
Desolation in immaculate public places,
Lonely reception room, lavatory, switchboard,
The unalterable pathos of basin and pitcher,
Ritual of multigraph, paper-clip, comma,
Endless duplication of lives and objects.
And I have seen dust from the walls of institutions,
Finer than flour, alive, more dangerous than silica,
Sift, almost invisible, through long afternoons of tedium,
Dropping a fine film on nails and delicate eyebrows,
Glazing the pale hair, the duplicate grey standard faces.

had a routine. Before heading to work at 4pm I would smoke a joint. Then I'd sit luxuriously among the mountains of cake-smeared plates, teapots full of leaves, dirty cups, saucers, spoons and knives, and, like in my grandmother's house in front of the coal range, make toast. I'd lavish it with butter and marmalade and consume slice after slice (I wasn't getting enough to eat at home) accompanied by a giant pot of strong tea. Then, rocket-fuelled, I'd wash out giant, gravy-caked pots and greasy pans full of congealed beef and lamb fat and scrub, dry and stack crockery, till 11pm without a break.

Hospital porter

I worked briefly - actually most of my jobs were brief - as a porter in a small hospital in Hove. I wheeled patients to surgery, x-ray or blood tests, brought unconscious ones back from surgery, and once took a well wrapped amputated leg down to the incinerator in the basement.

Painter and decorator

Back in London I got taken on by a decorating firm. I was only there for one job but it went on for weeks. It was a housing estate in Vauxhall made up of dozens of identical flats. We'd paint the outside windows and doors on fine days and the insides on rainy days. All the other painters were Irish.

Painting and decorating is probably the least skilful of the trades and the least respected but, like everything, it has its own artistry. I learned how to wield a wide emulsion brush all day long with strong and elastic wrists; how to store oil paint brushes in water during breaks and at the end of the day so they only needed cleaning when the job was finished; how to 'cut in' - sweeping the brush down the putty without getting any on the glass, and how to get more of the paint on the walls than on myself. But I didn't take up my workmates' habit of drinking pint after pint of beer every night and coming into work hung-over and nauseous.

The best bit of the job was lunch - the same every day. Eggs, bacon, chips, fried tomatoes, fried bread and mushrooms and a couple of mugs of strong sweet tea, followed by a roll-up and a read of the *Daily Mirror*.

Even after I started eating natural and organic food, once in a while - especially when I was doing hard manual work - I'd treat myself to a fry-up, right until the English café more or less disappeared from the streets of Brighton. It could cheer up my darkest moods and celebrate my sunniest ones.

Drug dealer

Early in 1969, age 20, I was living in Tulse Hill in South London. I'd started eating health food – things like wheat germ and muesli – and learning yoga from a book. I had a bedsitting room (bed, cooker and sink) and my friend Mick and my ex-girlfriend Mary lived next door. Mary - a pre-Raphaelite beauty - had been my first lover but, young and foolish, I had taken her for granted. I look back now with tenderness and regret that I was such an ill-educated and careless boyfriend.

I was mostly unemployed but happy enough. Saturdays I used to take the bus into Brixton and shop in the West Indian market for strange vegetables that I didn't know how to cook.

One day I went to North London to visit a friend from University – someone I'd last seen sitting on the carpet in the midst of a tornado-strewn room, thirty hours without sleep, rummaging through every scrap of paper and rubbish for the hundredth time in search of a packet of heroin he was convinced was hidden somewhere.

I met his sister Sue there and spent the night in her West Hampstead flat - a one-night stand that went on for weeks. Sue was a beautiful, sharp, North London Jewish girl and I was always just a little bit afraid of her. She had a business selling flared velvet trousers and I was quickly seduced by her hippie chic lifestyle. We went to clubs and parties, spent Saturdays roaming through Portobello Road market buying finery, and smoked a lot of dope.

Her entrepreneurial bent had already led her into small scale dealing and before long I'd slipped into it with her. With the two of us encouraging each other, the business grew and soon we were buying one pound weights of either Lebanese hash or African grass. Our suppliers were cool and laconic West Indian guys who within twenty minutes of a discreet phone call would turn up in ankle length black leather coats and sunglasses to deliver the goods. We'd sit on the floor, weighing it out into half ounce and ounce packs (14/28 grams) and then sell them to a wide array of customers - first friends, then friends of friends, then eventually, strangers.

Once a week I'd put on a brown double-breasted suit that I'd bought in Swinging London's Carnaby Street and catch the Pullman train from Victoria Station to Brighton. I'd tuck a brown carrier bag full of my wares beneath my seat and, like P. G. Wodehouse's Bertie Wooster, tuck in to a kipper breakfast delivered to my table by a uniformed waiter. My friend Steve would meet me on his Triumph Bonneville motorbike and drive me from customer to customer, always staying long enough for a smoke and a gossip with old friends.

Steve loved his bike with a passion but he was a swift-thinking pragmatist. We were sitting one afternoon in a friend's house in Clarence Square, when someone knocked on the door with a stricken expression and told Steve a lorry had just reversed over his bike. He leapt up, shouted "gimme a hammer", and started smashing up what was left of the bike. Better to get insurance for a write-off than a long, drawn-out repair claim, he said.

For a short spell the dealing felt very sophisticated and I loved the feeling of money in my pocket. But then things started to turn bad. Strangers would appear in the street late at night, yelling up to our second floor window and demanding weed. This was a time when possession of even a small amount could mean a jail sentence and - for what we usually had lying around – that could be several years. More and more often I'd be stricken by fits of paranoia in the middle of the night and – in an inverted version of Sue's brother – rummage through the flat hopelessly trying to collect up and dispose of all the spliffs from ashtrays and the packets of weed lying on tables, in drawers and even under the bed – terrified that we would be raided at any moment.

Sue and I weren't getting on, things were spinning out of control and I realised I was on a downward path of self-destruction. One day I just left, barely saying goodbye, and when I got back to my room in Tulse Hill I wept with relief. I felt like Mole in *Wind in the Willows* who'd walked out of his happy home at the first whiff of Spring and, like a faithless lover, only realised what he'd lost just in time to rescue it.

Film artiste

I'd moved back to Brighton, living a hand-to-mouth life, cadging from friends, even going hungry at times. Then I heard something wonderful. They were making a film – *Oh What a Lovely War* - and they needed hundreds of soldiers. Not only was film extra work paid better than any I'd ever done, but they fed you all day long. Even more, they had to give everyone a precious Film Artistes Association membership. Normally, you needed a union card to get work but you'd never get a card without having work in the first place. Catch-22.

I was so keen that I even cut my shoulder-length hair to First World War squaddie stubble. For days we lounged around in scratchy khaki uniforms and ate and ate from the mobile canteens. Every so often we'd line up in ranks to sing Pack up Your Troubles (in Your Old Kit Bag) and Oh, Oh, Oh

What a Lovely War.

Soon after that, I got a day's work on a Roger Moore movie. It was just one scene. I was a demonstrator trying to push through lines of police. It felt just like a real demo and got pretty rough, with the police extras as determined to stop us as we were to break through. How easy to manipulate people with roles and uniforms.

Carry on Camping was the proud swansong of my film career. For those who don't know, the Carry On films – part of many older Brits' childhood - were cheaply made, rough and ready films, full of bad jokes and infused with that typically 1950s British innuendo that makes sex seem ridiculous and mundane. But they are much loved, mostly because of the extraordinary cast. It wasn't till I got on set that I realised how odd-looking, almost grotesque, they were in real life. String-thin Richard Hawtrey, obese Hattie Jacques, Sid James with a creviced face like a dried out mudflat, and tiny, bubbly, squeaky, perky, cockney, Barbara Windsor. The scene that everyone remembers is when her bikini top bounces off during a keep-fit class taught by sneery Kenneth Williams, although typically for Carry On, no breasts were seen in the film.

It was a different scene that terminated my film career. I was one of a bunch of hippies dancing in a field to a rock band. Horrified by the noise and the counter-culture threat, Hattie Jacques and Kenneth Williams drove round on a flatbed truck spraying us with water to drive us away. Actually it was barely a spray, more a light mist.

There's a lot of politics from the top to the bottom of the film industry and the lowly world of the extras was no exception. Anything above and beyond a basic extra role was due a bonus, in this case 'wet money'.

"They owe us," one guy shouted. "We're not working any more till we get it".

After a stand-off, the Film Artistes Association union rep was called in and an hour later he turned up in a dubious trilby hat and a crombie coat the same colour as his yellow, nicotine stained moustache.

"We'll soon get this mess sorted" he said as he disappeared into the director's caravan.

Some time later he reappeared, wobbling as he came down the caravan steps, and slurring his words. "No deal, sorry", he said - as trustable as a five ace pack.

"They've paid you off and you're drunk," our agitator shouted. "Everyone who refuses to work come and make a stand with me" and he stomped off to the side, ready to man the barricades.

Five minutes later when it was still just him and me, the director said 'You're both fired'. As the Union rep took our precious cards back, I felt like Dreyfuss being drummed out of the French army, epaulettes ripped off, sword broken over my commander's knee.

"You'll never work in the film industry again", the rep said.

He was right. I did apply and got a place at the London School of Film Technique with ambitions to become a director, but my local authority refused me a grant on the grounds that I'd wasted the money they'd given me to go to University [for UK students reading this, just a reminder that in those far-off golden days we received grants - fees and living expenses - and didn't have to take loans that hung around our necks like millstones for ever after].

There was a small coda to *Carry On Camping*. I got a phone call the next morning. Clearly not yet informed that I was an ex-extra, a woman asked if I had a set of motorcycle leathers for Ringo Starr to wear in a movie that was shooting that day. It was Sunday, she said, and all the costumiers were closed. I briefly considered going to a café in Penge where I knew the bikers hung out but they were an intimidating lot and I decided discretion was the better part of valour and stayed at home.

7. BACK TO MOROCCO

The road of excess leads to the palace of wisdom

William Blake

Now twenty-one, with a short back and sides haircut from my stint as an extra in the film *Oh What a Lovely War*, I set off, alone again, for Morocco, still carrying the camera that I'd planned to sell on my previous abortive trip. This time I made it safely through Spain and crossed the magical strait from Algeciras to Tangier. I didn't stay there but took buses first to Tetouan and then to Chefchaouen in the Rif mountains.

I arrived during Ramadan and once again had the feeling of entering a different world and a different age. In the early morning darkness a procession of drums and horns passed beneath my window, waking the town for *suhoor* – the pre-dawn breakfast. I didn't observe the fast but as evening fell I would sit in a café with my bowl of harira soup and plate of dates, copying my fellow diners as they held their spoons poised, waiting for the cannon to fire to signal sunset.

In between I would climb the hills around the town or go down to the river to swim and read on the rocks. There is a blessed stillness and beauty in Chefchaouen with its clear mountain air, gushing streams, flowering trees and blue and white painted houses. I met no other foreigners, and as I wandered the tracks past small farms, I could have been living in Biblical times, passing robed farmers leading donkeys piled high with brushwood or dried grasses.

In the evenings I started going to a café where young Moroccans hung out, smoking kif and drinking tea. We British are great tea drinkers, some of the thirstiest in the world, but we can't compete with countries like (mostly) teetotal Morocco where no event is complete without it. A fat bunch of fresh mint, unfeasible quantities of sugar and a handful of Gunpowder Green tea are packed into a silver swan-neck tea pot. In elegant hotels a snowy white cloth will be provided to hold the burning handle while pouring, but in a café, under a shaded tree, or in an orange-blossom filled courtyard, the blessed arrival of a tray of tea is accompanied by the search for a scrap of paper or rag.

There is ceremony in streaming the tea from a great height so that it froths in the glass, then pouring it back into the pot to circulate the tea without bruising the mint. In Setti-Fatma, in the foothills of the Atlas Mountains, Ali the mountain guide once told me that kif is good for everything that ails you except that it rots your teeth. I said I'd never heard that, then laughed when I remembered how kif smokers drink sugary sweet tea from morning to night.

In the café in Chefchaoeun I made friends with a handsome young Berber called Mohammed and we talked for hours. I told him about my camera, how good it was and how I wanted to sell it. Maybe it was my childhood attachment to it, or else my experience of bargaining, but in true Moroccan fashion I inflated its value. He kept making me promise it was really worth that much and I kept reassuring him it was. In the end, we struck a deal – hash for the camera. He told me I could sell the hash for a good price to other travellers when I got to Marrakech. I handed over the camera and he gave me one large block sealed in plastic and a smaller piece which we broke a bit off and smoked - to great effect.

I was sitting on the bus the next day, its engine revving, the last passenger getting on and fumbling for his ticket, when someone banged on the window right by my head. It was Mohammed, waving his fist and shouting that he'd taken the camera to Tangier and it hadn't been worth what I said it was, that I'd cheated him, and he wanted his hash back. I just kept looking ahead, blank-faced, holding my breath until the bus door closed and with a clash of gears and my sigh of relief it headed off on the long road towards Marrakech.

I didn't unwrap the big block until a couple of days later when I was sitting with a Turkish musician called Ahmed. He and I had picked up a few dirhams playing (him on darbouka drum, me on vaguely Arabic-sounding violin) at a Moroccan birthday party and the opening of a tourist leather goods shop. When we tried to smoke the hash we discovered it was just pressed henna - a common trick. I should have laughed, remembering the self-righteous look on Mohammed's face, but I was in despair. I had virtually no money and no realistic way of getting any. But I trusted Ahmed and when he told me to give him the hash I did. That evening he thrust a fat wad of dirhams into my hand. He'd sold it to a couple of American tourists. He'd even smoked some with them and they had waxed enthusiastically about what 'good shit' it was.

I spent a month in Marrakech, more or less living on the street. I'd found the cheapest place in town to sleep - a shared room with no beds, just grass mats on the concrete floor. For a few centimes I'd lay myself down, wrap myself in my hooded burnous robe, rest my head on my rucksack and instantly fall asleep as all around me farmers in town for the market, smelling of sour milk and goats, snored and snuffled.

In the morning I'd buy a warm loaf of dark Berber bread, split and stuffed with melting *smen* - Moroccan preserved butter. Then I'd buy a kilo of small sweet oranges which I'd carry in the hood of my burnous. For the rest, I mostly ate street food - barley porridge with yoghurt, barbecued skewers of fatty lamb or hard-boiled eggs dipped in cumin salt, always with copious bread to bulk them out. Daytimes and evenings I wandered the souk, walking miles, making friends with shop and stall holders, drinking tea, talking, playing or listening to music, cadging cigarettes and coffees.

As I write this, I have to admit I'm a bit puzzled by the person I was then - feckless, reckless, purposeless, hedonistic. I don't judge myself harshly (though others might) but instead wonder why I lived like this. I know I was driven by powerful urges – to travel, to seek adventure, to do exactly what I was doing and not what others wanted me to do. And I was in the company of lots of people my own age who were happily doing much the same, though looking back I think I might have been doing it more enthusiastically than most.

I spent a cold Christmas in Marrakech. It rained a lot and the streets, my shoes and the hem of my burnous were always muddy. Ahmed and I heard about a Christmas Day celebration but it wasn't easy to find. Just like teenagers on a Saturday night back home, searching for a party that might or might not exist at an address we weren't sure of, Ahmed and I roamed the dark and empty souk with a barely legible street name scrawled on a bit of paper, until miraculously we found it. There were maybe fifteen people sitting in a circle round the walls of a small room – hippies and young Moroccans. As musicians, Ahmed and I were welcomed in and given cushions and the best places to sit.

Through this long stay in Morocco, my violin was my passport and my magic key. In its dark red case, lovingly covered by my mother in sticky plastic, it somehow stayed safe and sound, wherever I went and however many buses I got on and off. And wherever I went I was welcomed because of it.

A bowl of mahjoun was passed around. A mixture of ground nuts, dried fruit, butter, spices and kif, mahjoun is both delicious and treacherous. Eating cannabis can be formidably more powerful than smoking it, and getting the dose right is tricky, especially when mahjoun is so moreish. The 19th century French writer Théophile Gaultier wrote a meticulously remembered account (https://urbigenous.net/library/haschischins.html) of his hallucinatory trip at one of the monthly meetings of the Club des Hashishchins, a cannabis-eating gathering attended by writers such as Victor Hugo, Alexandre Dumas, Charles Baudelaire and Honoré de Balzac.

After Ahmed and I had played, and as the effects of the mahjoun started to course through me, I had the illusion that this party was being held in my honour, as though it was my birthday. I watched the proceedings with the beneficent eye of a wise king as people talked and smoked and a girl undressed and sat naked in the centre of the circle looking confused until a big bearded American guy covered her with a blanket.

When we finally left in the early hours, the temperature had dropped, and as we walked back through the dark and shuttered souk a light snow began to fall.

When I tired of Marrakech, I travelled a hundred miles West to the sea at Essaouira. I shared a room with a laid-back American called Russian and we began to lead an almost domestic life. We bought a clay brazier and tagine cooking pot and shopped in the market for charcoal, vegetables, olives, bread and more spices than we could possibly use, enticed by the sculpted piles of cumin, turmeric, coriander and paprika. Late in the day we joined the regular gathering on the ramparts of the old Portuguese fort to watch the kaleidoscopic sunset.

Every few days we'd buy dried poppy heads from the Berber herb and magic stall and boil them up. The tea wasn't powerful but it had that warm dissolving effect that I recognised from the times I ate opium at University. One of the carpet sellers told us he had a special recipe that he would make for us. He wrote the name of some seeds we needed and told us to buy a hundred grams plus the usual poppy heads from the Berber stall. We drank the tea when he made it and went our separate ways.

Most days I would buy myself a treat from the cake shop – a round almond biscuit – and I really loved them. But when I tried to eat one after drinking the tea, it gummed up my bone-dry mouth and I had to slip down an alley and dig it out with my finger. That was the last clear memory I had for the next twenty-four hours.

Russian and I came to in our room mid-morning and started trying to piece together what had happened. I'd get flashes of memory - sitting in a room, or arguing with someone, or not being able to play my violin. I went out into the town and grabbed hold of anyone I knew and asked them if they'd seen me. Yes, they said, you were acting strangely, you seemed obsessed with finding something, you just sat there without saying a word for hours. Then we found out the small black seeds were belladonna – also known as deadly nightshade, death cherries and the devil's berries. Another dodged bullet.

The beach and dunes at Essaouira went on for miles, wind-whipped and deserted apart from the occasional camel train. One day we walked further than usual and came across the crumbling ruins of a castle (inspiration for Jimi Hendrix's song *Castles Made of Sand* after he visited the following year). Past that was a river and a broken bridge and then endless mimosa, thuja and eucalyptus forests. Amidst the dunes we came across two naked French girls – both called Francoise. We sat with them and shared a joint, then I decided to swim. Still retaining my last shreds of Englishness, I spent ages trying to tie a piece of cloth into a swimming dhoti as the girls laughed. It came off when the first wild Atlantic wave hit me and from then I stopped bothering.

Big Francoise and little Francoise were living in a communal house in a nearby Berber village called Diabat and the next day Russian and I moved in. Thus began the most magical time of my life.

American Jim funded the house and whoever had money chipped in for food. Typically, I soon ran out of cash and from then on until I left Morocco three months later was a guest of this wonderful communal generosity. I had no illusions about my violin playing but since the only other music was one Led Zeppelin tape ('Squeeze me baby till the juice runs down my leg') and a tinny cassette player that kept running out of batteries, I paid my way as court musician.

It was a typical Berber village house with a couple of rooms facing a dirt courtyard. The rooms weren't big, but as many as a dozen of us lived there, sleeping on piles of cushions spread out on the floor. We cooked, ate, went to the beach and played together.

The winding path to the sea passed through a million suns of mimosa flowers whose golden dust coated our hair and clothes. The air was full of the smell of thuja and eucalyptus, and the earth was carpeted in spring flowers. What seemed like paths petered out amidst small dunes and it was easy to get lost. Some days we never made it to the beach but picnicked in the forest.

We'd made a temple space with a bone white camel skull resting in the crook of a tree and mirrors that turned and flashed in the breeze, and would spread out blankets, incense, food and fruit amidst the flowers.

Most days two of us would take the long walk into Essaouira to shop. After loading our sisal baskets in the market, our reward was a coffee and a cake in the square and a catch-up on who was new in town. Then we trekked back again, along the road, over the broken bridge and river, the coarse rope handles of the heavy baskets cutting into our shoulders. Opening the door into the courtyard was like returning home to family, with hugs and murmurs of delight as we unpacked the shopping and handed out treats of fresh fruit and chocolate. We were in love with ourselves and with each other, in love with our youth and freedom.

Smells and sounds evoke the most sudden and moving memories and even now can throw me back to those times. The frankincense and myrrh that we bought in the market and threw on the glowing coals of our cooking fire; the rose and amber oils we bought from the Berber stall in the market; the thuja wood crafted in the workshops of Essaouira, mingling with badly cured goat leather and the sounds of beaten brass; the fish and diesel and crying gulls at the port; the cumin and roasting lamb from the brochette stalls and the frying fish that seduced me away from my vegetarianism.

I always passed the fried fish stall when I went into town to shop and every time overcame the powerful urge to buy some. Then one day my legs took the decision for themselves and I could resist no longer.

Ricardo and Jamie

Our little community got even better when Americans Ricardo and Jamie joined us. Olive-skinned Ricardo combined a prince-like dignity with refined campness. Always calm, always kind, never flustered, his every breath was a cultivated performance. Jamie, a dancer, was wilder and naughtier. There was a little hillock outside the house where one of our neighbours tethered her baby donkey. Jamie christened it Mimosa and every time he left the house would run towards it, hands fluttering camply, crying out "Mimosa darling", and begin hugging and stroking it in an unseemly way as the village women screamed with laughter and the old lady would rush out of her house and beat him off with a stick. Some nights Jamie and others would use one of our two rooms for a variety of sexual activities that I was too prudish to join in with.

One morning, at the height of Spring, Dutch Jos and I went to order flatbread from the black woman who always dressed in snowy white robes. We nervously edged by her chained up semi-feral dog into the low room where she squatted, baking bread on a hot stone. We held up four fingers, knowing that one of her children would deliver the loaves to the house while they were still warm. On the way back we bumped into Brahim the Casablancan who took us to his house filled with a motley collection of Berber hippies and travellers and gave us four tabs of acid – two for us and two extra for Jamie and Wendy.

The four of us took the acid, gathered our things, bought milk from the goat lady, and headed for the woods. Mimosa trees exploded in waves of light as we walked on carpets of spring flowers, past rings of fairy mushrooms. The air was full of whisperings and hints of movement that vanished when I turned to look. We lost the path and followed wild pig tracks until we reached a clearing and could go no further. I lay on the vibrant ground, staring up at the trees, their leaves shimmering in the sunlight. We were there for a long, long time as I tuned in to the throbbing silence that lay beneath all sound.

Eventually we roused ourselves, retraced our steps and found the path. I lingered behind the others until they were far ahead. Alone now, I became fully alive to the smells and sounds of the forest. I climbed high into the crook of a eucalyptus tree and hung there like a koala bear, as the tree gently swayed in the breeze, feeling the hair on my body growing into a thick, furry coat.

A raucous noise broke the spell. Round the bend, along the path below me, came Brahim, bashing a brass tray with a lump of wood, leading his troupe in a dance down to the sea. There was his young friend from Casablanca in a sharp suit, shiny shoes and trilby hat, crazy Mohammed, a Moroccan girl who'd run away from her family, Bernard the French muscleman with his flowing blonde hair, and a couple of American girls. They didn't see me and I waited until the sound died away, then slid down from my tree and followed them towards the ocean.

In my white jellaba, holding a branch I'd picked up, I came into the open at the end of the path, feeling like Gandalf with his staff. I passed Bernard lying on the sand being caressed by the half-naked Moroccan girl. He smiled and waved as I passed him and climbed over the last dune and there was the wild Atlantic Ocean, crashing onto the miles of beach, smashing up the pebbles, swallowing up the land. In the distance I saw figures dancing and jumping amidst the waves and foam, disappearing and reappearing in the seething mass. I strode towards them, whirling my staff, but when I got close I found only danger and chaos. Mohammed, whom we'd christened the hungry lion, came bounding naked out of the waves, roaring with an energy that matched the ocean, and started picking up rocks and throwing them wildly through the air.

I retreated, climbed a sand dune and sat crossed legged with my eyes closed, trying to shut out the confusion, until my stillness was shaken by a familiar noise. Along the beach came a camel train, each animal following the one in front, swaying as it planted its splayed feet in the soft sand, and on top of each camel sat one of Brahim's family. He was at the front, still banging on his brass tray, behind him the little suited boy in his shiny shoes, clicking his fingers, and then the rest of them, whooping, blowing flutes and waving saucepans.

As the sun lowered, I made my way back along the path and found my friends in the temple in the woods. In the centre, on a multicoloured blanket, rosy, pink, plump of flesh and biting into an apple, lay a very naked Wendy (by Renoir). At the top of the highest limb of the dead tree, Jamie danced to the sky, a golden circlet around his brow and bangles and bracelets jingling on his wrists and ankles. A Moroccan in a holiday fez and holding a bunch of wild red flowers, wandered past and sat with us.

We returned slowly to our little white house in the village and found our household gathered on the hillock to watch the sunset. The sky turned a thousand colours and as the sun disappeared they grew even more intense and condensed into a band of fiery gold over the sea. Then a deep-blue blackness slowly swallowed it up and the bright stars began to burn.

Back at the house a fire had been lit in the courtyard. Trays strewn with flowers were filled with fruits and cheese laid on pieces of heavy brown bread, and dressed in our finest clothes we celebrated the beauty of Spring.

We didn't give much thought to what the villagers thought of us. On the surface they were accepting and friendly, selling us bread and goat milk, smiling when we passed each other and otherwise ignoring us. Our careless flamboyance and nudity would have been impossible among Arabs but Berbers seemed different.

But accepting as they were, in the long run we did the village of Diabat no favours. The unspoilt forest and village we loved so much became soiled and dirty within a few years, and the drug use became darker. And as happened so often, we hippies and travellers, playing in the unspoilt and tolerant places that we found, were the unwitting spearhead of mass tourism. In the case of Diabat that eventually meant a luxury resort and two golf courses.

Eid-al-Adha, celebrated on the last day of the Hajj pilgrimage to Mecca, was marked by a mass slaughter of sheep, their decapitated heads lying in piles through the village, blood trickling into the dust. The smoke and smell of roasting meat lasted all day. Then as it got dark, the camel puppet and the entire population of the village came out. I say puppet but it was the size of a real camel with two men inside the hessian sack body, and a long neck topped by a camel skull whose wired jaws were worked by the men inside. It lunged and snapped at screaming children as the villagers waved flaming torches. Then it came for me and I yelled in genuine terror, to the sound of crazy laughter.

One evening we made mahjoun and I ate too much and lay on my bed, wrestling through a dark night of the soul. What was I doing, wasting my life like this, purposeless, seeking only fun and pleasure? My family, my ancestors – useful, hard-working, committed to great causes – rebuked me and I writhed in shame. Maybe it was a sign that this phase of my life was drawing to an end. The next day I went down to the river, the shallow river where we bathed, washed our hair and played like children. An American sadhu lived down there on a blanket. He was stern and censorious and his words echoed those that had coursed through me the night before, but that harsh voice was what I yearned for. He appeared as a character in my short story *In Rahani.*

There were also signs of darker days ahead for our little community. One day, weary after a long beach session, we turned into the woods to walk home. American Margaret decided to stay awhile. We were at the edge of earshot when we heard her scream. We raced back and found her lying on the sand with a knife wound in her back. Someone had crept behind her as she laid out her Tarot card deck and slashed her. It took an hour to get a car near enough to take her to hospital where she was sewn up and allowed to come home. The next day the police arrived in force. We were to stay in the house, they insisted, and not enter the forest or go to the beach. But the house had no toilet and we normally used an area we had assigned ourselves in the woods. I watched as little Francoise pleaded with one of the police to let her through and when he bluntly refused, she hoisted her skirt, squatted down and crapped right in front of him. When we woke the next day, the police had disappeared.

One fateful day French Bernard came back from a visit to Casablanca. He'd met an English sailor and told him about Diabat. The sailor gave him some liquid acid – straight from a dropper bottle into his mouth. As it came on, he realised he had to get out of the city and jumped on a bus. He couldn't look at anybody, he said, because their faces were distorting, so he fixed his eyes on the back of the driver's head until the driver stopped the bus and told him to get off.

"It was crazy man," he said. "Too strong, crazy strong."

The next day we returned from the beach, salty and sun burnished, ready to eat and relax, when the door into the courtyard opened and the English sailor came in. We knew who he was because he wore a string vest and was covered in tattoos. As he went from person to person he just said "Open up", and like obedient lambs, most of us did.

It was OK. We'd had acid before and we had our routine. Gather blankets, fruit, drink, incense, something to smoke, dress in our finest and head for the forest. We barely made it before the first wave came on and my 36-hour trip started.

We were in the forest a long time. None of us knew how to get back to the village. French Giles started to build a fire although I yelled out to him to stop as I was afraid it would set fire to everything – the sand, the trees, the blankets, us. Then the full moon came up. Clouds swam past it at great speed, now veiling it, now letting it blaze forth, and the village dogs began to howl.

The forest had always had something strange about it. By day, it was benign, just a feeling that something or somebody was behind me, whispering, then slipping out of sight as I turned. But this night it felt like malevolent spirits were abroad and we huddled together for comfort.

Mustafa kept appearing to play tunes on his one-stringed guimbri bass before jumping up and thundering off again. Once he leaped up to swing on a branch where Giles was nestled, bringing both crashing to the ground. The Dutch girl had black insects crawling out of her skin and big Francoise said she was going away to die (she didn't). A crippled Moroccan appeared and stamped out the fire, whispering and muttering, then settled back in the shadows to watch. Mustafa came back saying "Si ça descend ça va, mais si ça remonte ça va pas" [if it goes down it's OK but if it goes up it's not OK] and speaking of a great heart beating in the sky and threatening to take him away.

We spent much of the night there, unable to leave. When we finally made it back we found scenes of mayhem. The sailor had passed through the whole village, thrusting his dropper at anyone he came across – farmers, children, elderly widows. Many had instinctively opened their mouth and had been dosed. Some had gone to hospital. Somebody had jumped off a roof. This was like the madness that overcame medieval villages when contaminated rye gave rise to ergot poisoning or Saint Anthony's Fire.

We stood on the hillock. Beautiful English Gail kept appearing, looking for cigarettes, sensuously stretching herself and speaking of thunderstorms. The moon and the distant lights of Essaouira blazed, the lighthouse beam swept through the sky and life everywhere crackled, whispered, hummed and buzzed.

When daylight came I couldn't stay there any longer. I grabbed Jos – my closest friend after Russian left, tall, sweet, soft-bearded Jos – and we went down to the river to bathe. But just as we got there, two bulldozers started up with a roar. Like savage animals they began to eat up the river bank, gouging great holes, turning wildly with crashes and grunts, churning the beautiful river into seething mud.

We left and headed for Essaouira. We found that a whole section of the ruined bridge had collapsed overnight and now there was only the narrowest parapet for donkeys and bicycles and people.

I had some English pounds that I'd religiously kept through thick and thin and I needed to change them to dirhams because I knew I had to get away now, get home as soon as possible. The banks were closed and we were sent to a Jewish family of money changers. Their sitting room was stuffed with plush velvet sofas and armchairs covered with transparent plastic and every surface was thick with gilt and glass ornaments, looking like they were about to melt at any moment. The family's features were exaggerated to the point of caricature – maybe because of my altered state or because of the in-breeding that happens in small, centuries-closed communities. Back in the street, every smell was foul, every face ugly, every activity meaningless. I saw rottenness and corruption everywhere and yearned for something clean and simple, like a shaven-headed Buddhist monk in a saffron robe, radiating peace and simplicity. I begged Jos to help me get back to the village.

When we reached Diabat there was a knot of people standing on the hillock.

"What's happening?" we asked.

"Fabian is freaking out in the bushes," big Francoise said and pointed. There below us, in the midst of a thorny thicket, a naked Fabian was silently writhing, legs and arms thrashing and twitching like a dying insect, as people bent over him trying to hold onto his bloody limbs.

Finally, as the second night fell, I was able to sleep. When I woke at dawn and went outside to pee I looked down and saw my urine had turned to deep brown. I knew immediately what it was – hepatitis (A), just like the French couple who had passed through the village a couple of weeks before. I checked my eyes in a mirror and saw that the whites had turned yellow. When I shat my stool was almost white, the bile not excreted but building up and turning my body and mind bilious.

Within two days, nearly everyone I knew had packed up and gone, but I was too ill to move. I was nauseous and couldn't eat. A Moroccan guy told me that I should drink my own urine. Another said I had to get some greasy, deep-fried Moroccan doughnuts, boil them in vinegar and eat them. I couldn't contemplate either. Once, I started to vomit and the fluid was bitter acid which turned back into my lungs and I thought I'd choke to death.

There were just two others left in the house, but as they were still shell-shocked, I wasn't getting much help. I lay on my bed, too weak to move. By now my face and skin were dark yellow. The others wanted to take me to hospital but – true or false – it had a terrible reputation. The rumour was that people who went there never came out, and I was scared.

I got it into my head that I had to take the next boat home to England or I would die in this remote and lonely place. It sailed in two days time from Casablanca, two hundred and fifty miles away, and there wouldn't be another one for a month. The night before I'd have to leave I couldn't sleep. I knew it was impossible. I'd need to walk the two miles into town, sit on a bus for hours, find a room and get to the boat the following morning and I could still barely lift my arms.

In the morning I dragged myself out of bed and was slumped on the step facing the courtyard when the outside door opened and a young woman came in.

In khaki shorts and a khaki shirt so tight her breasts threatened to burst the buttons, she wasn't dressed like anyone I'd seen for a long time. Her hair bunches, strong white teeth and freckles made her look like she'd stepped out of a 1950s American milk advert.

She took one look at me and said, "God, you look dreadful".

I started mumbling something pathetic about buses and dying and home when she said, "I've got just what you need".

She rummaged in her small knapsack and brought out a catering-sized jar of Marmite*.

Neatly and matter-of-factly, she found some wood and squatted down (now threatening to burst her shorts) to build a small fire, boiled some water and made me a strong, hot, salty mug of Marmite. As I sipped it I felt heat building up in my stomach and spreading through my chest and belly, arms and legs, kicking every cell of my body into life.

A few minutes later I stood up, gathered my paltry belongings, walked the two miles into town, got on the bus to Casablanca, found a room for the night, and in the morning climbed the gangplank of the boat to Southampton. Whoever she was, I felt like she'd saved my life.

---

* For those who don't know, Marmite is a black, salty yeast spread, uniquely British (although the Australians have an inferior – sorry – version called Vegemite). It is spread on bread or made into a drink and the name has entered the English language to describe something that people either love or hate. I loved it. When I was studying Chinese medicine, Ted Kaptchuk, one of my teachers, told us a story about when he was in Macau (then a Portuguese colony on the Chinese mainland) in the 1970s, studying Chinese medicine. He was suffering from some lingering illness and nothing would shift it – not acupuncture, not herbs and not Western medicine. Then his landlady told him that the only thing that would help him was rice from his own village. He tried to explain to her that they don't have paddy fields in Brooklyn, but I think the idea can be interpreted more flexibly, and in this case Marmite was indeed 'rice from my own village'.

I went back to Diabat two or three years later with Jenny, my future wife. I met some of the Berbers I knew from before and learned a little more about the sailor's story. They told us he'd been paid to deliver several bottles of liquid acid to Ibiza. Somewhere on the road he'd started taking it and went crazy, travelling down through Spain and into Morocco leaving a trail of havoc in his wake. In a fitting finale, they told me that the day after he left Diabat he was killed in a road traffic accident on the road to Agadir.

It was when I lay on my sickbed in Diabat that I came across a book that was to help change the course of my life. Read on to find out what and how.

8. CHANGE OF DIRECTION - INFINITY FOODS

Nothing is as powerful as an idea whose time has come
Victor Hugo

In April 1970, aged 21, after several months in Morocco, I landed on my parents' doorstep (I had nowhere else to go) dressed in a grubby Moroccan robe with long-hennaed hair, black kohl eye make up, festooned with beads, stick thin and a dirty yellow jaundiced colour from hepatitis. As soon as I could, I went to see Rab.

I'd fallen for sharp, funny Rab not long before I left for Morocco - fallen in a most romantic way. We'd never consummated the relationship (she had a distant boyfriend at the time whom she dangled in front of me whenever we got too close) which made the intensity of my feelings all the stronger. I wrote to her a few times while I was away – letters full of coloured drawings of suns, moons and stars, stuffed with dried mimosa flowers and scented with patchouli oil. I told her how much I yearned to see her again, though in truth I can't have yearned that much since I wasn't in any hurry to leave Morocco.

I assumed as I stood on her doorstep - the sexy world traveller returned, still clad in native costume – that she would throw herself into my arms. Instead, the reception was not warm. She made it clear that I was a person she no longer wanted to know, and within the first few minutes told me she was going out with an engineering student.

It had only ever been an infatuation but it hurt and compounded the misery of the long symptom tail of hepatitis. I couldn't seem to get my health or spirit back and my doctor had nothing to give me. Week after dreary week I lay low, lacking appetite for food and life. Being weak and ill for a long time changed my reality and I started to think of myself as an invalid.

One weekend, my brother and a couple of our friends set off to drive to Wales. At the last minute I decided to join them, even though I was afraid I wouldn't be able to keep up. We slept in a cottage close to Cadair Idris mountain, and the next day climbed to the top. I was soon winded and my legs felt like I was wading through mud, but I didn't want to turn back and sit on my own in the car for hours on a cold and grey day, so I plodded on – one heavy foot in front of the other. As we reached the top, the clouds cleared and I could see for miles over the landscape below, laid out in woods, fields, and valleys. I found what looked like a giant's seat and as I sat there and surveyed the world, something inside of me changed and I felt a thrilling surge of opportunity. It still took me many weeks to regain my strength but I'd realised I was no longer sick.

I found out later that Welsh bards used to sleep at the top of Cadair Idris in search of inspiration. [see short story *On Cadair Idris* in part two]

It was while I lay ill and fearful in the Berber village of Diabat that I'd come across a book that changed the course of my life and offered me a path back to health and wellbeing. *Zen Macrobiotics* by George Ohsawa (macrobiotics = 'big life') promised that I could transform and heal myself by harmonising yin and yang through diet - eating simple and plain whole foods enlivened by Japanese soya sauce, seaweeds and miso.

I already knew about brown rice. My friend Steve and I had heard about a mysterious ten-day brown rice diet at University. For some reason we thought we had to eat it raw. We lasted 36 hours – painfully crunching on tiny mouthfuls – rather than the ten days that were supposed to change every cell in our bodies.

Now I was recovering in my family home where there wasn't much chance of following a macrobiotic diet, what with my mother constantly offering me cheesecake to 'build me up'. So I moved back to Brighton where I'd enjoyed my brief University career. At first I had nowhere to live and for several weeks slept under the kitchen table of a friend of a friend. I thought nothing of it. I'd slept in all kinds of places in my travelling days, but I still bump into the owner of the kitchen from time to time and with a bemused look he never fails to tell me he'd thought I was the biggest loser he'd ever met.

I lived on the dole (welfare) which I supplemented by making bead necklaces and multi-coloured, densely crochéed bags. I sold them at the Wraggle Taggle Workshop run by my lovely friend Karen (with whom I later wrote a cookbook - *Nature's Foods* - https://peterdeadman.co.uk/writing/natures-foods/).

I decided to revisit the ten-day brown rice diet and took myself, a big bag of rice and a tiny tent to the slopes of Chanctonbury Hill, ascribed mysterious powers because of an ancient ring of oaks at its top. I cooked my rice over a wood fire, seasoned it with gomasio (toasted sesame seeds ground up with salt), meditated and didn't speak to a single person for ten days. I was in search of healing, clarity and simplicity and I read my way through Basho's *Narrow Road to the Deep North* and books on Buddhism. After a few days my knees swelled up and erupted into red, flaming boils full of pus. I chose to believe this was a discharge of the poisons I'd accumulated over my years of travelling, or perhaps just a Job-like affliction to be endured, and I stuck it out. Whatever the cause, my legs were back to normal by the tenth day.

My last trip to Morocco had been full of delights, but it was undercut by an anxiety that I'd never find a meaningful path in life. Now, on this solitary retreat, I began to get a sense of having found my purpose and it was something to do with macrobiotics.

I took it into my head that I should move to London and get a job in *Seed* – the only macrobiotic restaurant in Britain. The Sams brothers, Craig and Greg - both later to become famous in the UK's natural food revolution - were polite but turned me down, perhaps because I was still yellow.

I realised the only alternative was to start a restaurant of my own. It was a brave ambition as I had no money, no experience and only the most primitive cooking skills, but I had fire in my belly now.

To start earning and saving money, I went back to the trade I was most comfortable with – painting and decorating – working for Braybon & Sons, an old family firm in Brighton. At the same time, I realised I had to stop smoking cannabis. It was such an ingrained habit with me, and such an essential and unquestioned ritual among my friends, that it took me a long time to recognise that it had started to make me feel bad – depressed, negative and fearful - whenever I smoked it. I was proof of Einstein's definition of insanity – doing the same thing over and over again and expecting a different result. Maybe this time, I thought, as I accepted a joint passed to me in our comfortingly communal smoking circle, it would return me to that high, happy and inspired state that it used to. Instead, each time I would feel myself sinking rather than flying.

In the end I cut myself off from just about everyone I knew and stopped using cannabis. I barely touched it again for nearly a decade. I did test it once or twice during that time, but I immediately felt myself slipping back into that dark world. It wasn't until many years later, on a sunny Greek beach, that I smoked a little neat grass and dove naked into the clear blue sea. I twisted and turned like an eel, like a sleek porpoise, intensely present, free, my spirit soaring. That was many years ago now and I have continued to use it since, but in a much more conscious way - rarely, never contaminated with tobacco, always sativa-dominant plants grown organically under sun and rain, and always consciously connecting to music, creativity, friendship and the beauty of the world.

I still had no idea how I might set up a macrobiotic restaurant, though. Then serendipity struck. A mutual friend, Jim King, introduced me to Ian Loeffler. Lanky, long-haired Ian had just moved to Brighton with his girlfriend Jenny. Miracle of miracles, he was also set on opening a macrobiotic restaurant. We bonded straight away, with shared intention and unstoppable power. I don't remember ever having a disagreement with him, right up until the end.

Ian Loeffler

I have been incredibly lucky in my life in finding the right partner for the different projects I have worked on, and Ian was the first. When two people come together in this way, they can create so much more than the sum of their two parts.

Ian had a small amount of cash – insurance from a road accident – but nowhere near enough to rent and equip a restaurant. I had nothing. Jim King now pulled off another catalytical act when he told us about The Crypt, a restaurant rented out by the Sussex University Student Union on campus. It had been a greasy hamburger joint until the people who were renting it did a moonlight flit and now the union urgently needed someone to take it over before the new term started.

We assured them we were honest and reliable and knew all about running restaurants. These students were in a pickle and no match for our passion and they rented it to us dirt cheap.

Ian's money, topped up by a small donation from my parents, was just enough. We borrowed a van and drove to Copenhagen to buy ancient cast iron cooking pots, thrown out from farmhouse kitchens in favour of modern non-stick and aluminium. We spent a day in the market there and returned with a van full of pots, crockery, carpets and cushions.

We had a week to get the echoing restaurant space ready and we set to, equipping the kitchen, building floor level tables and scraping years of accumulated grease off every surface. It seemed like a strange kind of fate, though, when a year later we had to decontaminate a filthy old fish and chip van to sell tempura at Glastonbury festival, and then a year after that when we moved into a fish and chip shop in North Road and transformed it into the second incarnation of Infinity Foods. We were natural food warriors fighting back against the agents of grease.

In those days, I used to use the *Yi Jing* (*Book of Changes*), China's nearly 3000 year-old book of divination, and we named the restaurant Biting Through after hexagram 21 ("Biting Through has success"), printed fliers and opened for lunches only. The first day we ran out of food. By the second week we were cooking over a hundred meals a day – scoops of stodgy brown rice, lentil or red bean stews, sauteed vegetables, wet-cement-like muesli and apple pies with leathery crusts. But we had a few secret ingredients that made it all work. First, we were cheap and our portions enormous. Eat one of our lunches and you didn't need to eat again that day. Second, students – being young – have forgiving, cast iron digestions. Third, we were hip. We played great music, joked with our customers and from the very first day attracted volunteers who were happy to sit and slice carrots, serve at the counter or wash up. We were a community, we believed in something, and even if the food wasn't great, the experience was infectious.

That's not to say it wasn't hard. Anyone who's worked in a kitchen knows what it's like. We started at eight in the morning and pretty much ran non-stop till lunch was over at three. Then we ate together, cleared up and – from a few weeks after we first opened – got ready to do it all again for supper. We dragged ourselves home at midnight, resurfaced in the morning and started over.

After a while students and university staff began knocking at the kitchen door, wanting to buy brown rice, wholewheat flour or muesli. There were health food shops in town but their few real foods were expensive, packed in tiny bags and hidden behind shelves laden with vitamins and supplements. It was like when I was a child and the only place you could buy olive oil was at the chemist for cleaning your ears.

The obvious next step was to open a shop, but once again we had no money. We were selling meals at rock bottom prices and barely broke even, only paying ourselves enough to cover rent and basic necessities.

Then one day Andy the Anarchist came in for his regular vegetable chopping stint, dreadlocks tucked under a rasta hat and an everything's-wrong-with-the-world expression.

"What's up, Andy?" we said.

"My auntie died."

"Oh man, we're so sorry. Were you close?".

"No it's not that, I hardly knew her. But she's left me some money. I wish she hadn't. You know I don't believe in private property. I don't know what to do".

There was a long silence.

"Er ... maybe we could help you out Andy. We could take it off your hands if you like."

"Would you really do that for me? That would be fantastic".

So with Andy's money and donations from various parents, I went looking for a shop. I hunted for weeks, doggedly but with a growing sense of gloom as there was simply nothing we could afford. Then at last I found a tiny shop hidden away on a quiet residential road opposite St. Nicholas churchyard[3]. I saw it on a Friday morning and knew - in my bones, in my marrow - that this was the one. I ran to the estate agent who regretfully told me he'd just let it to someone else.

I spent the weekend in a ferment. How could this be? That shop had to be ours and I burned with frustration and disbelief. On the Monday morning I rang the agent – just in case.

"Actually," he said, "I've just now put the phone down. The person who took the shop sadly died of a heart attack over the weekend and it's back on the market".

We opened early in 1971. We bought an old blue Commer van and ran it up to London and back, filled to the roof with sacks of grains and beans, nuts and dried fruit. We took delivery of Japanese seaweeds, crafted bamboo casks of miso and gallons of tamari soy sauce. We built rudimentary shelves, found an old-fashioned till and hung an OPEN sign in the window.

The first Infinity Foods, 54 Church Street Brighton

For a year we ran the shop alongside the restaurant with a crew of full or part-time workers and an ever-changing flock of volunteers.

How did we manage the business? First, we were all friends, and work and community were one and the same. Second, nobody was in charge and everyone took the same (paltry) pay. Decisions were consensual and taken by whoever was most committed to the cause at any one time. And thirdly, we shared a common vision of transforming ourselves, our community and the planet with simple, healthy, organically grown, mostly plant-based foods. It ticked a lot of boxes – fairness and food justice, respect for nature, support for small farmers, egalitarianism and more.

In 1975, a few years after we opened, we formed the Natural Foods Union with a handful of similar business scattered across the country. When I rediscovered our mission statement recently, I was struck how much of it is as relevant today as it was then.

NATURAL FOODS UNION

We believe that the food we eat is an important factor in the way we live. A diet which is wholesome, simple, non-destructive (to other creatures, other men and our planet) and inexpensive, is a desirable social goal. We believe that by eating thus, our physical, mental and spiritual health will improve, since we cannot truly feel a separation among them.

The NFU is a brotherhood of natural foodstores, restaurants, suppliers producers and growers who share the above ideals. The NFU sprang from a desire to buy co-operatively to reduce prices and to influence growers and manufacturers to improve the quality of their produce.

The Intentions of the Union

To present an alternative to the supermarket - and most 'health food stores'. To do this we will strive to provide food of the highest quality at the lowest price we can. By high quality, we mean: unrefined organically grown where possible, ecologically sound, if processed, to be processed in the most natural way, and free from additives. We wish to provide food direct from its source, the earth, nourished by the sun, rain and elements, rather than from factories.

To promote revolutionary medicine - and help create a healthy people freed from dependence on drugs, drug companies, hospitals and doctors. To do this, we want our stores to become focal points for the exchange of experiences and ideas concerning natural medicine(ie - herbalism, Acupuncture, Massage, Yoga, Macrobiotics and other diets).

To present an economic alternative to the food industry - and make good food available to everyone. We are attempting to replace the economic system behind the food technologist and the businessman-farmer, supermarket and health food empire, by using methods that are non-exploitive of the consumer or environment. NFU traders operate on a lower mark-up, buy co-operatively in bulk, prefer to sell in bulk and pack the food themselves in simple bio-degradable, recyclable containers(hessian, cellophane or paper).There are no great profits being made, The primary concern is the spreading of life-giving food. As we obtain more and more of our supplies from local and small producers, the money that passes through our hands is used to directly support them in their efforts, rather than big artificial food combines. We can use our communal buying power to directly encourage other producers to improve the quality of their products, by presenting them with an attractive market.

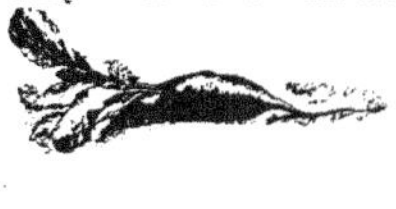

To demonstrate that it is possible to eat simply, lower down the food chain, and spend less. Individually, some items in our shops are more expensive than their counterparts because of the care taken in their manufacture and/or growing. However a diet based on whole grains, vegetables, beans, seeds, nuts and fruits, with little or no animal food, can incorporate the higher quality foods without being expensive. We wish to do away with the concept of a healthy life only for the affluent.
To support farmers who are enhancing and protecting the land. Most modern agricultural methods are destructive and exploitive of the land, and the consumer of the food raised on it. We are supporting and actively convincing new farmers to use proven farming methods which promote a living soil.
To encourage a return back to the land. To assist people in a better use of the land, through the use of waste ground, allotments and back gardens. To learn about wild edible and medicinal plants.
To revive interest in traditional British foods and develop their uses.
To see the introduction of new crops which could grow here and make Britain more self sufficient.
To distribute information about the foods we use-and the philosophy behind them. To describe them honestly with a clear statement of the ingredients, origin and any processing used, and to praise their true qualities. We are not interested in vague sales promotion and unfounded claims.

Listed below are the shops which now form the Union, hopefully this list will grow and grow. We will be able to help people who wish to set up shops, co-ops, restaurants etc., by giving them details of suppliers and sharing our experiences. Through unity we will become stronger and more effective in our work. Because of the size and nature of our shops, there is more communication than in most others. We hope to develop this by responding to your criticisms and opinions, and we hope you will use our services and support us in our work

HARMONY FOODS 191 FRESTON ROAD, LONDON W 10 (01 969 1644)
HARVEST 31 BELVEDERE, LANSDOWN ROAD, BATH (0225 23407)
INFINITY FOODS 54 CHURCH STREET, BRIGHTON (0273 29386)
SESAME 128 REGENTS PARK ROAD, LONDON NW 1 (01 586 3779)
ARJUNA 12 MILL ROAD, CAMBRIDGE (0223 64845)
CERES 269a PORTOBELLO ROAD, LONDON W 11 (01 229 5571)
COMMUNITY SUPPLIES 28 PRINCE OF WALES CRESCENT, LONDON NW1 (01 485 8213)
THE HAELAN CENTRE 39 PARK ROAD, CROUCH END, LONDON N8 (01 340 4258)
ON THE EIGHTH DAY COMMUNITY WHOLEFOODS, 111 OXFORD ROAD, ALL SAINTS MANCHESTER (061 273 4146)

But for now, the old-fashioned dangling bell on the back of the shop door barely ever rang. Nobody knew we were there and in any case hardly anyone understood or wanted what we were selling. To bring in a little income, we used the van to run a removals service, hefting pianos and wardrobes up narrow staircases. We might have been skinny almost-vegans but we'd built up strength, manoeuvring one hundredweight (50 kilo) sacks of rice and lentils down into the tiny basement and even, once in a while, 100 kilo bags of hazel nuts from China. Buying in bulk like this and repacking into small bags was our way of keeping prices down for our customers.

We baked heavy sourdough bread and bought our own stone grinder to mill flour and peanut butter. We did everything we could to make our food enticing, but we still had too few customers and weren't making any profit (it helped a bit, though, when we finally discovered the difference between mark-up and profit). We lived above the shop in two tiny bedrooms and an attic room too low to stand up in, and we ate from the shelves or at Biting Through so our food and accommodation were covered. But we were barely able to pay ourselves. We needed a plan.

That's when we heard about a free festival coming to a farm near Shepton Mallet* (and hard on its heels a music festival in Reading) and decided to try our hand at mass catering. If we did this right we could make enough money to tide us over for at least a few weeks. We loaded the van with a hired marquee, gas powered laundry boilers (to cook rice and lentil soup), all the bits and pieces we needed to cater to the crowds, and seven large calor gas bottles.

We arrived in the still empty fields at Shepton Mallett, overlooked by St Michael's Tower perched on distant, misty Glastonbury Tor. As we set up the marquee and the kitchen, a small pyramid stage took shape. Then the crowds came.

We worked day and night with a constantly swirling shift of helpers, collapsing for a few hours sleep under the tables or in the spaces between the cookers. We served thousands of meals – muesli for breakfast, and brown rice, lentil soup and vegetables for the rest of the day until the early hours. I'd slip away occasionally to try and catch a bit of music but it was as though a cord woven from duty and worry tethered me to the kitchen and tugged me back. That's how I missed David Bowie's set.

We'd bought a cheap fish and chip van, scraped off archaeological layers of grease and sold vegetable tempura from the open hatch. On the final day of the festival, the tempura team, crazed from lack of sleep, went off piste, roaring around the bumpy fields, hot oil pitching and rolling in the fryers, yelling out "tempura for dope".

---

* This was the second Glastonbury Festival. For those who don't know, Glastonbury is the most famous and biggest festival in the UK, maybe the world. To give an idea of its range, I was performing there in 2007. While the Arctic Monkeys played the main stage in front of tens of thousands of ecstatic fans I was far over on the other side of the site learning stone age flint knapping.

We had a day to rest and recover, then packed up the van and headed straight to the first Reading Music Festival to do it all over again. After the hippie vibe of Glastonbury it was a shock to see gangs of young men pogo-ing and throwing beer cans full of urine at each other but we just carried on, churning out meals, getting filthier and more disreputable by the day.

Cooking at Reading (me on left and D.)

When we got back to the shop we half-heartedly unpacked, moving the mostly unused (we massively over-estimated) calor gas cylinders into the basement kitchen for safety, meaning to take them back the next day. But we were annihilated with exhaustion and they stayed there for the next two days.

I was sitting behind the desk we used as a shop counter, wondering if any customers were going to jangle the bell, when the air around me filled with pretty little flowers of flame. There must have been a bang but I don't remember it. My first thought was that a petrol tanker had exploded in the street and I ran out the back into the tiny yard, only realising later that I'd burst through a locked door. But the air in the yard was still burning and that's when I figured it must have been a nuclear bomb. I'd been waiting for this since the age of thirteen when my family sat around the radio during the Cuban missile crisis, thinking the world was about to end in thermonuclear war.

Finding no refuge in the yard, I shot back through the shop and out into the street. The whole shopfront and the basement windows had been blown out and I could see straight into the basement kitchen where flames were licking round the calor gas cylinders. I realised that if one of them had blown and done this much damage, the rest of them exploding would bring down the whole street. Yet I was unable to act. To go down into the kitchen and drag them out felt like suicide.

Among the numerous friends and helpers who used to hang out at the shop was Austrian Bruno. He ran the Open Café community centre in town and was permanently zoned out on tranquillisers. Now Bruno appeared from nowhere like a superhero, weighed up the situation and plodded down the outside stairs into the kitchen. A passing off-duty fireman was willing to risk his arms by standing with his back to a solid wall and grabbing the cylinders when Bruno yelled out to take them. Between them they cleared the kitchen.

It wasn't till hours later that I found out what had happened. There were four guys in the kitchen when it blew up. They were friends of friends but one of them knew us well enough to be cooking a meal. Someone had sat on one of the gas cylinders and it had started leaking. Calor gas is heavy so it sank, which is why they didn't smell it. When he rested a hot pan on the floor, the gas rose, ignited on the cooker and the kitchen exploded in searing flame and flying glass. All four of them went on to need facial surgery.

The strangest thing for me to understand was that in the seeming seconds it took me to get out to the road, they had completely vanished – whisked off to hospital by passers-by. That and the fact that we never saw or heard from a single one of them ever again.

The local evening paper splashed us over their front page (inaccurately claiming it was firemen who saved the day), with a picture of Jim King (left) and three Infinity workers incongruously smiling.

We went on to cater at more festivals, including Bickershaw in 1972 where the Grateful Dead played. It rained for days before and during the festival, turning the whole site into a bog. During the night, a toilet block slowly upended, spilling a flood of sewage down the slope into people's tents as they slept. The final morning, as I surveyed the site – empty now apart from discarded tents and one or two people curled up in the mud in plastic bin bags,

Hand Tailoring Bernard Luper

Evening Argus

SPECIAL

SATURDAY, JULY 3, 1971 3p

LARGE RANGE OF DRESS FABRICS 25p PER YARD WADES WESTERN ROAD, BRIGHTON

Train crash —dead children are named

BRITISH RAIL engineers today continued their priority investigation into last night's train crash in which two children died and 400 youngsters had a "miraculous" escape.

Chester Police this morning named the two dead children as Catherine Sylvia Clarke, 10, of Birmingham, and Wayne William Dandy, 11, of Kingstanding, Birmingham.

The children were on their way home from Rhyl, the North Wales seaside town, on what for many had been their first day ever by the sea.

Then the 10-coach train hit a bridge at Waverton, near Chester and the last coach — carrying about 50 children—was derailed and dragged along the line for several hundred yards.

Many of the children were flung clear from the toppling coach.

A British Rail spokesman said: "The children seem to have had a miraculous escape."

DETAINED

Early today, four adults and two children were detained in Chester Royal Infirmary and Wrexham Hospital.

Mr Dennis Stanley, 39, who saw the crash, said "I was coming up the road from the fields when I saw the train coming down the line. I was about 50 yards away. When first I saw it, I shouted 'Christ, look at this train, it isn't half motoring.' hen I saw the back carriage whipping.

"It then hit a bridge and debris flew everywhere. I ran along the line and I heard screams. A woman came along towards me and said: 'For Christ's sake, help me.'

"I climbed on top of the ...

Firemen remove gas cylinders

FOUR HURT IN HIPPY SHOP BLAST

FOUR MEN were taken to hospital with severe burns after a blast at a hippy food shop in Brighton town centre last night. The explosion ripped out the frontage of the ground and basement floors of Infinity Foods, a macrobiotic food shop in Church Street in the early evening.

A large plate-glass window on the ground floor was smashed and a brick wall in the basement damaged.

Cause of the blast was a leaking Calor gas cylinder, one of seven stored in the basement. The other six were removed by firemen.

The four injured men were in the basement when the explosion occurred. All four were taken to the Royal Sussex County Hospital with burns to their hands, arms, feet and face.

Members of the commune who run the shop in Church Street, Brighton, stand beside the tarpaulin-covered window shattered by the explosion

Hijackers fly—with £40,000 ransom

A HIJACKED U.S. Boeing 707 airliner took o from the Mexican city of Monterey last night, apparently for Lima, Peru, carrying two hijackers—a man and a woman—who had been given a $10,000 (£40,000) ransom to release the passengers.

Officials at Monterey, 625 miles north of Mexico City, said the plane took off just after midnight (BST), with the pilot and co-pilot and a stewardess on board, as well as the two hijackers. All 103 passengers had been allowed to leave the plane.

NITRO

The hijackers who had identified themselves as Robert Jackson, a U.S. citizen, and Alicia Sanchez, originally ordered the plane to fly to the Caribbean island of Trinidad, but just before take-off said they wanted to go to Lima, officials said.

They were said to be armed with at least two guns and a bottle of nitro-glycerine.

The plane, belonging to Braniff International Airlines, was flying between the Mexican Pacific resort of Acapulco and New York when the two staged the hijacking over San Antonio, Texas. It flew back over the border to land in Monterey just after midday.

BRITISH ANTIQUE EXPORTERS LTD
Urgently require
DOUBLE DIAL CALENDAR CLOCKS

almost indistinguishable from the primal ooze - I saw a Boy Scout troupe single-filing through the mud. I went up to the leader, immaculate in shorts and long socks, and asked him what, on God's earth, they were doing there. "It's the nearest thing to a disaster you could find in peacetime," he said, "and I wanted my boys to see it".

It was that summer that Ian went back to Glastonbury Festival – this time for fun. The days passed and he didn't return. There was no word from him and his girlfriend Jenny was confused and angry. One night she came to my room and asked if she could share my bed.

Beautiful Jenny, quiet and serene, had been a part of my life for the last couple of years, ever since I first met her and Ian. She studied in the library every day for her Psychology degree, came to Biting Through for lunch, and was always helping out with whatever needed doing, bringing order to chaos. We spent a lot of time together – Ian and Jenny and whoever else was living and working at the restaurant and shop - and she and I often talked. Yet I'd never thought of her as a possible partner – she was with Ian and that was that. Then she appeared in my bed, and although we slept fully clothed that night, by the next day I was fiercely attached and praying she and Ian were finished. Thus began the most important relationship in my life – one approaching its fiftieth year as I write and which has blessed me with two

Jenny

beloved daughters and three beloved grandchildren. Without Jenny the rest of my life would have been utterly different.

By the time Ian returned it was too late, and anyway he wasn't in a good state. He'd taken too much acid at Glastonbury and had become detached and floated away. Although he was puzzled about what had happened with Jenny it didn't seem to register deeply, even though they'd been together for years. He carried on living with us above the shop, strange as that was, but his behaviour became more and more erratic. If I was working at the restaurant or had gone to London for supplies, I might return and find the shop closed in the middle of the afternoon and full of strangers smoking weed, some of whom Ian was giving money to from the till. In the end he just disappeared and we didn't hear anything from him for many years.

Some time around Ian's disappearance, Robin Bines turned up. He started by working at the restaurant and slowly became more and more central to Infinity. For me, he became the partner I sorely missed in Ian and we worked together in harmony for years.

Robin

I'd been looking for a stable and loving relationship ever since I was a teenager. But even though a couple lasted for a year or two, I was emotionally immature and selfish and they ended unhappily. But opening the restaurant and then the shop, following a plain macrobiotic diet, not using drugs or alcohol, committing to something greater than myself, had settled me. Now, being with Jenny brought a new and delicious stability to my life. I was hooked and in love.

We'd been together for a couple of years when we decided to get married. It wasn't an obvious decision as most of our friends in long-term relationships hadn't bothered, but my mother kept pushing us and in the end it seemed like an opportunity to have a party and get some much-needed gifts.

As non-believers, a church wedding was out of the question (and would have been incendiary for my equally atheist but very Jewish mother), and the plain functionality of a registry office certificate seemed inadequate.

We'd made friends with an inspiring couple who ran a biodynamic farm near Forest Row in Sussex and supplied the shop with vegetables and eggs, and they suggested an Anthroposophical wedding. We weren't into Rudolph Steiner's philosophy but this seemed to offer meaning and ceremony, although its unfolding religious base took me by surprise. We met with the immensely tall, sonorous Adam Bittlestone, ordained priest in Steiner's Christian Community.

He informed us solemnly that in addition to the human guests at the wedding, a heavenly host would be present as well, and that we each had to pick a mentor from among our friends to act as a bridge between these two parties. At the height of the ceremony, Adam bound the two sticks that we'd been asked to bring with a red ribbon, and what with the expectations of both human and celestial witnesses and the binding, we were well and truly married. It seemed that as the years passed the door and we went through the well-worn difficulties and challenges of a long term relationship, the bond often stretched to its limits but remained unbreakable.

Jenny made herself a skirt from a length of Liberty's silk-satin which she wore with a Romanian peasant blouse and a pair of (so fashionable!) Clark's open-toed sandals and I wore an Afghan waistcoat and a home-made shirt. My father kept sipping from a hip flask of whiskey at this strictly teetotal event, and the macrobiotic wedding cake was as heavy as a stone and reeked of cold pressed corn oil. Such had been our relative poverty that wedding presents of a pair of sleeping bags, a good cooking pot and a hi fi were treasures.

By this time we were living in a beautiful house a few miles outside Brighton, large enough for ten of us. We ate together every evening around the farmhouse kitchen table, taking turns to cook on the coal-fired Aga range. It was in the garden shed of that house that I co-wrote my first book, *Nature's Foods*, with my friend Karen who lived with us.

Karen perfectly embodied the rural hippie movement that was flourishing in America at the time – homesteading, dungarees, co-raising children, re-learning the old crafts of animal husbandry, food growing, pickling and preserving, weaving and quilting. Together, we tried to interpret Japanese macrobiotics through the lens of both British and American rural traditions, and in the spirit of the times the book was hand-drawn and illustrated by Karen. I can't pretend I don't squirm now at some of its more naïve passages but it was a creature of its age.

Nature's Foods was published by Unicorn Books (and later by Rider) a small bookshop run by big Bill Butler and his partner Mike. A gay, radical, cowboy-hat wearing poet and publisher, Bill nursed our book into being at the same time as being prosecuted for obscenity for publishing *Why I Want to Fuck Ronald Reagan* by J.G. Ballard. Along with Public House bookshop –

home to yet more revolutionary literature and recently visited by beat poets Allen Ginsberg and Lawrence Ferlinghetti – Brighton was shaping up to be a beacon of the counter-culture, of which Infinity Foods was a key part.

After the wedding, we decided on a first honeymoon in Wales (to be followed, later, by a trip to India). This coincided with a small festival on the Welsh border that Infinity was catering for and which we'd visit on the way.

D. took charge of the festival planning. He'd been part of Infinity for a couple of years and lived with us in Burgess Hill. He was conscientious, a touch obsessive and very hard-working. He had a passion for smoking pipefuls of hash every evening, lying on his bed listening to music through headphones and eating giant bowls of muesli. Now, organising a complex festival catering project for the first time, he took to walking around with a clipboard, constantly jotting down notes and muttering to himself. He seemed more intense than ever, but the rest of us had been distracted by running the shop and preparing for the wedding, weaving flower garlands and hand-sewing wedding clothes, and our attention was elsewhere.

When we arrived at the festival on our way to Wales, the marquee and kitchen were already set up. D. had hired an enormous truck and parked it so that its snub nose thrust through one wall of the tent. In the middle of the night, he climbed into the cab, switched on the headlights and started up the engine. People jerked awake in their sleeping bags strewn across the floor, some lying right up against the massive tyres. Over the roar of the motor we could hear D. shouting that he could run us all over if he felt like it. It took patience and time to coax him out of the cab but even then we didn't realise quite how far out on a limb he'd gone.

We stuck to our plans and set off the next morning into a cold and wet Wales, trudging the damp hills and finding a chilly welcome in pubs that fell silent as we English strangers walked in. At a bleak and deserted crossroads on the third day we saw a red telephone box and decided to ring the shop to see if all was well.

"D's gone completely crazy," Robin said. "He's run off with the cheque book. You'd better come home".

We postponed our honeymoon and went back. D. had reappeared with the cheque book but his behaviour had become more and more erratic. He stalked the house day and night, jumping out from behind doors, shouting and doing kung fu kicks. One night he burst into our bedroom, switched on the light, yanked the light fitting out of the ceiling, turned abruptly on his heel and strode out again. We didn't know that he had a history of bipolar disorder, didn't even know what it was, and we were out of our depth.

He was spouting so much gibberish that we stopped listening. There was one phrase, though, "oinkers in the bushes", that he kept repeating, though we had no idea what it meant.

Early one morning, when we were still asleep, the doorbell rang. I opened it blearily to find a gang of drug squad officers on the doorstep. Flashing ID, they swiftly spread out and searched the house – thoroughly and successfully. I had long stopped using any drugs but the others hadn't and they found weed and hash and cannabis plants in most of the rooms.

Later that day, as I was in the garden, our next-door neighbour called me over to the fence. She was sorry about the raid, she said, but she had warned us. The police had asked to use one of her upstairs rooms to watch the house. She couldn't refuse, but she had told D. Then it clicked. The oinkers (pigs/police) were hidden in the bushes. He'd done his best.

The police laid charges. Two of the household fled back to America and another got away with a warning. D. was sectioned to a mental hospital after attacking a policeman in the street in London and didn't have to appear in court, so all the weight fell on me. My name was on the lease and everything that happened in the house was my legal responsibility. I was facing nine charges and at worst looking at several years in prison.

I had to meet with a probation officer who would submit a report on me to the magistrate before the case came to court. I struck lucky. My very English probation officer was a committed follower of Mazdaznan, a Zoroastrian religion which believed the Earth should be restored to a communal garden where all could converse with God. He was a vegetarian and practised breathing and 'glandular' exercises and he really took to me. *Nature's Foods* had just been published and when I gave him a copy, he was beside himself. He believed me when I told him I was pure in heart and lung, though I had to let him down gently when he tried to convert me. I did agree to try out one of his exercises though. He had me sitting on a table, crossing and uncrossing my legs rhythmically, and turning my head from side to side while reciting a nursery rhyme.

When the case came up, his report was so glowing that the magistrate let me off with suspended sentences on all counts.

When the lease on our little shop expired, we had to move on. We found an old fish and chip shop nearby and, like Hercules in the Aegean stables, set about cleaning it of decades of grime. One of the challenges we continually faced was never having enough money to employ people to do the jobs we knew nothing about. That meant we had to learn them ourselves, and right now that meant building, carpentry, shelf-building, decorating, plumbing, rewiring and more. It was an education that has stood me in good stead throughout my life.

A couple of years after we opened, we started to notice a striking new customer. She'd blow into the shop on a whirlwind. Big hair, big sunglasses, big skirt, and a floppy sack of a handbag, shedding flurries of paper and make-up. She was always in urgent need of things like aduki beans or oatmeal as she'd sold clean out of her home-made face-packs.

Who was this crazy woman? She'd set up between two funeral parlours in Kensington Gardens, a cobbled pedestrian street directly opposite Infinity, abandoned by the tide as first the 1950s and then the 60s passed it by. It had a London East End market feel to it and the threadbare businesses were just getting by on low rents and meagre takings. Rose's Ladies Outfitters with its fading post-war coats and dresses on wobbly mannequins; the discount wallpaper shop, window posters forever announcing "Silly Sale, Closing Down, Everything Must Go"; and now this - some kind of cosmetics shop, orange box shelves held together on a shoestring, pots full of vegetable detritus.

I remember standing with Robin, young and cocky entrepreneurs that we were, wisely predicting that she'd be out of business in a couple of months. Then she disappeared, gone and forgotten as our own business grew at measured pace, takings and reputation rising steadily year on year.

But then we started seeing Anita Roddick's face on hoardings and in newspapers. The Body Shop was no longer just a shop but a franchise, with branches in New York, Boston and Montreal. I went to take a look at the one in the high street and found shrink-wrapped baskets of foot scrub and exfoliates, smelling of popsicles, coloured like spangles, and selling like hot cakes.

Many years later, just one of the old traders remained in Kensington Gardens, still selling rolls of remaindered cotton, silk and satin. I went in to buy something garish and silvery to make a samba outfit and we started talking about how long he'd been there and about the old days.

"Do you remember that woman, Anita Roddick," I asked. "How she opened up her first shop just opposite you and how she seemed the woman least likely to succeed".

"Sure" he said, and he told me that she came to see him one day and asked to borrow some money to open a second store. She'd been round all the local shops and no-one had been willing to lend her anything. She'd finally taken four thousand pounds from Ian McGlinn, a friend of a friend, for 22 per cent of the business. The story goes that she wrote to her husband who was crossing Patagonia on a horse but the letter took too long to arrive, as did his reply, "Whatever you do, don't do that". McGlinn eventually sold his share for 146 million pounds.

Within a few years, Kensington Gardens had become the heart of Brighton's hip North Laine community – full of small, alternative businesses, grandfathered by the presence of Infinity Foods.

When the timber shop next door came up for rent in 1976, we took it on and transformed it into a bakery. Beneath the decades of old lumber in the basement we found it riddled with dry rot – the worst kind. Through one of the hottest summers of the century I was down in the depths, hacking the walls back to bare brick and the floor to earth, then searing every inch with a paraffin powered flame thrower before dressing in wellington boots, a boiler suit, mask and helmet and coating the ceiling and walls with black, sticky and foul-smelling Synthaprufe. Six months later we were finished.

The proud bakery building team (Nick, Peter, S., Eddie, Dave)

During my abortive year as a student at Sussex University, I lived in a guest house in Brighton's Kemptown and walked past The Pie Shop every day, nearly always stopping to buy a blisteringly hot apple pie. Inspired by this memory, we named ourselves Infinity Foods Bakery and Pie Shop. Guided by our baker, S. who'd learned his trade in prison, we bought a second-hand stone-floored oven, a dough mixer, a proving oven and a couple of pie machines. We developed recipes for a range of breads and pies (red bean and onion - with just enough tamari soy sauce and wakame seaweed to add umami savour - was a surprising hit) and opened with a flourish.

Barely a week later there was a 6am knock at the bakery door and I opened it to the now familiar sight of a gang of drug squad officers. Within seconds they'd arrested S. and whisked him away, and that was the last we saw of him.

I'd done small-scale baking before and had worked alongside S. for the few days we'd been open. Now I was chief baker and I loved it. I'd get up at five in the morning and walk through the silent streets – empty but for the occasional milkman - to the warm bakery. By the time the first Infinity workers turned up, I felt like I'd done most of a day's work, though I carried on through till the shop closed in the evening. [see short story *A Simple Man* in part two]

Overall I was proud of the way I was handling this unexpected turn of events, of stepping into S's shoes, and especially proud of remembering that I had to carefully weigh out one and two pounds of dough for small and large loaves - aware that selling underweight bread was one of Britain's oldest crimes. Unfortunately, I was summonsed to court for exactly that. I'd missed the point that dough loses weight in the oven as the water steams out. In front of the magistrate I did what I've often done in such circumstances and pleaded rank stupidity and ignorance. I escaped with a small fine and a warning, instead of the ancient punishment of being paraded through the streets and pelted with refuse.

In its small magazine section, Infinity Foods sold *Brighton Voice*, an alternative newspaper set up "in opposition to state power, locally and nationally". A local Conservative MP wrote to every newsagent in town advising them not to sell it because the collective which published it included "a number of left-wing extremists" responsible for "churning out deliberate lies and political filth".

In fact, the true political filth were the local fascists who took exception to the Voice exposing them, and waged a war of intimidation against the few shops which sold it. Public House Bookshop was firebombed twice, had its windows broken seven times, and its owner Richard Cupidi was assaulted inside the shop. We arrived at Infinity one morning to find a ball bearing had been fired through the plate glass window leaving a neat hole, and a 'friendly warning' popped through the letter box.

"Because Brighton Voice is a Communist front paper, shops which sell it have had their windows broken and other troubles. It is advisable therefore not to sell Brighton Voice in your [heavily underlined] shop." It was signed 11th Hour Brigade – an obscure fascist group. We had a meeting, agreed to carry on selling the Voice, and asked Paul Bonnett of Solstice Bookshop – also threatened – to teach us karate. In a room above the shop, we punched and kicked, fantasising destroying the fascists.

By now Infinity had grown. Not only had we taken over next door for the bakery, but we were renting a ramshackle, mostly wooden warehouse behind the two shops. We used it for storage and workshops that we rented out to friends.

A couple of weeks after we received the letter, when the shop was closed for the Christmas holidays, the warehouse burnt down. Arson was suspected but never proved.

A Friendly Warning.

Because "Brighton Voice" is a Communist front paper, Shops which sell it have had their windows broken and other troubles (Solstice Simple Supplies, Public House bookshop) It is advisable, therefore, not t sell "Brighton Voice" in your shop.

11th Hour Brigade.

A few days previously, Robin and I had stood in the shop trying to decide whether to renew the insurance on the building. The premium was expensive and we were short of money. We chewed it over for a long time and finally – but only just - came down on the side of renewal. That insurance money not only covered the thousands of pounds worth of food that was destroyed, but paid for rebuilding and turning the space into the Brighton Natural Health Centre charity.

The inspiration for the centre came from our original vision of 'healthy individuals, healthy communities and a healthy planet'. Diet was key and Infinity Foods served that need, but so were other practices that could help build health and physical and mental wellbeing – things that were rare then but normal now, such as yoga, tai chi, meditation and more. The Centre met that need (it was Robin who put in the hard work setting up the charity) and is approaching its 40th birthday as I write, assuming it can survive COVID lockdowns.

While our fire was never confirmed as arson, when the nearby Hanover Chapel was burnt down because it hosted the leftist Resource Centre in its basement, there was no doubt. But in another example of phoenixes rising from the ashes, it was rebuilt into the wonderful Brighthelm Community

Centre. Thus did the fascists contribute to the health and happiness of Brighton.

Infinity Foods mid-1970s (me in centre)

As the business grew, with an ever busier shop and a thriving bakery, so did the number of workers, and the harmonious and free-going mood of the early days started to dissipate. One reason was our slapdash attitude to taking on new people. We didn't interview anybody, and being a friend, or a friend of a friend, of someone who was already working there was sufficient qualification.

That's the way cliques develop – sub-groups that are more loyal to each other than they are to a shared vision. And the shared vision itself was becoming frayed. We had been idealistic about the transformative power of food, agriculture and healthy lifestyles. That had lent us a fierce dedication with an austere edge. It took us by surprise now that others had a more hedonistic approach that involved smoking copious amounts of cannabis, sleeping late, coming in to work when it suited them or not at all, playing loud reggae in the shop all day long (it took me years before I could listen to

Bob Marley again) and reacting to any suggestion that this wasn't really what Infinity Foods was really about as jackboot coercion.

Everyone – however long they had worked there – still took the same pay and decisions were communal but that didn't stop a widening 'us and them' split – compounded by the fact that three of us (Robin, Jenny and myself) technically owned the business.

Our meetings started to be both endless and toxic and I wasn't smart enough to realise that what appeared to be arguments about policy and decision making were more often about personal relationship. We caused each other a lot of unhappiness all round and in the end we three partners decided that if the workers didn't believe that at heart the business was a co-operative, we'd better make it formal.

In 1979 we founded Infinity Foods Co-Operative (I was already practising as an acupuncturist and Jenny had recently become a mother so Robin did all the heavy lifting again) and have over the business to it. One of the features of this kind of co-op is that nobody owns it, not even its members. Should they ever make the decision to shut down, all the assets would have to be donated to another co-operative with similar aims.

Infinity Foods is approaching its 50th birthday. It provides ethical and reasonably well-paid employment to around 130 people. The retail shop in the centre of Brighton is now embedded in the city's culture. It provides a vast range of natural foods, has the finest organically-grown fruit and vegetables in town - wherever possible bought from local producers - and all through the day, breads and other baked goods are wheeled into the shop from its in-house bakery. A little out of town, the Infinity warehouse ships products all over the UK and it's no longer a surprise to wander into some tiny village grocery and find Infinity Foods own products on the shelves.

I had a memorable experience many years ago. I went to London to hear Gary Snyder and Wendell Berry read their poems at the Barbican. I'd been a fan of Snyder ever since I encountered him as Japhy Ryder in Jack Kerouac's books, but Wendell Berry was a revelation. Wikipedia describes him as a novelist, poet, essayist, environmental activist, cultural critic and farmer, and he's a Christian into the bargain.

He introduced one of his poems by talking about the Sabbath, when he ventures beyond the boundaries of his farm and into the woods. For six days a week his eye is attuned to tasks that need performing – a fence post to be repaired, the hay to be brought in, a field to plough. And as he enters the untamed world of nature, he can't at first let go, noting an untidy pile of fallen branches or an untamed patch of briar. But slowly the workaday world slips from his shoulders and he can allow himself simply to be.

It was like this for years after I left Infinity. Whenever I went through the door, I'd see an unfilled shelf, a drooping notice, an unattended till, and start fretting. Now I can go in, do my shopping, and forget that this shop was once the passion that consumed my life.

Infinity Foods now

From Nature's Foods (illustration Karen Betteridge)

9. AFGHANISTAN & INDIA

On March 3rd 1974, Flight 981, a McDonnell Douglas DC-10 incoming from Istanbul crashed into the Ermenonville Forest outside Paris, killing all 346 people on board - the deadliest plane crash in aviation history. One week later Jenny and I sat on a McDonnell Douglas DC-10 at Paris airport, waiting to take off for Istanbul. As we taxied to the runway we saw the ground staff crossing themselves.

We had a friend – Hugh – who'd disappeared then reappeared many months later with the very best of traveller's tales. He'd bought a horse and a gun and trekked across the deserts and mountains of Afghanistan. We had a honeymoon due to us and decided to follow in his horse's footsteps. Our planning was erratic. I tried to copy my father who, whenever he travelled somewhere new, always learnt some of the language. I bought a hardback notebook with thick, creamy, unruled paper and started writing down Farsi words and phrases, drawing maps and making notes on customs and diet. However, it never occurred to me to try sitting on a horse.

We took trains and buses across the width of Turkey, the long straight road swept by icy winds coming off white-capped mountains. In one freezing hotel we bought firewood and rented a tin-can stove that plugged into the room's chimney. We sat by it long into the night, drinking pot after pot of Turkish red tea from long, small glasses.

Close to the Iranian border, we spent a filthy night in Agri. First the sewage system failed in our Russian-style hotel and the floor of the cement block toilets floated in a sea of urine and faeces. Next, as vegetarians, we hunted in vain for something to eat – driving on, heads down, through the empty streets as the wind pierced our thin hippie clothes. In the only open restaurant we ordered soup and bread. As we sat waiting, I heard a hacking sound coming from the kitchen and peered in to see the cook squatting on the muddy, bloody floor, chopping bits off a sheep head and throwing them into the soup pot. We left hungry and took to our hotel bed. How much more endurable things are, though, when you have a friend to cuddle up to.

We passed through the Turkish border the next day and moved on through Iran – every day another bus. In Tehran, we talked to young lads with baby moustaches who complained bitterly about their lives and how they could never meet girls. They burned with sexual frustration.

In Mashhad we arrived during the frenzied peak of Ashura, a ten-day mourning for Husayn ibn Ali ibn Abi Talib, martyred in 680CE. Gangs of men, dressed all in black, with holes cut out of the chest, shoulders or back of their shirts, marched by silently – whipping themselves bloody with chains. As we watched, the atmosphere grew tense and we were warned to leave.

The Afghani border post was like a set from The Good, the Bad and the Ugly, with no sign of life apart from swirling dust and a couple of dogs stretched out in the shade of the customs hut. Eventually a guard appeared, yawning and hitching his trousers up to his fat belly, and stamped our passports. Then we waited for hours until the mail van came by and we rocked around on stuffed mail sacks in the back as it took us into Herat.

That night I strolled down the main street, passing stalls piled high with pyramids of oranges and dates and lit by hissing paraffin lamps, pools of light strung along the dark road like jewels. I heard the clip-clop of a horse and there, appearing out of the darkness, riding down the middle of the dusty street like the leader of a guerrilla army, came a turbaned rider dressed all in white, carrying a rifle, two bandoliers strapped across his proud chest, a knife at his waist, his snowy-white horse hung with embroidery and tinkling bells.

In the Southern city of Kandahar we befriended Abbas who claimed to be a prince from Mazar-i-Sharif. It was easy to believe as he held himself with dignity and easy command. We sat in the flowering garden of our lodging house, watered by cooling irrigation channels as Abbas rolled us a joint of Afghani hash. I'd not smoked for years and it was so strong I could barely stand. When, at last, we could move we went for a walk out of town. Along the roadside, gutters ran with streams that all kinds of filth had been thrown into and in which vegetable sellers stood their lettuces to keep them fresh.

We were by now used to passing women dressed in head-to-toe burqas, their eyes barely visible behind a mesh screen, and it was a relief to come across an encampment of nomadic Kuchi people, the unveiled women decked in golden jewellery.

But as we watched them from a distance, something changed. For years I'd loved to travel and see new things but suddenly I realised that I'd had my fill. I no longer wanted to just be a pair of eyes, an outsider spying on other people's colourful lives. From now on, when I travelled, it would be to learn something - and later to teach.

It wasn't long before the opportunity arose. In Kabul we began to lose confidence in our planned journey. Whenever we turned down a side street we'd see someone wagging a warning finger then drawing it slowly across their throat. Then we heard that four young French travellers had had their throats cut in a hotel in Kabul the week before.

I was already feeling unmanned and out of my depth in this land of guns, knives and male honour and it was hard to know if we were being threatened or warned. The ever-present air of menace began to tell. So when we met a traveller who'd been studying in McLeod Ganj – home of the Dalai Lama in Northern India – and he told us it was just a few days away by train, we decided we were too soft for this confusing country, reset our compass and headed for the gentler world of Tibetan Buddhism.

We took an ancient, groaning bus through the Khyber Pass and into Pakistan. Looking down from terrifying hairpin bends, we saw women far below slapping and beating clothes on the river bank amidst a sea of blossoming almond trees. And in a last goodbye to the Wild West we reached Darra, where every corner shop sold guns and half the guns were AK-47s.

McLeod Ganj, two thousand metres up in the Dhauladhar range of the lesser Himalayas, was a single street village with one hotel, a few shops and a couple of restaurants. A little way above the village is the Old Palace, so-called because it was where the Dalai Lama first lived after fleeing from Tibet. We rented a simple room there, bought a cooker, a couple of cheap pots and some basic foods – shrunken red beans, cracked lentils full of dust and stones, broken rice, flour, and a few vegetables. This high up in the foothills, food was expensive and of meagre quality and for some basics like cooking oil we had to apply for a ration card. I lost so much weight in the three months we were there that I looked like a famine victim, and when we hit Delhi three days before our flight home I did nothing but eat, drink mango milkshakes and shelter from the vicious pre-monsoon heat.

A good half hour's walk down the mountainside (everything here was up or down) is the Tibetan Library. We signed on to study the Lam Rim – a three month course in basic Buddhism with a Tibetan flavour. We walked there every morning after breakfast and sat in front of our teacher, Geshe Ngawang Darjay, solid and plump in his maroon and saffron robes, as a young monk interpreted and we took notes. The early part of the Lam Rim is designed to evoke in the student a passionate commitment to escape the wheel of birth and death.

For the first week we meditated on the inevitability of death so that we truly understood the fragility of human life. We visualised death sitting on our shoulder, ready to strike at any moment. When we had fully grasped this, we moved on to the reality of death, visualising our own corpse rotting in the grave. That was a grim few days. Then we spent a week meditating on the rarity of being born into a precious human body. The Lam Rim compares it to a blind turtle swimming in an ocean that covers the whole earth and on which a circle of rope floats with the currents. Once every hundred years the turtle rises to take a breath and the chance of its head passing through the rope is the same as the chance of being reborn as a human.

There are six realms in the Buddhist Wheel of Life – human, animal, hungry ghost, hell, demigod and god. Only the human realm offers the right balance of suffering and intelligence to provide both the motivation and the tools to escape the wheel whose turning is fed by ignorance, hatred and delusion.

While some Buddhists interpret reincarnation into these different realms literally, for others it describes the emotional and psychological states we churn through, sometimes from moment to moment. The animal realm is characterised by ignorance and driven by naked instinct. The hungry ghosts are consumed by need and greed - insatiable hungers and thirsts that can never be satisfied. The hell realm is one of intense suffering, and most of us will pass through it at some time in our lives. The demigods are forever at war; they are powerful and wealthy but burn with jealousy of the gods who have more than them. In the heavenly realm the gods enjoy every pleasure, but though their delights seem endless, they are, like everything else, conditioned and impermanent, and eventually they are sucked back down into one of the lower realms. There is no permanent happiness or satisfaction to be found in the turning of the Wheel of Life. Only when we are able to move beyond states that depend on external conditions, the Buddhists teach, can we step outside the wheel and be free.

Towards the end of our study, we formally took refuge in the three jewels of Buddhism – Buddha, Dharma (teachings) and Sangha (community) - and were given Buddhist names.

At the library and in McLeod Ganj we were surrounded by Tibetans, many of them monks. We turned prayer wheels amidst clouds of incense smoke, drank yak butter tea, watched the monks clapping their hands in theological debate, and heard the belly and chest vibrating roar of the twelve-foot long dungchen horns echoing through the valley.

After spending the morning studying, we'd climb back up to the village, where we'd stop for lunch – vegetarian noodles or momo dumplings - or climb further to the Old Palace and cook a simple meal of rice and dhal.

Most of us – travellers and locals alike – got ill at one time or another. In my case it was mild dysentery and I went to the Tibetan medicine doctor to get treatment. We'd watched her from afar as she taught her students the art of urine diagnosis, holding glass vials of pee up to the sun and discussing its colour, clarity and smell.

In my case, she simply asked a few questions, took my pulse and prescribed three days of medicine – large round balls of foul-tasting compressed herbs that I had to chew twice a day. The fourth day I was better.

One afternoon, two young New Zealanders appeared at the Old Palace. Andy had been suffering from dysentery for weeks but they'd decided to keep going without resting up, keen to get to McLeod Ganj. He was in a bad way, thin, weak and passing blood and mucus. We told his friend Peter to call the Tibetan doctor. She promised to come up from the village to see him that afternoon but she never showed. I went down the next day and asked her again, but again she didn't appear. We bought some antibiotics and glucose and tried to feed them to him but he kept getting worse. On the third day we went round the travellers staying in the Old Palace and raised enough money to hire a jeep to take him twenty miles down the mountain to the hospital in Kangra. Peter and I laid him onto a stretcher in the back of the jeep and a terrible journey began. The road was potholed and he was mercilessly thrown around. He stank and whenever we stopped, clouds of flies descended on him in seconds.

For reasons we didn't understand, the jeep couldn't drop us directly at the hospital and we had to carry him uphill through the bazaar on the stretcher. Though he'd lost a mass of weight and his angular bones stuck out, he was tall and heavy. I was weak and I struggled. Every twenty metres or so we had to lay him on the ground to rest, and now not only the flies but a swarm of curious, silent onlookers crowded round. The relief of finally handing him over to the staff in the cool, clean American-funded hospital was overwhelming. I left him tucked up in crisp white sheets and, satisfied, began the long winding journey back up the mountainside. The next day I bumped into a weeping Peter in McLeod Ganj. Andy had died just an hour after we left him. He is buried in the church of St. John in Dharamsala.

After a few weeks in McLeod Ganj, we were offered the rare opportunity of an audience with the Dalai Lama. I'd seen the long queues of Tibetans, many bedraggled and filthy from long pilgrimages, who passed reverently in front of him. Some had followed the Tibetan tradition of prostration - stretch out full length on the ground, stand and step forward to where the tips of the fingers reached and repeat endlessly over enormous distances. They offered their kata – a white cotton scarf bought for the occasion – and he would bless it and hang it round their neck. It took maybe twenty seconds before they were urged on. We expected the same treatment.

But the small group of us, all foreigners studying at the Tibetan library, was ushered into an audience room. Then we heard the slap of sandals on the stone floor and this muscular, beaming, earthy man walked in and talked with us for over an hour. His main message was that whatever religion (or none) you held, the most important things were kindness, considerateness, unselfishness and being a good human being. He laughed a lot, answered everything we asked without a trace of otherworldliness, laughed some more, and then we were shaking his hand and leaving. I was dazzled and inspired and walked on air for days. I don't believe he is the reincarnation of the previous Dalai Lama, and I'm not sure he does either. What I think I saw was someone who was thrust into an almost impossible situation as a child and who, through his Buddhist education and practice and his own authentic personality, grew and grew into it until he became what I would call a true person.

As the 4th century BCE Chinese *Guanzi* says, "The complete mind cannot stay hidden in the body. Rather, it takes shape and appears on the outside. It can be known from the complexion of the face. When people meet someone whose appearance and mind are full of positive energy, they will feel happier than if they had met their own brother ... His words without words will sound better and further than the vibrations of an eight-sided drum. When the complete mind appears on the outside, it shines brighter than the sun, and people recognize such a person easier than their own children."

When Jenny and I flew back to the UK, we were committed to continuing the Buddhist life.

10. BUDDHISM

Ever since I was a teenager I'd been lured by the 'mysterious East' with its tales of reincarnation, karma, enlightenment, mountain hermits, yogic esotericism and magic powers.

Then, when I was 20 and living in London, I stumbled across the Friends of the Western Buddhist Order (FWBO) founded by Sangharakshita – a quietly charismatic, austere and very precisely spoken English monk – on his return from many years in India. Known as Bhante (Venerable Sir), he taught meditation and Buddhist philosophy classes in a basement in Monmouth Street, London.

Though my first class was a nightmare of knee pain and a frenetically unquiet mind, I fell for Bhante's teaching. I was also mightily impressed by his work in India, collaborating with Bhimram Ambedkar to convert the Dalits (Untouchables) to Buddhism and thus, at a stroke, allowing them to step out of the bitter and oppressive Hindu caste system within which they were the lowest of the low and subject to endless humiliation.

When Bhante invited me to visit him in his house in West Hampstead, I was pleased, flattered and uncertain. We talked, he cooked me a meal and I felt cared for. When it turned out that he expected me to sleep in his bed, I wasn't really surprised, any more than I was when he initiated a sexual encounter. I'd never slept with a man before, nor have I since, but in those days I was open to most of what came my way.

Not long after, he invited me to stay with him in a country cottage he'd rented, but when I got there I discovered that I'd been supplanted in his affections by another young lad. I was surprised, but the feeling quickly passed, in fact my strongest memory of that weekend was Bhante's cat which he fed on oat flakes, peas and Ovaltine powder. He was very proud of this carnivore-to-vegetarian conversion, quite unaware that the cat spent every waking minute stalking the garden, chomping on mice and voles.

I drifted away from Buddhism soon after, until the overland trip to India Jenny and I made a few years later. When we returned to the UK we wanted to carry on our Buddhist practice and as there was a branch of the FWBO in Brighton where we lived, it seemed natural to join the community.

I meditated every day, went on retreats and was well on the path to lay ordination when rebellion stirred in my soul and I quit. I'd tried so very hard to carve myself into a kind and compassionate person, constantly battling and trying to transform the anger, frustration, unkindness and other 'unskilful' emotions that welled up inside me. That and sitting in devotional pujas, desperately trying to squeeze out feelings of reverence for various Buddhas and Bodhisattvas. I was exhausted by the effort.

With relief, I left Buddhism behind and almost immediately discovered Gestalt therapy. Its understanding that true change occurs when we fully allow and explore our feelings – whatever they are - was a great liberation. I know that Buddhist teachings encourage us to observe the rise and fall of emotions without becoming attached, but that may not be the same thing as really feeling them in all their bloody intensity.

A final reason to leave the FWBO was its disapproval of couples, especially heterosexual ones. Jenny and I were committed to each other and we began to feel our relationship was unwelcome.

I am a committed humanist and – the semi-religious devotional aspect apart – that is what first attracted me to non-theistic Buddhism. I have reflected, though, on the different approaches to suffering in Buddhism and Christianity. It is really quite extraordinary that the central figure of Christianity is the son of God, tortured and nailed to the cross in agony, a man with a loving and then mourning mother who becomes a religious icon in her own right. This roots the story deep in the rich and messy human experience of family, love and grief and – in the best of Christianity at least – a heartfelt and generous response to individual human suffering. In Buddhism, by contrast, all suffering is rationalised as being caused by ignorance, greed and hatred, and the individual's experience of it, its unique shape, colour and taste, seems of no great importance. Of course compassion is a central tenet of Buddhist philosophy but it feels to me like a more detached and impersonal response.

As the years passed, I found myself increasingly drawn to Daoism, especially the early Daoism of the *Daodejing* and *Nei Ye.* The Daoists were great observers of life, fascinated by nature and free of the limiting beliefs that led religion to deny the evidence of its own eyes and seek to destroy those who refused to do so. The late and great Sinologist Joseph Needham attributed the extraordinary advancements of early Chinese science, astronomy, mechanics and medicine to this clear seeing. Observed reality is dismissed as illusion in Buddhism and a fascination with it is a hindrance to the task of dwelling in the unconditioned. Yet while a pregnant emptiness (Dao) lies at the heart of Daoism, so do the 'ten thousand things' (i.e. all phenomena) that endlessly spring forth from the Dao. This allows us to experience the emptiness beneath manifestation while loving the manifestations in all their beauty and variety. As the *Daodejing* says (Gia Fu-Feng and Jane English version):

> The nameless is the beginning of heaven and earth.
> The named is the mother of ten thousand things.
> Ever desireless, one can see the mystery.
> Ever desiring, one can see the manifestations

So what of my sexual experience with Sangharakshita? I value it as an experience that did me no harm. When I entered a prolonged period of therapy and turned over every stone deep in my psyche in search of the pains and traumas that might crawl out from beneath them, I discovered plenty – and many surprising ones. But of this event there was no trace. To me, aged 21, it was an interesting but unexceptional experience, though it was not so for everyone. Years later I met an ex-member of the FWBO - one of 'Bhante's boys' - who had struggled with suicidal impulses ever since. Sangharakshita died in 2018 and his Wikipedia page has a section on his sexual misconduct, an indelible stain on his legacy.

I also value the experience for the insight it gave me into the sexual power of the teacher/guru. Where the student is confident, has ego-strength and enters into such a relationship willingly and with awareness, there may be no great harm. Both parties get what they want. The guru gets sex, usually with a younger partner, and the feeling of vital power that goes with it, while the student gets the perks of being singled out in the eyes of the teacher and their peers.

However I think it rarely happens this way. Most students who get sucked into such affairs are vulnerable and suffer as a result, and many gurus use their power – sexual or otherwise – abusively, causing long-term damage.

It has been my good and bad luck to experience or witness from a distance a variety of gurus and masters over the years and I have a real distaste for how most of them operate. They included the Maharishi Mahesh Yogi (John Lennon's *Sexy Sadie*), Guru Maharaji, Bhagwan Shree Rajneesh, various qigong teachers and of course Sangharakshita.

It left me profoundly allergic to the guru game, a feeling only deepened by the recent steady drip of tales of the sexual shenanigans of famous Buddhist and yoga teachers. It's exactly the same psychology that allows priests and other powerful individuals to get away with sexual abuse, and enables politicians to lie through their teeth and speak nonsense while their followers hold them up as founts of wisdom. It seems to me that many of us are terrified of self-determination and carry an empty space inside, just waiting to invite a religion, a belief, a guru or a master to lodge in it and make us feel whole. [see short story *Callie and the Guru* in part two]

It's also a curse for most gurus who, because of their own vulnerability, social ineptness and stunted emotional intelligence, create a world where they stand alone at the top of their little hill and have no peers to tell them when they're talking rubbish, nobody to bring them down a peg or two, nobody to help them laugh at themselves, nobody to relieve the loneliness of their elevated status.

I have learned untold amounts from many teachers but I have no illusion that they are other than variously flawed humans. The ones I respect most are open about that, never allowing their students to put them on a pedestal and remaining sincere and authentic throughout.

11. CHANGE OF CAREER AND ILLNESS

After we got back from India I returned to working at Infinity Foods but my heart was no longer in it. I'd relished co-creating the shop, with its ever-rolling excitements and challenges, but I didn't want to be a shopkeeper for the rest of my life.

Also, I wasn't feeling great and it seemed that for the second time in my life travelling had made me ill.

For years I'd been bursting with energy, able to work from early morning till late at night. Before leaving for India we'd been living in a tiny caravan a few miles outside Brighton. It sat on the edge of an old market garden – a third of a UK acre – that we'd been granted use of by the owners of the stately home it was attached to. Robin had restored it as a vegetable plot to supply the shop but he was away on his own travels now, and I took on the horticulturist role. I knew nothing about it but I read every book I could get my hands on.

I started work soon after dawn – sowing, planting, hoeing, harvesting - and only put my tools away when night fell. In the evenings we would read books by candlelight – mine on vegetable growing and Jenny's on herbal medicine, and as I lay down to sleep I was already impatient for the morning. The sun always seemed to shine and it was one of the happiest summers of my life.

But now I was exhausted by mid-afternoon. On days when I wasn't working, I'd collapse into bed after lunch and sink into a long, heavy, stuporous sleep. I'd lost a lot of weight in India and had a mild attack of dysentery but that didn't seem to account for how I was feeling. Several days of tests at London's Hospital for Tropical Diseases couldn't find anything wrong with me either.

The reassurance that I wasn't dying cheered me up for a while, but then my condition began to worsen. I was feeling tired all the time, fuzzy-headed, achy, dispirited. I'd lost my libido and my joie de vivre; my get up and go had got up and gone and I was depressed. I tried everything I knew to fight it, practising yoga and meditation for up to two hours a day, and eating as carefully as possible. I let go of a lot of my responsibilities at Infinity Foods and set myself to undemanding work in the packing room – filling bags of brown rice, muesli, beans, lentils, nuts and seeds ready for the shelves.

At the same time I was going through a crisis of uncertainty about my future, with no idea what to do next· This went on for several months. We were now living in a flint-walled cottage next to the vegetable garden and on days off, after my morning yoga and meditation, I'd take long walks through the woods and onto the Downs* – trying to pace myself back into clarity and strength, but I only ended up exhausting myself.

Then one morning I had an epiphany. It was suddenly so obvious - I would become an acupuncturist! From macrobiotics, I'd learned a little shiatsu – traditional Japanese massage based on the channels and points of acupuncture. That, combined with a long-standing fascination with Far Eastern traditions, had led me to this point and I was again filled with the fire of certainty and purpose. I was inspired by the thought that I could help heal people with nothing more than a handful of acupuncture needles, as well as teach them some of the dietary and lifestyle changes that I had been working with for years.

In 1975 acupuncture was barely a profession in the UK. There was one practitioner in Brighton and – serendipitously – a three-year course had recently started up in East Grinstead, twenty miles from my home. I went for an interview and was accepted.

Like many 'wounded healers', especially in the field of complementary medicine, one of the driving forces behind my decision was the need to solve my own health problems. Just as when I had hepatitis and turned to a

---

* The South Downs are a range of rolling chalk and flint hills that extend along the South-East coast of England. They are dotted with hill forts and ancient burial mounds. I wrote this poem after a mid-Winter walk.

Downs, Winter

Northern light, tin-grey, bright.
Cold wind burns, earth turns.

Bushes bow To fields of stone.
We harvest crops of flint and bones.

Briefest day, then dark returns.
Life of men, earth turns.

macrobiotic diet after realising that Western medicine had nothing to offer, I now hoped that Chinese medicine would help me through this new challenge.

East Grinstead was a centre for all kinds of wackiness. The Scientologists had their HQ there and the town hosted centres for the controversial Opus Dei, the Rosicrucian Order, a Mormon temple, a Rudolph Steiner school and a clutch of dowsers and druids.

I was keen to study again, happy to start something new, and hopeful that somehow – maybe by osmosis – I would get through the illness that seemed determined to pull me down. But studying acupuncture proved to be more difficult and challenging than I expected.

There were only four books in English and the long tail of the Cultural Revolution meant that China was still firmly closed. As the proverb says, 'In the country of the blind, the one-eyed man is king', and the principals of the three colleges then in the UK, with only a smattering of knowledge between them, were now presenting themselves as experts. As my time at college passed, however, I began to realise that the front they put up masked their ignorance. I wonder if any of them ever said the honest words, "I don't know".

It was only in my third year that the first solid information from China became available in English and I rapidly fell in love with the clinical, theoretical and philosophical beauty of the medicine. I was also fortunate in having one wonderful teacher in my final year of college. As the years passed, Giovanni Maciocia became my friend and colleague. He led the seminal trip to China I joined in 1981 and together we taught a post-graduate course on our return. We also organised the first ever (1984) visit of Chinese medicine doctors to teach in the the UK, and when he died in 2019, I helped plan a memorial gathering (https://www.youtube.com/watch?v=iJiSFc5hCEw) for him, struggling to speak when it came to saying how I felt about our friendship, how grateful I was to him, and how I missed him.

It was a reflection of the infancy of the profession that I began to teach first year students as soon as I qualified. I was happy to do it though. I was was on a mission to help them dodge some of the energy sapping confusions and contradictions of my own education.

At the same time, I started to practise acupuncture – both from my house and at the college clinic. However, I felt desperately under-qualified and clinically unsure of myself, and this was compounded by the absence of any meaningful supervision or mentoring.

In these early days (and even today), most Western practitioners benefitted from the fact that acupuncture is very forgiving. It has a powerful enhanced placebo effect which means that many patients will improve, whatever the skills of the practitioner. After all, how often does a stranger ask you intimate details for up to an hour – questions that even your mother never asked, look fascinatedly at your tongue, go into a seeming trance as they take your pulse, then engage in a mysterious ritual of needling and herb burning? We also know now that piercing the body triggers a host of physiological reactions, including endorphin production and parasympathetic stimulation, almost irrespective of where the needle is inserted. I'm not suggesting that superior skill doesn't produce better outcomes, far from it, but simply that most acupuncture will help most people to some degree and sometimes trigger extraordinary changes.

I'd only been working in the college clinic for a few weeks when a new patient came in. She was in a bad way – depressed, exhausted, overweight and generally unhappy with her life. I didn't have a clue what to do and however much I believed in the power of acupuncture, I doubted that a few needles could make much difference, especially in my inexperienced hands. I chose a simple and safe treatment, using only four needles (Neigian P-6 and Zusanli ST-36), and she left.

The East Grinstead college was ruled by a Dutchman called Dick van Buren. One of his strange habits was to only treat patients once every six weeks, something I think he must have picked up from homoeopathy since it was never part of any acupuncture tradition I've ever heard of (when I was in China, treatment was given daily or every other day, and even in the UK, weekly was the norm). So it was weeks later when I looked at my list and saw, with a sinking heart, that this woman was my eleven o'clock patient. When she came into the treatment room I had a moment of confusion - this was definitely not the woman I'd treated weeks before. But before I could say anything she was advancing on me with an adoring look in her eyes, both hands held out to clasp mine.

"I don't know what you did to me," she said, "but you've changed my life".

Since I'd last seen her, she'd left her husband, lost 14 pounds in weight, bought a new wardrobe and been chosen as her party's candidate in the local elections. All of this, she was convinced, was due to my treatment.

Most acupuncturists are familiar with outcomes like this. We can't pretend to know exactly what has happened but it's unwise to take pride in the result, in part because it means we have to take similar responsibility when patients fail to improve or get worse.

It wasn't until I went to study in China in 1981 that I started to feel any real confidence in what I was doing and it had been touch and go whether I'd ever get that far as I nearly fell at the first hurdle.

Van Buren had passed several of his chronic 'sink' patients on to me – ones who'd been coming to him for years without making any real progress. Most of them passively accepted the change, but one woman was furious. Conditioned by his fawning clinic managers, his patients had been led to believe that he possessed almost magical powers - despite the fact that they often didn't seem to be working on them. In the case of this woman, being demoted to a mere beginner like me was deeply insulting.

It was just before my fourth ever session at the clinic that I was told Van Buren 'wanted to see me in his office' (what intimidating words of power those are).

"What's this I hear about you making making all your patients worse?" he said.

These were dreadful words. They froze my heart and shattered my already fragile self-confidence. I could barely speak but managed to squeeze out something like "What do you mean", while inside I was thinking that this was the end and that I had no future as an acupuncturist.

He had a pile of my case notes on his desk and picked up the top one. "Mrs ... he said."

"I know about her," I managed to say. "She's furious that you stopped treating her. I'm not surprised she's complained."

He just grunted.

I didn't want to hear any more. I was totally demoralised and on the point of leaving, perhaps abandoning acupuncture for good, but with my last shreds of bravado I asked, "Who else do you have there?"

He looked at the next case sheet.

"Mr ...."

"But last time I saw him he seemed happy enough with my treatment".

He grunted again, and, gaining confidence I asked, "Who else?"

He started flipping through the notes and that was when I realised that he hadn't read any of them, and that – as I'd believed – the patients I'd treated were contented enough. The fact was that I despised him and he probably knew it, since I didn't idolise him like most of the other students and staff. This was his way of punishing me.

My initial disillusion had come in my first year. My father needed prostate surgery but the consultant was unsure if it was safe because of a pre-existing heart condition. Still believing in the wonder-working powers of Van Buren whom I'd only met once at my interview, I set out to persuade my father – a sceptic – to come for an appointment and an opinion on whether acupuncture could help his prostate. He finally and reluctantly agreed, probably to please me as much as anything else. I met him on arrival, but as a first-year student wasn't allowed into the treatment room and waited outside. He emerged half an hour later, white-faced with anger.

"What happened," I asked?

"He didn't speak to me once", he said. "He didn't even ask why I was there but started talking to his students about the colour of my knees. He put some needles in and left the room, came back after a bit and took them out without saying a word, turned his back on me and was halfway out of the door when I reminded him I'd come for an opinion about my prostate. He just said, 'eat less cheese' and shut the door on me."

I was mortified. I knew my father's sense of pride and how insulted he was. I also knew he never ate cheese.

I hung on working at the college – treating patients and teaching - for the rest of the academic year. I felt a strong loyalty to my students and tried to convey to them my excitement at discovering a Chinese medicine that wasn't just mystical obfuscation (Van Buren's stock response to any question about his endless contradictions was, "Ah well, it's not easy of course but when you know as much as me ... "). However when I came in on the morning of my students' end of year exam to find that he'd replaced the paper I'd carefully prepared with one of his own, one that bypassed everything I'd been teaching them for a year, I walked out. I vowed never again to set foot in that dark and gloomy building, seemingly impenetrable to sunlight (a resolution I kept for nearly forty years), and that I would never, ever, work for anybody else in my life.

Don Juan, the Yaqui sorcerer, tells Carlos Castaneda (in *The Teachings of Don Juan*) about the inspirational power that comes from having a powerful enemy. It's true. For many years I was driven to learn and study as much as possible in order to be as little like van Buren as possible and to strive to become everything that he wasn't.

Finally, however, I owe him a debt of gratitude. Unlike his colleague Jack Worsley who had set up one of the other colleges and who offered his students an all-embracing version of acupuncture that didn't allow them to read any books on Chinese medicine, Van Buren was a magpie. He had no respect for other people's work and would absorb anything he came across into college handbooks that he then copyrighted. That meant that his students were exposed to a mass of information that seemed to trigger a passionate desire in some of them to make sense of it all. The result was that several eventually became leaders in the field.

It was in recognition of the challenge of studying acupuncture that I founded *The Journal of Chinese Medicine* in 1979. I'd qualified as an acupuncturist the year before, but it took several months to build a practice and I had a lot of free time. During my years at Infinity Foods, I'd got used to translating ideas into action, so I appealed to friends and colleagues to write articles and put the first few issues together in my bedroom – laboriously typing them out, correcting my numerous mistakes with Tippex and getting a designer friend to create titles with Letraset (stick-on letters). It was a thrill and a relief to buy one of the first (very expensive) electric typewriters with a tiny screen where you could check the last few words you'd written before OK'ing them. Not too long after that (what excitement!) I bought an Atari personal computer with word processing software.

For many years we counted our subscribers in the low hundreds and the journal barely broke even. But the numbers slowly increased, the range of our authors expanded to include the world-wide Chinese medicine community, and the JCM is now the longest-lasting (40+ years) and most reputed journal in the field.

When I wearied of editing articles, I was supremely lucky to find a replacement editor (and good friend) in Danny Maxwell. And just this year – halfway through lockdown – I passed on the business to people who I believe will carry it forward with a new influx of ideas and energy.

When I returned from China, early in 1982, Brighton's *Evening Argus* gave my trip a centre spread. It was rare in those days for anyone to visit China, let alone to study, let alone to study acupuncture. And in my first experience of the power of the media, within hours of publication my phone started ringing and didn't stop for months. I quickly adapted my clinic room into a Chinese-style multibed, with three curtained-off couches. I employed a nurse assistant (she was also an acupuncture student) to keep an eye on patients, take the needles out and make appointments. In that way I could treat up to twenty patients a day.

The more I practised, the more I enjoyed it. Chinese medicine responds to the patient as an individual rather than a disease. It concerns itself with a much wider range of possible symptoms than modern medicine and that means we often have to ask patients a good deal about themselves in order to understand their disorder, what might have contributed to it and how to treat it. And the more patients we see, not only do our treatments become more precisely tailored and effective, but our understanding of human life grows.

I'd brought a vigorous style of needling back from China with me, having been astounded by the results it achieved, and it didn't go down well with some of my more fragile British clients. Most Chinese patients I'd been treating – many of them labourers and peasants - were tough and stoic, since daily life demanded more resilience than in the UK. People were often cold, ate simply, performed hard physical labour (women as well as men), walked or cycled long distances daily, used advanced wrestling techniques to get on crowded buses, and endured pain in a way we had largely forgotten. For example, I saw teeth extracted in the street without anaesthetic, while back home it was normal to numb the gum to reduce even the discomfort of the injection. It took me a while to learn that I had to adapt to the different physiques and emotional vulnerabilities of my patients.

I treated up to eighty patients a week for a couple of years, building valuable clinical experience – one of the most precious treasures in any kind of medicine. Then I began to ease off as the demands of teaching, editing a journal and spending time with my family competed with the demands of the clinic.

As for my illness, it continued for about eighteen months after I returned from India and then went into remission, but it has never completely disappeared. I had periods when all of my previous energy came back (for example when I managed the building of Infinity Foods bakery during the summer of my second year at acupuncture college), but the disease still lurked deep inside and resurfaced to different degrees again and again - as it does to the present day.

Two people gave me valuable advice. The first was Michio Kushi – a macrobiotic teacher and inheritor of George Ohsawa's mantle (the founder of macrobiotics). I must admit I lost my respect for his dietary wisdom after an embarrassing seminar when he tried to persuade the audience that a young man's long nose came from eating too many cucumbers (in fact he hated them). However at an earlier seminar I approached him for advice. I'd barely started to explain what ailed me when he simply said "more exercise" and dismissed me. As the years passed I realised how right he was and how profoundly important appropriate exercise is for building strength and health*.

The second was Dr. John Shen (https://peterdeadman.co.uk/uncategorized/dr-john-shen/) – the smartest doctor I've ever met. He just asked a couple of questions and felt my wrist pulses.

"Nerves too tight", he said in his unique take on the English language. "Before, always working, working, working with tight nerves. Get too tired inside."

I learnt a lot from that, though it took me a while to absorb the lesson. I held a picture of myself as someone who could work flat out whenever I was enthused by a project, and if my energy dipped and I was forced to stop, I couldn't wait to get back to my customary hundred per cent and tire myself out again.

The downside of my belief in responsibility for my own health was that for many years I felt that if I was ill, it must be my fault – that I was or wasn't doing something necessary to get well. The upside was that I was powerfully motivated to take care of my diet, practise qigong (see Chapter 18) assiduously and learn to manage my energy even while doing my best to enjoy life as fully as possible.

It was only a couple of years ago that I finally had a series of blood tests at a German clinic and they came back positive for both acute and chronic Lyme disease. It seems likely I'd picked it up in India in the 1970s, in the foothills of the Himalayas.

For people with chronic fatigue, exercise may have to be mild or very mild – even just breathing practice - but like most things, a commitment to regular practice will reap rewards. And more generally, finding the right exercise for each individual is really important – something I discuss in my book *Live Well Live Long: Teachings from the Chinese Nourishment of Life Tradition*

12. CHINA

It was December 1981, and though the temperature outside was -5°C, the stove in the heart of the large, bright clinic room threw out welcome waves of heat. This was in honour of our status as foreign students, and without us there would have been no heating. Nanjing lies on the South bank of the Yangtse river and was therefore 'officially' warm, and subject to tight coal rations.

We had no such luck though in restaurants, theatres or the Medical University. We sat in unheated classrooms with the windows inexplicably thrown open. Like every Chinese person, we soon learned to dress in fat layers of clothing topped with padded army greatcoats. Even so, it was only the ten minutes of table tennis every tea break that kept my blood moving.

In the clinic, a kettle simmered on the stove, and in a side chamber two large sweet potatoes were slowly baking. Dr. Xiao would ceremoniously thrust them into our hands – still hot – as Vivienne and I left at the end of morning clinic.

Dr. Xiao (left), nurse Mei, Tao and Vivienne

We always began the day seated around the table, drinking tea and chatting. There was Dr. Xiao, our teacher, broad-faced, energetic and excited by the novelty of having foreigners to teach and show his skills off to. Next to him, Dr. Lin, short and fierce, was quick to defend Dr. Xiao if she ever thought we were disrespectful – which usually meant asking too many questions. Dr. Lin had been forced to retire as a surgeon after developing a tremor, and now specialised in ear acupuncture. Xiao Tao, our boyish, bespectacled interpreter, soon became a friend. He bridled at being called Xiao (little), especially as his best friend and fellow interpreter – just a few months older – was Lao (old) Jin. Tao clearly thought he deserved the honour of an upgrade, and one morning appealed to Drs Xiao and Lin and Nurse Mei. They looked him up and down for a long time, carefully measuring and weighing him, then shook their heads.

"Not ready yet", they said, though to his embarrassed pleasure I started calling him Lao Tao away from the clinic. Mei rarely spoke to us but when she chatted with the doctors I saw no trace of hierarchy or status, a quality that seemed to pervade the whole hospital.

And finally there was myself and Vivienne, my fellow student.

One of the many privileges we had as foreigners was access to the Friendship Store - forbidden to ordinary Chinese - where we could buy all kinds of luxuries. One day I bought a tin of Peach Blossom Tea, the most expensive one on the shelves, and took it into the clinic. The reaction was extraordinary. Everyone had a story about this famous tea. Dr. Lin's auntie had once tasted it in a teahouse in Shanghai; Mei's father had told her about it with the wistful hope that one day she would be lucky enough to savour it. Dr. Xiao explained that the tea bushes were planted in-between rows of peach trees and that the tender tips of the tea leaves were picked only when the peaches came into blossom, so that the tea was infused with the most delicate flavour. When it was ready and we raised our cups to first smell and then taste it, there was a reverential silence.

The next day, and every day afterwards until the tin was empty, we sat and drank peach blossom tea before our patients arrived, and every day the same conversation was repeated. The same stories were told and enjoyed and the same instructional lecture given by Dr Xiao - prolonging the pleasure and squeezing every last drop of enjoyment out of it.

Another purchase I made at the Friendship Store was a beautifully packed box of dried Longyan fruits. They are highly prized in China and ascribed the ability to nourish blood and refresh and calm the spirit. I had asked Tao about the best gift to make to one of our lecturers. I assumed she would appreciate chocolates or flowers, but Tao said definitely not and that Longyan was the correct and most traditional gift. And as he said it, I realised that Chinese people hardly ever ate sweets of any kind.

Within an hour, the five beds lined up along the clinic walls were full, and several patients waited their turn to see the doctor. On one couch, a worker had rolled up his two pairs of trousers and two pairs of long underwear to reveal a winter-pale leg, and the nurse was fixing a big slice of moxa stick to one of the needles I'd inserted*. She lit it and the comforting smell of the burning herb filled the room. On another couch a woman lay, the needles in her belly twitching in time to the pulse from an electroacupuncture machine. On the couch closest to the stove, an elderly woman was receiving treatment to restore movement to her stroke-paralysed limbs, while patients with migraine headaches, period pain and sciatica had already come and gone.

When it was her turn, the next patient was called to the consultation desk. Dr. Xiao asked precise, targeted questions and took a long look at her tongue. Then she rested each wrist in turn on a small blue cotton cushion with the name of the hospital printed in faded red characters. We fell silent as Dr Xiao spent an age gently pressing her pulses, as though playing a fine musical instrument, then asked us to feel them ourselves and tell him what we found. Finally, he sat back, gathered himself, and spoke.

"This disease is sinusitis, not frontal headache. The patient has suffered from it for seven years since catching cold. It is made worse when she drinks alcohol or eats too much greasy food. Also when she gets upset. The pattern is phlegm-heat in the Stomach channel. Now what points should we needle?"

Moxa is made from dried artemisia vulgaris herb and is used to warm acupuncture points or larger regions of the body. There are various ways of using it. The loose dried herb might be fashioned into small cones which are placed on acupuncture points, lit, and removed when they start to burn the skin. Or larger cones can be used and burnt on top of slices of ginger, aconite cakes, or salt (for example filling the navel with salt and burning large cones of moxa on top so that the salt radiates its heat deep into the abdomen). Moxa is also tightly rolled into cigar-shaped sticks, sometimes mixed with additional herbs, and these can be used to warm larger areas such as the lower abdomen or back. For this patient, a fat slice of moxa stick was pierced and placed over the needle. It would take around ten minutes to burn down, during which time the heat would be conveyed deep into the acupuncture point through the needle.

Then - as always - he gave advice. "No more rich food. And you must stay calm; worry achieves nothing. But it's OK, we can help you. Just come regularly for a while and you will get better."

"That's right, you listen to the doctor and do what he says," shouted one of the waiting patients, drawn up as close to the table as possible to hear every word. "That's what the doctor told me and now my piles are almost gone."

After the first few weeks I was trusted to needle some of the patients. At the beginning, Dr. Xiao was confused. "You know a lot of Chinese medicine theory," he said. "Very good! But you know nothing about needling."

It was true. I had watched in astonishment as he plunged needles into acupuncture points – far deeper than anything I had ever seen in my three years of training in England. Sometimes – as he pushed a needle two centimetres below the eyeball into the socket, or beneath the ear lobe so far into the head I feared he would spear the brain, he reminded me of one of those circus performers who used to lock his assistant into a box and pierce it from all sides with long swords. And unsurprisingly, the patients felt it, sometimes shouting out with the intensity of the sensation. At the beginning though, when I needled them, they complained loudly that they couldn't feel anything and these foreigners had no idea what they were doing. The treatment may sound brutal, but it was a revelation to me how powerful acupuncture could be, as patients – often with severe and intractable disorders – got better in front of my eyes.

The morning we first drank the peach blossom tea, I was treating a fourteen year old girl with crippling asthma, brought to Nanjing by her parents from the far reaches of Jiangsu province. Because they could only stay in town for a fortnight, we treated her every day. I had given her regular acupuncture and was just finishing injecting a solution made from human placenta into acupuncture points on her back when the clinic door burst open and a young man staggered in. On his back was his brother whom he'd just carried up three flights of stairs (the hospital had no elevator). Dressed in filthy olive green work clothes, this tough-looking peasant was clutching his right ribs and groaning in pain.

After asking the brother a few questions, Dr. Xiao didn't hesitate in his diagnosis – biliary ascariasis (worms in the bile duct). This normally rare disorder was common among peasant farmers and was passed on by eating raw vegetables from fields fertilised with human manure – one of the secrets of

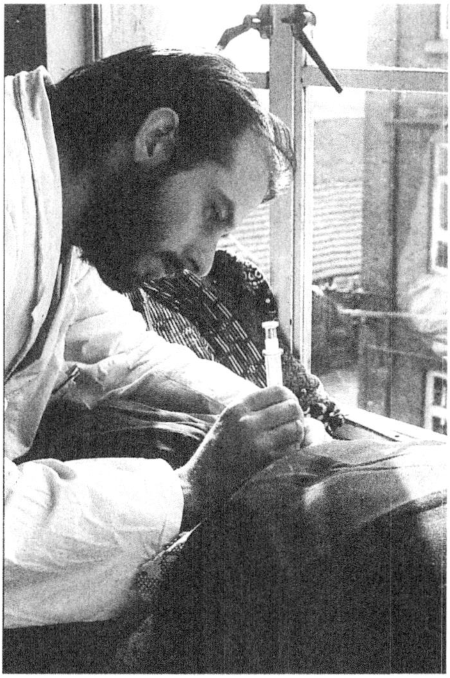

China's millennia-long history of sustainable agriculture. When the worms travel from the gall bladder along the biliary duct it causes a pain just like gallstones, which some say is the worst the human body can suffer. This man had been in agony for thirty six hours, his brother said. He hadn't slept in all that time, just cried out day and night.

Dr. Xiao took an acupuncture needle and inserted it next to the patient's nose, pushed it through the flesh towards a point below the eye, and started twirling it vigorously.

"This is an empirical treatment," he said. "The needle sensation has to be stronger than the pain."

True to his words the patient stopped holding his ribs and started pointing at his face in astonishment. Thirty seconds later, he was snoring.

Just as with treatment for gallstones, acupuncture can relieve spasm in the bile duct almost immediately and relieve the terrible pain. The hospital I was working in had gone further, pioneering acupuncture treatment (daily for ten days) to eliminate gallstones, and we had been proudly shown a display case full of hundreds of dishes of expelled stones of varying sizes. For worms, though, once the pain had been relieved, the patient would be sent to the herbal medicine department.

A few days later a woman shuffled into the clinic, bent over with her arms shielding her chest. She worked in the market and had been lifting a two hundred pound basket of vegetables when her colleague suddenly let go of the other side. She'd sprained the muscles in her chest so badly she could barely move and had to be treated sitting up. Dr. Xiao selected the point called Inner Gate on both wrists (a point well known for preventing travel sickness and with a powerful influence on the chest) and needled right through the forearm, between the bones, towards the point Outer Gate on the opposite side (because the pain radiated from the chest to the back), until he could feel the tip of the needle just below the skin. After ten minutes of twirling the needles, he removed them and asked her to move her arms. With a growing expression of disbelief she did so, first gingerly, then wildly - copying Dr Xiao as he jumped up and down excitedly waving his arms around. But as he leapt, his spectacles fell from his breast pocket and crunched beneath his feet when he landed, and though it wasn't enough to deflate his joy at her magical recovery, I felt a real pang of sadness.

I knew how Dr. Xiao – indeed how most Chinese people – lived. He owned a couple of suits, a fountain pen, maybe a spare pair of spectacles, a bed, some basic furniture, a TV, cooking pots, a few books and a bicycle - and that was it. It was poverty, but apart from the Party apparatchiks who might as well be living in the clouds, so different were their lives, it looked to me to be an equally shared poverty.

Almost the first thing I did when I arrived in Nanjing was to buy a Flying Pigeon – a heavy, gearless bicycle. It was said there were four and a half million of them in Nanjing at the time, and the first morning I set off to ride to the hospital I stood waiting for a gap in the endless, swirling river of bikes. It was rush hour and I was there for nearly ten minutes before I understood no gap would appear, so – taking my life in my hands – I closed my eyes and rode straight into the flood, which parted to envelop me. This was Daoist free flow in action, I thought, but the gory pictures of dead cyclists, crushed by lorries, or by the few cars on the road, and posted as warnings on street corners, brought me back to earth. A bicycle was a big purchase for the average Chinese person. From that very first day when interpreter Tao took me to the bike shop, he made me promise that when I left I would sell it to him for what we both understood would be a very good price. I loved riding everywhere in the city, and if anything needed fixing – tyres pumped, brakes tweaked – there was a bike repair man squatting on the pavement every hundred metres or so.

I'd flown into China in December 1981 with a group of fellow acupuncturists to attend The First International Course on Further Studies in Acupuncture and Moxibustion (the Chinese love long and grand names). I was thirty-three years old and a seasoned traveller. I'd journeyed overland to India and hitched my way across North Africa, but I'd never experienced a culture shock so deep as during my first days in Nanjing. Sitting on the bus from the airport, watching the thousands of blue or green clad cyclists thronging the streets, I realised I couldn't see a single shop. It took a few days for my eyes to adjust to the muted colours of the stores and absence of advertising. And when, after several weeks, we went to see a Chinese opera version of Wu Cheng'en's famous 16th century novel *Monkey (Journey to the West)*, the brilliant colours of the silk costumes were almost blinding.

Throughout my three and a half months in China I felt like a sponge, soaking up every scrap of knowledge in the clinic and University. I'd already been in acupuncture practice for three years and had a thousand questions. It was the same out walking the streets, watching intently, trying to understand, and photographing the endlessly fascinating life around me. I spoke barely a word of Mandarin and had to mime everything I needed. On my next visit in 1992 there was no lack of people happy to help and to practise their English, but in 1981 the fear still lingering from the Cultural Revolution meant that nobody would dare speak to me in the street.

It was also a hard time. For the first week I felt like I'd landed on another – greyer and much colder - planet. I had left behind my wife Jenny and two young daughters and I missed them with a pain that grew by the day. Phone calls were almost impossible (I only managed one during my whole stay) and letters slow. One day in clinic we were treating a young child. It was at the peak of my home sickness and I began to weep. The doctors looked at me with astonishment and Tao had to explain that I missed my children. Even then their faces betrayed incomprehension. It was normal in these times for many Chinese, including doctors, to be sent to work in far regions of China, leaving their families behind – sometimes for years – apart from a few short days during Chinese New Year when most of the population returned to their homes.

When the opportunity arose to make this trip to China, I knew I had to seize the moment. I recognised that it was the springboard for my future career in Chinese medicine*. But leaving my family was incredibly hard. Natasha was just six months and Susie three – old enough to understand and to miss me. In the days before I left, I recorded hours of bedtime stories, and in China I managed to record and send a couple of tapes full of news and reminders of my love. And it was tough on my wife, managing two young children alone, especially during what was called The Big Snow – one of the coldest Decembers ever recorded in the UK. I had read quite a few of Carlos Castaneda's books (how much fact and how much fiction is blurry) about his training with a Mexican Yaqui sorcerer. Don Juan told Carlos that in our closest relationships, we are connected to each other by invisible fibres. When we part, these fibres stretch and cause us pain. This is exactly what I felt as the weeks passed. The fibres connecting me to my family were being pulled taut and I could feel it in my belly. One day, about halfway through the three and a half months, it got so bad I just stayed in bed, in the grip of feelings I had no control over. Then, suddenly, it felt as though the fibres snapped and I was free. I still missed my family and yearned to see them, but it was no longer painful and I could truly enjoy the time I had left on this precious adventure.

On crisp mornings, soon after dawn, I joined the tai chi and qigong practitioners in the frost-sparkling park to do my practice. I was happy to rise early as there was nothing to do in the evenings. By eight or nine pm the city was dead, the streets empty, and there was barely a single restaurant open.

One evening a group of us went to view the famous Yangtze River Bridge. It was a longer walk than we expected and by the time we headed back it was cold, dark and raining. We realised we'd missed our hotel supper and looked, in vain, for somewhere to eat. Then we found a tiny restaurant, still open. It was icy cold inside and the floor was littered with chicken bones and gobbets of phlegm (at that time people spat anywhere and everywhere). The only dish they could offer us was sweet and sour fish. I was dreading it, having sampled the British high street version – drenched in a bright orange

---

* There is a tide in the affairs of men, which, taken at the flood, leads on to fortune; Omitted, all the voyage of their life is bound in shallows and in miseries." *William Shakespeare, Julius Caesar.*

sauce flavoured with harsh vinegar and sugar. What was worse, a seemingly endless amount of time passed with no sign of our food. We were all miserable – sitting in wet clothes, hungry, unable to get warm, barely speaking to each other. Then, at last, the kitchen doors opened and the chef came out with one of the largest whole, cooked fish I'd ever seen. It had been baked so perfectly that its sweet and sour coating had caramelised the skin into a crisp delight and when we cracked it open the flesh beneath was tender and sweet. With great bowls of steaming rice and flash-fried vegetables, it was one of the best meals of my life.

The fourteen of us did find comfort in each other, but it wasn't always plain sailing. For example, there was a small contingent of Italian Marxists who were the quickest to respond when we were asked if we wanted to take Christmas Day as a holiday.

"We don't believe in Christmas", they pronounced - and that was that.

In the end we only worked in the morning and gathered in the cavernous restaurant of our Soviet style hotel for Christmas lunch. There had been extended negotiations with the kitchen. It was a feast, we said, and we wanted roast chickens (they had no turkeys), roast potatoes and boiled carrots.

"Potatoes?", they asked. "For a feast? And boiled carrots?".

"Yes, carrots", we said. "And potatoes – they're our rice. And we have these special puddings we brought all the way from England.".

Carrots were a treat as vegetables were incredibly scarce, apart from the ubiquitous Chinese cabbage. Open-topped trucks carried them in from the countryside every morning and piled them up on street corners. They hung everywhere, drying, from balconies, power lines and telephone cables.

Anyway, we waited and waited and waited, and drank and drank and drank (we were introduced to a deadly Italian drinking game). Then, emerging from the kitchen, three waiters appeared in single file, ceremoniously carrying the Christmas puddings (it's a British thing). They'd been boiled dry and their plastic wrappings had melted into them."

No," we said. "Pudding last! As agreed!"

There was another long wait, then things looked up when they appeared with four fat golden-brown chickens. We were so hungry, even the platters of boiled (not roast) potatoes and boiled carrots looked good. But under their tempting skin, the chickens were half raw. The kitchen had been too embarrassed to admit they didn't have an oven, and they'd tried to fry them whole.

We did have one chance to enjoy a proper Chinese banquet. All the foreign students (mostly African and Asian) in Nanjing had been invited and were spread around a vast hall – the seating carefully planned, with six Chinese and six foreigners sitting alternately round the circular tables. Our Chinese hosts replenished our three glasses (beer, wine and mao tai white spirit) whenever we took a sip, and piled food into our bowls with their chopsticks as soon as there was the tiniest space. Then the top dignitary at our table rose - at which point we all rose too – and proposed a toast to international cooperation and friendship between our countries. This was followed by a whispered discussion among the foreigners, and one of us was prodded to stand and return the favour. A few minutes later, the number two Chinese dignitary at the table rose and was responded to by another one of us. With twelve toasts per table, the evening began to take on a hysterical quality, but any relief that it was over was short-lived as the Number One Chinese Dignitary at the feast started working the room. As he approached each table we bobbed up like jack-in-the boxes for another toast. Soon, this carefully structured arrangement started to break down. I needed a break and went for a wander holding a glass and discovered that any time I got near one of the other tables, everyone would immediately stand up. Soon, we were all at it. Then, suddenly, without a moment's warning, presumably at a secret sign, every single Chinese person in the room got up and staggered off home. No after dinner stories, jokes or confessions – it was as though a balloon had burst and we were stranded with nothing to do but crawl home ourselves.

Several years later, I was invited to dinner at the Savoy Hotel in London to meet a couple of high-up Chinese medicine officials. It was another heavy eating and drinking occasion and we three British acupuncturists present were determined to make the most of it. By the time we reached the dessert we were very merry, and Julian Scott decided to tell a story that we all knew and loved. It was a slow process as every sentence had to be translated into Chinese. When he got to the meaty part of the story (we knew what was coming) we started to laugh and by the punchline were falling off our chairs. But throughout – from the first word to the last – the grim expression on the faces of the Chinese guests didn't change a whit.

To listen to the story, and understand how surprising that was, here is my retelling of it: Attack of the Killer Moxa https://www.youtube.com/watch?v=UkGAWkzXnI4

I came back from China inspired and burning with the desire to share what I had learned. With three friends who had been in China with me (soon to be labelled the Gang of Four*), I started teaching a post-graduate course in the UK for students who had completed their acupuncture education - an education that from our new perspective had more holes than substance. We held our first planning meeting over an elegant English tea in Fortnum & Mason's in London, and given the success of the course which ran for several years, I adopted the habit of launching all new ventures in similar style. Within a couple of years, I was teaching all over Europe, and after *A Manual of Acupuncture*, the textbook I co-authored came out, the invitations widened to take in North America and Australia. For many years, I fulfilled the resolution I'd made on the edge of Kandahar, to bring meaning to travelling by studying or teaching.

Just over a decade after my first visit I went back to Nanjing, this time on my own. I'd qualified in the UK as a Chinese medicine herbalist and relished the opportunity of working in the internal medicine and gynaecology departments. As a favour, I'd helped out with editing *Chinese Acupuncture and Moxibustion* - the latest English language textbook published in China - and the College had offered me free tuition as a reward. When I walked out of Nanjing airport I saw two things – a camera crew filming my arrival and two Chinese men approaching me with widespread arms and smiles of delight on their faces. As I was clasped in a double embrace, two thoughts went through my mind. First, Chinese don't hug. Second, I know I helped with a couple of chapters of the book, but a film crew? Really? Then one of the huggers said, "Please go back into the airport and come out for a second take. We are filming a typical greeting for foreign students who come to Nanjing," which was one of the least believable things I ever heard in China.

This time Nanjing had changed. Restaurants were opening by the day to a cacophony of firecrackers, people were dressed in colourful clothes, and

---

* Maybe an unfortunate name. The Gang of Four were four leading Communist Party officials who rose to power during the Cultural Revolution but were later imprisoned for treasonous crimes. Our gang of four was made up of Giovanni Maciocia who led the group to China, Julian Scott, Vivienne Brown — my fellow student at the hospital, and myself.

best of all, they wanted to talk. There were still countless bikes, but now the car lanes were beginning to fill up.

Once again, I soaked up the precious information I was receiving every day in the clinic. And I lived like a king – China still being incredibly cheap for Westerners. I could afford powerful tuina massages whenever I wanted, I ate fabulously, and my teacher, a professor in the internal medicine department, was happy to come to my room in the evenings to give me private lectures for just a few dollars.

My spell in the gynaecology department helped me develop a small speciality in my clinic back home. Chinese herbal medicine can be really helpful in treating gynaecological disorders and infertility. One of its many strengths is that it fills a major gap in orthodox medicine by helping to regulate the menstrual cycle, for example if it's too early, too late, too heavy, light or painful etc. In Chinese medicine this is understood to be essential both for women's wellbeing and to help treat and prevent other gynaecological disorders and infertility. As a reflection of my commitment to this branch of medicine, I co-edited and published T*he Essential Guide to Acupuncture in Pregnancy & Childbirth in 2006,* and *Female Infertility & Reproductive Gynaecology: A Comprehensive Clinical Manual of Integrated Chinese Medicine and Biomedicine* in 2020. However, I slowly began to realise that although I had attended numerous post-graduate seminars and worked in the gynaecology department of a large Chinese hospital, I'd never once been taught anything about male disorders. When asked why I liked treating women, I used to joke that it was a relief to treat diseases I knew I wasn't going to get, but now I started to tune in to how many men were, often silently, suffering with disorders such as chronic pelvic pain, infertility, enlarged prostates, erectile dysfunction and more. And that these disorders were largely ignored by my Chinese medicine colleagues and often downplayed by men's doctors.

My experience of sitting in a men's circle at a qigong camp cemented my feelings of affection towards men, and my awareness of how much hidden suffering we endure. That was my motivation to explore the treatment of male diseases by Chinese medicine and I began to write and lecture on them whenever I could. It also led me to write a rather graphic story. [see short story *Spunk* in part two]

I practised Chinese medicine for about twenty-five years, then made the difficult decision to stop. I yearned to be a free agent again – untied to a diary that determined where I had to be at any given part of the day. I was also suffering from compassion fatigue. I had been drawn to Chinese medicine through a love of its philosophy, its theories and its time-tested practices, but strangely – all the time I was at acupuncture school – I never quite realised that I would be spending my days alone in a room with suffering patients who needed my help. I am reminded of my daughter who went to all the childbirth classes and read all the books, but said that she hadn't really grasped - until the moment she held her son in her arms - that she was actually going to have a baby.

It's not that I didn't enjoy caring for people, more that it increasingly became an effort. And I was beginning to be pulled in different directions. One was my late-blossoming music career. Rough and rowdy late nights don't lend themselves easily to the demands of practice. The other was a return to my original inspiration – as far back as Infinity Foods – which was to offer people the knowledge and tools to take care of their own health. I became more and more committed to my practice of qigong, began to teach it, and started lecturing on *yangsheng* (the traditional Chinese wisdom on how to live a long and healthy life). That eventually led to the writing of *Live Well Live Long: Teachings from the Chinese Nourishment of Life Tradition.*

A Manual of Acupuncture

In 1990, I was approached by a publisher (Churchill Livingstone) who wanted to commission a book on the acupuncture points to add to their list. I turned them down on the grounds that there were already too many on the market. But then a colleague (Julian Scott) pointed out that this was simply a sign of how in demand they were, and I began to think about producing something radically different. I knew I couldn't do this on my own, both because of the daunting size of the task and because I didn't read Chinese, so I invited two friends, Tim Martin and Mazin Al-Khafaji, to join me. Between us, a vision began to take shape.

One of our first decisions was to publish the book ourselves, in order to have control of the creative process. Tim dropped out early and Mazin and I worked on harmoniously. We expected to be finished in around eighteen months but in the end it took eight years. Mazin already spoke and read Mandarin but he had to teach himself enough classical Chinese to translate from a wide range of ancient texts.

Acupuncture is a relatively new practice in the West and most practitioners don't read Chinese. In the absence of authentic source material, a host of unrooted ideas about the tradition had flourished and we wanted to lay down some solid foundations.

Our task was to study, sort, rationalise and interpret, and then to write commentaries based on our research. As this was going on, I started working with another colleague, Kevin Baker (surgeon, general practitioner and acupuncturist), on the locations and illustrations of the points, consulting every available text and drawing heavily on Kevin's anatomical expertise. For the illustrations, there was a particular style I was drawn to, and I spent many hours in bookshops leafing through medical books until one day I found the artist I was looking for.

We commissioned fifty meticulous core drawings and over the next three years I taught myself to use Adobe Illustrator, Photoshop and InDesign to transform these drawings into the hundreds of precise illustrations we needed (one or more for every acupuncture point).

I felt in my heart that we were creating something special and wanted every aspect of the book to meet the same high standard. I asked another friend, John Chippendale, to advise on typography. He was a strict taskmaster, rapping my knuckles whenever I wanted to put in anything unnecessary ("What purpose is that semi-colon supposed to serve?" he'd demand). I also had to learn the arcane language of the printing trade and source the right paper, card, binding, endpapers, ribbons and more.

Throughout one long hot summer I sat with a young friend, Jake Stephens, laying out the pages. Our aim was to make the book as user-friendly as possible. For example we might spend hours adjusting text and layout to ensure an illustration and its accompanying description ended up on the same page.

I know that much of this design work isn't consciously noticed by most readers, but I believe that the deep affection the book is held in is due, in part, to this subtle care.

Of course a project like this had its challenges. Progress was agonisingly slow since it depended on the three of us finding matching spaces in our busy week to work together. We also foundered halfway through when we realised that much of the translation work had to be repeated, since many of the nuances of Chinese medical terminology had been skated over the first time. That added another year or two.

In the final year, though, I was no longer dependent on anyone else's avail-

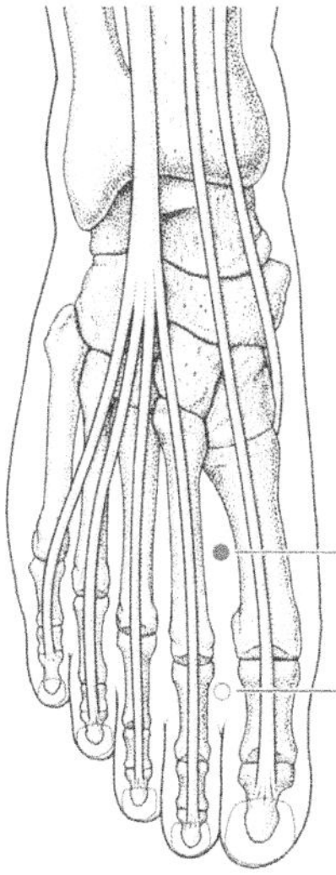

ability and I stopped all my clinic work and set to putting the book together. I became consumed by the need to finish it - increasingly fearful that I would somehow repeat my grandfather's failure to complete his vast five language encyclopaedia of law before he died. I also heard through the grapevine that some unnamed person in America was working on a similar book and that added to the pressure. I might have put in a twelve hour day, then wake in the night and realise that because of the time difference our unknown competitor was working on it right now, and I'd get up and take to my desk again. It turned out to be fake news, by the way.

During my years of acupuncture practice, I treated a number of patients in the throes of writing PhDs and I saw the mental and physical struggles they went through after years of mostly lonely work. One day, during that final year, I was struck with chest pains - severe enough to go to hospital. One of the great things about heart symptoms is that they rush you straight through, VIP style, instead of leaving you in the waiting room for hours.

We Brits love and esteem our National Health Service, for all its faults, and they did a great job of checking me over (and finding nothing wrong, apart from 'stress'). I did bridle, though, when the doctor kept asking my wife Jenny things like, "does he smoke" as I lay there, fully compos mentis. It was enough to give me a heart attack.

Anyway, everything comes to an end and the day finally came when I was able to cradle a copy of this precious book in my arms.

A Manual of Acupuncture has been the main acupuncture point text for students and practitioners for over twenty years, has been translated into several languages and published on a variety of digital platforms (thanks to Tom Kennedy), as well as in its original, door-stopping 675-page book form.

Norway

Over the years I taught all over the world, but one place I kept going back to was Norway.

Ever since my time in Israel as a four-year old, I'd yearned for sun, blue skies and warm seas and whenever I travelled for pleasure, I turned my back to the cold North. Then I was invited to teach in Oslo and over the next thirty years spent more than six months of my life there in four-day lecturing stints.

At first, going to Oslo felt like being dragged back to the 1950s. Restaurants served plain fish and potato or meat and potato meals, there were no late night corner shops and there was barely a black face to be seen.

As the years passed, however, I slowly fell in love with the country and made many friends. I presented one seminar in fjord country on the West coast near Alesund. From the small fishing village we could look up to high cliffs where waterfalls poured in ceaseless cascades onto the land far below. In Norway's poorest days, people had scraped a living on minute patches of soil on the sides of these cliffs, sometimes having to tether their children to the hut to stop them falling off.

One day we walked up to the flower-strewn summer pastures high above the village and had a Norwegian picnic. There were just four ingredients – a large leg of cured ham, a crate of beer, crisp flatbreads and a very sharp hunting knife. Another day we sat and ate our way through wooden barrels full of fresh crabs and shrimp.

I also taught in Tromso, North of the Arctic Circle, on Midsummer's Day. Of course I'd heard of the midnight sun but I'd not grasped its reality until the first evening I was there. A group of us had a dinner party on the broad balcony of an apartment overlooking the sea as the sun slowly set. Everything I'd ever experienced told me what would happen next. The sun would slip into the sea, the sky would darken, the air would cool and we'd move inside. Instead, time seemed to stop. The sun remained above the horizon as it slowly crossed the sky, and hour after we continued to bask in the warm sunshine. It felt like a party held in heaven. At three in the morning there were water-skiers and sun bathers in the bay beneath us and when I finally left at six, the sun was rising again.

I taught another workshop in the South of Norway in a converted barn, this time with my daughter Natasha along for the ride. In the morning I was woken by a bleary trumpet reveille. Looking out of my window, I saw a bedraggled crew – the late-into-the-night drinkers – standing to attention and solemnly raising the Norwegian flag. At first I thought it was a joke. I told them that the UK flag was more and more associated with the far right and – for me and my friends at least – with an embarrassing kind of patriotism.

"We are a small country", they said, "and we were controlled for centuries by the Danes and the Swedes and the Germans. Now we celebrate our freedom".

After a while, the poor 1950s-style Norway began to change as ever-growing oil revenues flowed in. Almost overnight, it seemed, it became wealthy, with high-end restaurants, beautiful art galleries and museums, and coffee shops everywhere. In these post-oil years, Norwegians seem to have it all (though like everyone they still often moan about their lot). Now richer than Sweden – long their domineering neighbour - they enjoy decent incomes, good schools and medical care, and a healthy lifestyle. Most weekends in winter, the trains and buses are crammed with cross-country skiers on their way to the beautiful forests and snow tracks outside the city.

A few years ago I took my children and grand-children skiing in Norway. A student of mine lent us her cabin and we hit the slopes in -25°C temperatures. Most of us had never skied before though we'd had one artificial slope lesson in the UK. I figured it couldn't be too difficult for someone like me who'd spent years developing balance and leg strength through qigong. Unfortunately, I was completely deluded.

The first morning we beginners practised on the nursery slopes, trying to learn the snowplough (to be able to turn and stop). But on the second morning, while I still struggled, my daughters graduated to one of the easier runs. I kept at it for an hour or two but eventually gave in when they urged me to join them. The ski lift dropped us at a steep and cambered slope. I nervously set off, but within seconds I was out of control and I made myself fall. This happened time and again and I could see my daughters getting more and more anxious and wondering what the hell they were going to do about their father.

I really hate embarrassing myself – truly hate it – so the next time I gritted my teeth and just kept going. Soon I was hurtling straight down, unable to stop or turn – faster and impossibly faster – hanging on for dear life, knowing that if anybody got in my way, one of us was probably going to die, as would I if lost control and hit a tree. It seemed to go on forever. I was taking off whenever I hit the slightest bump (and maybe my qigong did indeed stand me in good stead because I managed to stay upright when I landed), until the run eventually levelled off at the bottom. I slowed to a halt and was still standing there in shock when, minutes later, my daughters appeared, white-faced. They'd followed me down, expecting as they turned every bend to find my mangled body in the snow.

I decided downhill wasn't for me and spent the rest of the holiday doing safer cross-country skiing.

13. THERAPY – THE JOURNEY WITHIN

If you want to go down into the self, you'd better go
armed to the teeth
Paul Valery

In 1992 I returned from my second trip to China – this time seven weeks working in the Chinese herbal medicine department of a large hospital in Nanjing. In the last week I was there I caught a cold, and soon after I got home it turned into pneumonia. I had to cancel a keynote speech at a conference in the Netherlands, which was both embarrassing and disappointing. I resolved to do my best to prevent it happening again.

Years before, I'd learnt tai chi with a Chinese woman called Rose Li, though in truth she spent more of the class talking than teaching. I'd also practised meditation, Iyengar yoga and karate for varying amounts of time, so I had some background in Asian health, mindfulness and exercise practices.

This time I was drawn to healing qigong (pronounced chee-gong) and specifically to a book called *The Way of Energy* by Lam Kam Chuen. It was all about standing – a training method practised throughout the world of qigong and the internal martial arts. Standing qigong (*zhan zhuang*, also known as standing like a tree) starts with establishing a rooted, aligned and open posture and then focuses on releasing and relaxing whatever is tight and constrained, while the mind settles into the present moment and is absorbed into the body and (slow) breath.

Standing qigong is more challenging than it might sound. Holding stillness in this way can rapidly reveal and magnify what Chinese medicine calls stagnation or lack of free flow. This can be experienced as tightness and pain in different parts of the body, an almost irresistible desire to stretch and move, and mental and emotional frustration, especially if we are not used to dwelling quietly in ourselves without external distractions. However, through practice we can slowly train ourselves to stay soft and released and allow what the Chinese call 'qi and blood' (maybe think of 'all physiological processes and substances') to flow free and unobstructed.

I practised every day on the tree-sheltered patio at the end of our garden. I began to feel strong and full of energy and welcomed every new project and working invitation that came my way. Soon my life was full to bursting. I had a rich family and social life, a steady acupuncture practice and a journal to edit and publish every four months. I'd taken on a principal lecturer role in a Danish acupuncture college and was travelling there every month, as well other frequent teaching trips. Finally, I was co-authoring an acupuncture textbook. It seemed the more qigong I did, the more energy I had.

But slowly, things started to go wrong. I began to experience muscle and joint pain in different parts of my body and couldn't understand why. The more pain I had, the more qigong I did – always focusing my mind on where it hurt and trying to soften and dissolve it away. Then my neck started to twitch and go into spasm. If I allowed it to, my head would turn of its own accord and I'd end up looking backwards over my shoulder – usually on the right side – sometimes for minutes on end. This went on for weeks.

I began to feel stressed and tired. Travelling to teach became exhausting and swallowed up my precious weekends. I felt I'd built an enormous house of cards that threatened to crash down on top of me and I was struggling to cope.

Then one day, during my standing practice, I had an inspiration. For weeks I'd focused on releasing and softening nearly every part of my body as it made itself known through pain and soreness, but I'd not yet tried releasing my chest and heart.

So that's what I did. I opened my heart - and all hell broke loose.

It was like a chamber inside me had opened up and a tsunami of emotion poured out. This time when my head turned to the right I understood there was something there that I needed to see. Immediately an image came into my mind - a flat empty landscape with a single track railway line leading into the distance.

I turned away. I knew there was something awful there and I couldn't look. I felt unbearably strange and started to weep.

I rang Jackie Clements, the therapist I'd seen during a previous tough time in my life, made an appointment for the next day and hung on by my fingernails.

Jackie grew up in the remote Shetland Isles. She combined Scottish earthiness, a fey, shamanistic intuition, authenticity, and a willingness to accompany her clients wherever they needed to go – however dark. I sat in her peaceful garden room and told her about the railway lines and how I'd turned away and couldn't look any further.

"You're going to have to look now."

"I know," I said.

I took long, slow breaths to relax and empty my mind as I was accustomed to from working with her before. Sometimes it took a while to connect to the deeper self that lay beneath my rational mind, but now it was instant. When I turned my head, I saw the railway lines again and this time I looked long enough to see the dreadful place they led to. It was a concentration camp.

For the next three months I lived in two worlds at the same time. There was the normal world where I spoke to people, did my work, ate and slept. But it was tissue thin. Behind and beneath it was the world of the camps which I was compelled to return to, day after day, week after week – a place of fear and despair. Through the day I would feel this other world trying to burst through, like the alien in John Hurt's chest, and if I could, I would find a space – a spare room, my clinic in-between patients, Jackie's therapy room – to sit, close my eyes, and plunge back into that hell realm. For most of my adult life life I had invested great energy in hiding vulnerability and always felt shame about showing hurt, let alone crying. But now I wept every day, always in private or in Jackie's little therapy room, pragmatically purging my distress so that I could hide what was going on from everybody around me. Putting on a tough front was a hard habit to break.

I had one spell of weakness. I felt so desperate that I asked my doctor for medication and he gave me Prozac, but it made me feel so bad (I lay curled in a foetal position for hours) that I only took it once.

When I say weakness, I mean fear that what I was going through would destroy me. But apart from that one time, however bad things got, however strange, deep down I had faith I would get through. After all, I'd taken ferociously strong LSD several times in my life, looked madness in the face and survived, and I believed that I could survive this too.

It was also an incredibly interesting experience, much richer and deeper than any drugs I'd ever taken. I hunted for, and started to come across, references that gave me encouragement for this unknown journey I was on*. Robert Frost's "The only way out is through"; Christian theology's Dark Night of the Soul (the loss of faith and the journey into utter darkness in

---

* Also Andre Gide's "One doesn't discover new lands without consenting to lose sight of the shore for a very long time"; and Proust's "We don't receive wisdom; we must discover it for ourselves after a journey that no one can take for us or spare us".

the hope that something lies beyond it); and what became a kind of bible to me – *Alchemy and Mysticism* - a book of 17th century alchemical illustrations with annotations and explanations by Carl Jung[1].

The cosmic chaos unloosened by the initial procedures of the alchemical work[1]

Of course there was a part of me that wanted an explanation for what was happening. Inevitably, born just three years after the end of the war, I knew about the Holocaust. I'd first read about it when I was a teenager and the images of the piled up corpses had burned themselves into my memory. But none of my family had been involved, nor could I relate to it personally. I was a Jew because my mother was a Jew, and if I'd been in Germany that would have been a death sentence. But it had always seemed very distant from me. And I was an atheist, had never been in a synagogue in my life, and had been brought up without a single Jewish custom or practice – not even Friday night dinner.

A past life experience would have been one interpretation but I didn't

From *Alchemy: The Medieval Alchemists and Their Royal Art*, Johannes Fabricius.

believe in reincarnation. And anyway, with or without an explanation, I had no option but to deal with what was happening to me.

Slowly, as the weeks passed, the Holocaust visions started to fade and I began to think that I was coming out the other side. Then one night I had a terrifying dream. I was driving and the road started to cave in under my car. I was trapped in a narrow pit as the ground closed over my head.

When I revisited the dream at my next session with Jackie there was no car, just a hole in the ground reaching down into the darkness. With a sense of weary despair I knew I would have to descend into the pit but I didn't have the courage or the strength. Then Jackie offered to tie an imaginary rope between us, and knowing she would be by my side, I slowly climbed down into the darkness. At the bottom lay a prison vault and as I stared into the cells - one by one - each held a vision of horror. It was as close to unbearable as I had yet known but always there was Jackie's strong voice, "What can you see? Tell me what you see."

Then my Holocaust world ended as suddenly as it began. Sitting in Jackie's room the next week, I returned to the railway lines and followed them into the camp, but instead of the terrible scenes I'd been forced to witness, this time the camp was deserted, scraps of paper and ashes swirling in the wind.

Even though the world of the concentration camp had faded, I was still profoundly distressed and still weeping whenever I had a moment of privacy – often many times a day. The Holocaust turned out to be just the opening chapter of my journey and I had to draw on deep reserves of strength to carry on.

The next time I sat in Jackie's room, she invited me to go deeper.

I'd once done a weekend workshop with a shaman. He'd asked us to lie down, close our eyes, let our minds roam and look for an opening into the earth (the realm of the unconscious). We had to travel through it and at some point would discover our spirit animal. My mind took me to a place I'd once visited in Israel – a cave in the Ein Gedi nature reserve where the Bible says David hid from King Saul. I walked into the cave and as I reached the darkness at its back it turned into a tunnel and I began to fly through it at great speed until I popped out into bright daylight and found myself on a rocky slope. There, in front of me, was an ibex (mountain goat). I realise what this says about me but I was disappointed it was such a lowly animal. So I cheated. I decided that the ibex must be the guide which would lead me to my true spirit animal.

It trotted up the stony hillside, pausing and waiting for me to catch up, then at the top lowered its head with its curved horns, as if bowing, and there, suddenly, was a giant eagle. I entered into the eagle and flew.

Soaring above the earth and the hills I could see for enormous distances with crystal clear vision – sharp enough to detect a mouse moving in the rocks far below. And I felt a sense of exultation in my ruthless beak and talons, ready to tear and kill whatever came my way.

Now, in Jackie's room, I went back to that cave. I flew through the tunnel again and this time landed in a vast and bare desert. All I could see in any direction was sand and heat haze. I knew I was here to meet some kind of guide but I had no idea who or what and I waited nervously for a long time. Then I became aware of a figure, still a long way away, shimmering and wavering in the heat haze. As it approached, I saw that it was a man. Then as he came close I realised - no, it was impossible, embarrassing, the very last person I wanted to see. My guide was Jesus Christ.

Apart from a brief dabble with Christianity when I had a schoolboy crush on one of our religious education teachers, I was an atheist through and through. Not just an atheist but anti-religious and – since it was the religion I'd been most exposed to growing up in England – particularly allergic to Christianity.

But Christ it was and I had no choice. However, it turned out that Christ was the modest and silent messenger of a greater power as he ushered me into the presence of Jehovah, God the Father, seated on his heavenly throne and gazing straight at me. I stood there paralysed, with an intolerable feeling of shame and unworthiness, unable to even lift my eyes. I was being seen as I truly was and it was dreadful.

Thus began more than a year of hard and painful work – both solo with Jackie and in intensive weekends of group therapy. What it seemed I had to do, although the pattern only became clear when it was all over, was revisit every loss, every shame, every embarrassment – major and minor - that I had ever experienced. Some of them I knew about, in the sense that they were no surprise to me, while others whipped the ground from under my feet, like the session when I wailed for the loss of our first family dog, Lynx, friend and protector of my early childhood. This wasn't a case of discovering a new memory. I had always known about Lynx and half remembered how he used to stay close to me when I nervously joined the other children playing on the green in our quiet suburban road. And I knew that he had accidentally or intentionally been poisoned. But I had no idea this well of sealed-off emotion had been lying there all these years.

The route into the unconscious was often via dreams, and Jackie's preferred Gestalt therapy has a powerful way of working with them. Instead of recounting the dream in the past tense ("I was walking along the street"), it's told in the present ("I am walking along the street"). This quickly puts us back in the dream state and gives us the opportunity to creatively explore the dream, not sticking with the linear narrative of how it actually unfolded. And since every object, every person, every animal that appears in the dream comes from our own unconscious, we can inhabit any one of them and take it where our inner voice tells us.

One dream serves as an example. It was night and I was alone. From a side street a figure emerged, dressed in a long black cloak, face shadowed by a dark hat, a black jaguar padding by his side. The man and the jaguar exuded an overwhelming satanic power, the embodiment of pure evil, and as the jaguar leaped at me, I knew this dark power would annihilate me and I had no conceivable defence against it. I woke up with a feeling of dread.

Sitting with Jackie, I was scared to go back into the dream, but her simple invitation to be not the 'me' of the dream but the jaguar instead, turned it on its head. Now I felt infused with power and could overcome any difficulty in my path.

I worked on another dream – a recurring one I'd had for many years. I would be at some familiar place, usually my parents' house, where builders had arrived to dig up the garden. As I watched I would suddenly remember - with a dawning horror - that I had killed someone and buried them there and the body was about to be discovered.

In my latest dream, it was the shop floor of Infinity Foods that was being excavated. And as the builders dug, it was not one but many bodies that began to appear. Then I spoke, or maybe heard a voice, saying "so many shoulders".

When I recounted my dream to Jackie, in the present, and reached the "so many shoulders", she asked me to repeat it over and over to see if I could find out what it meant. I realised with a shock of recognition that shoulders didn't just mean the ghastly dead shoulders appearing beneath the pneumatic drills but could also be spoken as should-ers – so many 'shoulds'.

And the 'shoulds' were the key to unlocking the dream, my unconscious – as always - speaking to me in obscure and tricksy ways. I was thrown back to a painful time when the world of Infinity Foods had changed from the joyous experience of working and playing with friends into a nightmare of arguments, jealousy and mistrust. As the original founder, I was the main target. In response, I kept insisting that there were certain inalienable 'shoulds' that had to guide how we operated. I was determined to defend myself and sought alliances in what was becoming a factional war. Lacking sufficient emotional intelligence or leadership skills I lost friends and was deeply hurt by it. Sitting in Jackie's room, for the first time I let out the pain I'd toughened myself not to feel. But it wasn't just catharsis. I could see clearly, and feel shame for, the mistakes I had made. Not my principles, but how I had put those principles above people and ended up contributing to discord and unhappiness. It was a lesson I've often had to remind myself of.

There was a very strange ending to this session. Befuddled and a bit sleepy, as I often felt after emotional catharsis, I drove home, parked the car and walked up the short pathway to my front door, key at the ready. It was only at the last moment that I stopped short. I was at the wrong house – number 25 not 22 Cromwell Road – in the long terrace of Victorian houses where my family and I had lived for so many years. Then with a clutching sensation in my chest, I remembered the news story that was all over the media at the time. Fred and Rosemary West had murdered young women and buried them in the cellar and garden of their family house – 25 Cromwell Street - in the city of Gloucester.

I feel the need to say that this work wasn't a process of casual imagining, to entertain myself or please Jackie. I was doing it because I was desperate and if I wanted to be be free I had to continue. I was also pretty sure that conventional talking therapy just wouldn't touch what was going on for me.

I won't pretend I didn't find it interesting, though. A whole new world had opened up, and the unconscious – which of course I'd heard about but given little thought to – was revealing itself to be a deep well of wisdom and insight – forever bubbling up thoughts, feelings, dreams and images - invitations to explore which, like most of us, I had habitually ignored.

Without a dream, the route into the unconscious could be harder. I would start with long slow breathing, especially focusing on travelling into the distance with each outbreath. I would try to quiet my conscious and censoring mind, and if I was struggling, Jackie would ask me to tap the point directly between my eyebrows. I would be waiting for something – a memory, an image, a feeling – to appear. The difficulty was knowing what was important and what wasn't, since some of the most powerful journeys began with seemingly insignificant beginnings but then unfolded with unmistakable power and authenticity.

There comes an inevitable point in every therapeutic journey when we have to address our relationship with our parents and family, and it's usually a big pile of work. This phase began for me with a casual image that appeared as I sat, eyes closed, tapping my forehead, worrying that nothing would come and – as always - feeling like I'd have failed if it didn't. Then the memory of travelling to Jackie's - just a few days before, for a group session – drifted into my mind. I'd been given a ride and had sat in the back of the car with one of the other group members. I'd felt uncomfortable all the way but hadn't given it any further thought other than the fact that I always felt uncomfortable and anxious on my way to a session with Jackie, knowing that something deep inside would usually be knocking at the door, ready to be seen and heard.

Now, as I stayed with the feeling, it took me back to sitting in the back of the family car, my brother beside me and my parents in front. I felt powerless, a child in the world of adults. Jackie asked me to look carefully at who was in the car and choose which of these relationships I needed to explore. I knew it was my father.

In the weeks that followed I allowed all my sadness that my father had so often been my adversary rather than my friend, especially at critical points during my childhood years. When I put on weight aged twelve, he (athlete as he had been) barely hid his distaste. And when, aged sixteen, I began to rebel against my conservative grammar school, he was more scathing than any of my teachers. I remembered the time a friend of his was visiting our house. My father brought him into the room where I was reading and started talking about me as if I wasn't there.

"He's so arrogant, so stupid," my father said. "He thinks he knows more than his teachers," while my face and ears burned with shame.

At one stage he stopped talking to me altogether and as we sat at the dinner table would only speak to my mother, saying things like, "Please tell your son to pass the salt."

I realised that even as an adult, I felt awkward with him and watched from the outside as he and my brother shared an easy intimacy that I wasn't a part of.

Then, the grief turned to fury which I vented at the end of Jackie's garden. I wanted to move on, to let go of the past and be able to have a loving – or at least comfortable – relationship with him, but I couldn't force it out of me just by willing it. It was only when I'd fully exhausted the intensity of my childhood feelings towards him that the space arose for me to understand and forgive him as an adult.

Towards the end of this process, my parents took me to eat at a local Indian restaurant. I'd saved up everything I wanted to say to him and I went through it all with quiet determination. Whenever he tried to interrupt – whether to disagree, explain or try and stop me – I shut him down and told him to let me speak, and to his credit he did.

After this, things changed between us. I came to realise he'd done his best, having no model for fathering, his own father having died when he was very young. I could place him in the context of his own history and struggles. I understood how confused and resentful he had been when he saw me sneering at an education and a safe lifestyle that for him had been so hard won.

After his first stroke, I had to hold his hand to help him across the road and I felt a great wave of tenderness towards him. And just a couple of days before his third and final stroke, we sat in the family home swapping jokes. We laughed together more freely and happily than I'd ever remembered. He died one week later. [see *Picking My Dad Out of my Pockets* at the end of this chapter]

Since then, my love and appreciation for him has grown and I regret I cannot talk to him in a way I wasn't able to when I was younger. I would like to know how he felt about ageing, how he felt about his declining health, his heart problems, the successive strokes which slowly robbed him of movement and eventually speech. Outwardly he accepted them all with grace, patience and as much dignity as strokes allow. And I'd like to tell him how grateful I am for everything I learned from him, especially his commitment to equal education for all and his socialist determination to fight poverty and oppression. And I am also grateful that I could watch him paint and decorate the family house, mend broken plugs, plane wood, dig the garden and try his hand at anything that needed fixing. It served as a model to me – one which has given me great pleasure in my life. I always took these skills for granted until I realised that many of my friends, especially the younger ones (but not my daughters who can do just about anything!), don't have a clue.

The work I did on my father also taught me that I didn't want to repeat his mistakes with my own children (though I'm sure I invented some new ones of my own). Of course I might get angry with them or be challenged by some of the choices they made but I would always aim to stand alongside them in the world and do my best to understand and support them.

The Chinese have a great saying, "The last creature to discover water is the fish." We cannot see the sea we swim in and whatever ideas about the world and responses to it we absorb in infancy and childhood will be largely invisible to us because they are so familiar. Indeed, many of the subtle or gross pathologies ingrained in our family will have been passed on – unseen - to our parents by their own parents, and their parents before them.

As Philip Larkin wrote in *This Be The Verse*
They fuck you up, your mum and dad.
They may not mean to, but they do.
They fill you with the faults they had
And add some extra, just for you.
But they were fucked up in their turn
By fools in old-style hats and coats,
Who half the time were soppy-stern
And half at one another's throats.
Man hands on misery to man.
It deepens like a coastal shelf.
Get out as early as you can,
And don't have any kids yourself.

Every few sessions with Jackie, I would find myself back in the desert waiting for my Christ-guide to usher me into the presence of God – a kind of check-up to discover whether my work was finished and whether I could lift my eyes and allow myself to be seen without shame.

I failed many times, but increasingly, as I stood in the desert waiting, I became aware of a whisper of voices and a vague awareness of multitudes behind my back, urging me onwards. It dawned on me that these were my ancestors.

Every one of us has wounds. We don't have to have had obvious and extreme traumas in childhood - just having been a child is enough. Nothing bad had ever really happened to me and in most ways I'd had a comfortable and privileged childhood but I still discovered layers of unacknowledged hurt.

Most of us can live with these wounds, perhaps not knowing they are there, nor how much they shape and influence our life, relationships and patterns of behaviour. Many of us will ignore or repress them, maybe drowning them with addictive and distracting behaviours, or allowing them to diminish us as we age and they congeal into emotional disability. But some people – it's hard to say why - reach a point where the power of these wounds is great enough to break them down and they cannot function any more.

Carl Jung wrote something about men's lives that made sense to me - written at a time when gender roles were more traditionally defined. He said there comes a time in a boy's life when he has to actualise himself as an adult, a man; a time when he has to venture out into the world of work and career. In order to function he has to seal off any vulnerabilities, any unfinished business of childhood, which he cannot allow to interfere with this difficult task. But there will come a time, usually in middle age, perhaps when he has established himself and can afford to release the tight hold on what is buried, when that unfinished business demands to be addressed. We are increasingly aware that many men – including seemingly tough and successful ones – suffer (and usually try to hide) mental health problems, that if severe enough will result in breakdown.

This kind of breakdown – which of course is not confined to men - can be immensely destructive and lead to a lifetime of psychotropic medication, inability to work, addiction, family breakup, severe depression, self-harm and even suicide. But it can also be a gift - an opportunity to resolve some of the unfinished business of our early life, and to learn to know, accept and cherish ourselves.

For most of my adult life, I have worked in the field of health care, especially health promotion. One of the challenges, one that frustrates and baffles everyone who works in the field, is that even when people know perfectly well what they should and shouldn't be doing to look after themselves, many seem unable to do so. Most of us have made resolutions - to exercise more, sleep more, drink less, improve our diet etc. - yet struggle to keep to them. It's as though there is a part of us that wishes ourselves well and another part that is constantly working to undermine it.

Sun Simiao (581-682), the great Chinese doctor and teacher wrote, "Whenever people don't live out their lives or their life is cut short, it is always caused by not loving or cherishing themselves".

Identifying and resolving the lessons we have absorbed – especially those that tell us that we are unworthy, not deserving to be well and happy - is a challenging and heroic task, though. It requires stamina, courage and an ability to be ruthlessly honest, and it absolutely requires the means and good fortune to find the right person to help us in the work. There are no quick and easy solutions. I have sat for many hours in therapy groups and watched people wrestle over and over with emotional patterns which torment them, and their struggle can be as hard as climbing Everest.

But more than that, more heroic still, is that we are also doing this work on behalf of the ancestors who came before us, the ones who passed their pathologies down through the generations. If the idea of healing backwards through the family line sounds fanciful, we can at least accept that we carry the burdens accrued not only in our own lives but in theirs too.

And theirs were the voices I heard from behind me as I stepped out again into the desert – Larkin's 'fools in old-style hats and coats'. But though I couldn't see them clearly I had a strong sense that these weren't my English, Scottish and Irish working class forbears on my father's side but the intellectual middle European Jews on my mother's. [see short story *Testament* in part two]

So what about my mother? When I finally turned to her, Jackie quietly said that in therapy we usually start with the parent we think we have the problem with, but often that's the easier one.

My mother might be called a colourful character. She was incredibly gregarious, filling the house with friends and food. She had a ceaseless stream of lodgers, often Russians in England for short spells, who found staying with her on the outskirts of London more comfortable and cheaper (mostly free) than staying in a London hotel. The house was so full sometimes that Yevgeny the antique weapons dealer would have to sleep on a bed she made up for him in my father's garden shed, still full of rusting tools and smelling of dried grass and machine oil.

She was emotional, emotionally demanding, generous (often giving away money she couldn't afford) and very, very talkative in her thick accent which remained untouched by seventy years in England. I remember once flying to Israel with her. I sat with my daughters while she was in a different seat, next to a stranger. As we were getting off the plane she introduced me to this new best darling friend – this poor bewildered woman to whom my mother had poured out her entire life history - her childhood, marriage, career, father and family.

On her 90th birthday, she received phone congratulations from all over the world – from the people she had made an indelible impression on, worked with, invited to stay, fed and looked after. They loved her and thought her fabulous as she poured out the stories I had heard a hundred, a thousand times. I was mortified when I saw her approach a new person, clasp their sleeve like the Ancient Mariner and start to hold forth.

Better, for me, was her endless fund of Jewish jokes that I didn't mind hearing over and over. One went like this. A man riding on a train sits near a noisy group of elderly Jews. One of them would shout out a number and the rest would fall about laughing. After a while he approaches them. "Excuse my interruption," he says, "but what's so funny about these numbers?"

"They're jokes", one of them tells him. "We know them so well we only have to say the number, not the whole joke."

Itching to take part, to be welcomed into this friendly tribe, the man decides to try it out. "Twenty-eight", he says. Nobody laughs.

"What's the matter, why didn't you laugh?" he asks.

"It's the way you told it."

Jackie used the term confluence to describe a relationship where the clear boundaries between two people are blurred. I began to understand that this was the Eisenstadt curse running through my mother's family. Her brother Eliakim hanged himself soon after his mother died; hanged himself where his fourteen year old daughter and her younger brother would find him when they came home from school. My mother herself was bound to her father with indissoluble ties. When she left Palestine to live in England, they wrote to each other several times a week, and after she died I found an old leather suitcase stuffed with hundreds of those flimsy airmail letters that went out of use many years ago. They were in Hebrew and I couldn't read them.

A great part of her identity was bound up in her father and she would constantly laud his greatness – and in consequence her own reflected specialness – to anyone who would listen. He left behind an unfinished masterwork – a dictionary of law in five languages - and had made her promise to complete it for him if he was unable to. What she found when he died was boxes and boxes of scribbled notes. But the impossibility of the task didn't detract from the deep guilt she suffered for the rest of her life. She compensated for it, in part, by compiling and publishing a book about him – as he had for his own father.

This was Eisenstadt love, a love that was held up as the deepest and finest possible - to be so wrapped up in another person that there was no defining point where one ended and the other began.

And it seemed to me that though she loved my father passionately, and my brother of course, I was the one singled out to carry the Eisenstadt torch into the next generation. I'm not saying I didn't benefit from it in many ways. I received the full force of her maternal passion and was praised to the skies. But it took me a long time to understand that the uncomfortable feelings I had when she praised me like this were because she was praising herself even more.

I left home in stages from the age of sixteen, travelling for longer and longer spells before I went off to University. I needed to keep my mother at arm's length.

My parents appeared to be complete opposites. She with her great big throbbing Russian-Jewish soul, and he with his British coolness and reserve. Yet, as yinyang theory tells us, everything contains the seeds of its opposite. After my mother died (several years after my father), I found a stack of birthday and wedding anniversary cards to her from him. The cards themselves were frankly kitsch, but the sentiments he poured out were as romantic as could be imagined. They were passionate love letters – year after year into old age. It may just be an accident of fate but I only found one from her to him. It expressed her thanks for his help in producing the book about her father, because of course they both agreed what a great man he was.

As for myself I slipped comfortably into my father's English reserve and coolness when she threatened to swamp me, something I still do when anyone I meet indulges in similarly florid displays of emotion. Yet in other circumstances, other places, I am the one with the big emotions and social hunger.

We absorb parts of both our parents into ourselves, and one of the many tasks we face - to become what we might call 'a true person' - is to integrate them so that we are more whole, more internally congruent, more truly ourselves. The greater the gulf in our parents' personalities and emotional behaviour, the harder but more vital this task is.

The downside of my mother's inexhaustible sociability was that she demanded constant contact and – with a single word or just a tone of voice -

could make friends and family squirm with guilt for neglecting her.

When my father died she was bereft. They had been married for fifty-six years and he was the one she abandoned her country and her family for. But inevitably her mourning took over every inch of the emotional space. I had lost my father, yet such was her grief that I barely recognised my own until years later.

And when my mother suffered, everybody knew about it, everyone had to feel its depth and weight. I barely remember a single meeting or phone call after his death, until she herself died thirteen years later, when her first words were not, "I'm in agony", or "I'm suffering" - even before I'd had a chance to ask how she was. And it seemed to come with the expectation that I should be able to fix it for her; fix her grief, her loneliness, her arthritis, her insomnia and her existential pain. And if I couldn't, which was usually the case, I was left with the dreadful feeling that I was letting her down.

It was on a ten-day therapy workshop with Jackie, down in the sunflower-filled South of France, that I realised that I had also absorbed the Eisenstadt model of love between parent and child and that I would endanger the psychological health of my own daughters unless I could dig it out from the root. As the group sat in a circle around me on a burning hot afternoon, I acted out a ceremony as painful as any I could remember, one which I cannot share here, to cut this toxic tie.

The work I did on my mother was never 'finished' in the warm and happy way it was with my father, perhaps because he conveniently died, while she lived on for many years. Maybe it was too complex and I was still too tightly held in her bonds.

Yet as time has passed, as with my father, I am more and more aware how grateful I am to the lessons I absorbed from her. I too love excitement - company, parties, celebrations and food - and like her, I try to be generous. I am full of admiration, too, at how this stranger in a strange land forged such a successful career, bringing her phenomenal energy and appetite for people to her work of caring for the thousands of Russians she interpreted and cared for.

But I learned negative lessons from her too, as she became more and more crippled, first unable to walk, then unable to get in and out of bed and eventually even to leave her chair unaided. I decided to do my damnedest to look after myself and stay as strong, co-ordinated and fit as possible. As I lie in a warm bed on a cold morning, it is my memories of her pain that often help rouse me and take me out into the crisp clear day to practise qigong. And like my father, I hope to meet the sickness and death I inevitably face with gentle stoicism, not complaining all the way like my mother.

I had one final challenge during this period. I qualified as an acupuncturist in 1978 and – such was the way in the infant days of this profession – I not only began to practise in the college clinic but to teach and lecture first year students. I couldn't believe my luck. I would have paid for the pleasure of standing in front of a class, communicating what I'd learned about the wonders of Chinese medicine. Instead they paid me – and quite well. As the years passed, I taught more and more, travelling widely and often, always loving the chance to get classrooms of people to sit silently and listen to what I had to say (an astrologer might comment on the fact that I'm a double Leo with Pluto, Mercury and Saturn also in Leo, but I don't believe in astrology).

Then I had two hard trips in rapid succession. In Oslo, I had to lecture – six hours a day for four days - with flu. Then, just a few weeks later, the night before I had to present a weekend workshop in Sweden, I got food poisoning from some bad seafood. I managed to teach but it took all my grit to get through it.

Soon after, on one of my regular lecturing trips to Denmark, I was holding forth in front of the class when I began to feel very strange. My heart was thudding in my chest and I felt disorientated, unreal, outside of myself, unable to speak. I took ten minutes out, sitting and trying to slow my breathing. Then I went back and with what felt like a heroic effort managed to complete the day.

Later, I realised it was a panic attack, and for the next few months, teaching became a torture. I feared it could happen again any time and I'd start dreading the next trip I had to make, sometimes for weeks beforehand, for example when I had to fly to Australia and give three one day workshops in different cities. I even turned down a close friend's request to be best man at his wedding, partly because I couldn't face the thought of speaking in public.

I started reading accounts of stage fright and how it often happened to performers at the height of their careers. Because they were renowned, everyone who came to see them had high expectations. But however many glowing reviews they had under their belt, however many awards, they doubted themselves. They were suffering from what is called impostor syndrome, believing that they were undeserving of all the praise and that at any moment the audience would see through them. The terror was so great that many abandoned live performance forever.

I got through my stage fright myself, without Jackie's help. The revelation came one day when I left my acupuncture clinic after a long day with many patients. The clinic was in an unsavoury part of town; there had been break-ins and two murders over the past couple of years. As I walked round the corner from the clinic, I saw a man walking towards me and I went into fight or flight mode, preparing myself for an attack. I soon forgot about it until it happened again a few days later. Then again.

I tried to think it through. I rationalised that these were harmless and innocent passers-by so I must be projecting my own hostility onto them. And I saw that this sprang from the frustrations I'd suppressed during a long day of trying my best to be caring and supportive to a bunch of often trying patients.

That helped me realise that when I stood in front of a group of students, in fear that I would be seen through, unconsciously expecting their judgement and hostility, I was actually projecting my own feelings onto them.

So, as my trip to Australia approached and the anxiety built and built, I started practising a meditation I'd learned during my Buddhist days. It's called *metta bhavana* and the practice is to generate loving kindness towards ourselves (how hard that can sometimes be), then a friend, a neutral person, an enemy and finally all sentient beings in the universe. So I sat and imagined my class spread out in front of me and cultivated loving feelings towards them, day after day, until the lecturing was done.

Cause and effect can be hard to establish and I can't be sure that was the remedy, but from then on the fear abated and within a few months I was back where I started – in love with teaching. But there was a difference now. It became less about me and more about them - how could I best transmit the subject I loved so that they would understand it and love it too?

I spoke to a dear friend about this, a woman used to performing. She told me that in ancient Greece the actors put on masks so as to transcend their normal ego-laden selves and simply serve the play. The moment they stepped on stage it was as though something took them over and spoke through them. They called it 'the god entering in' and that was how I began to experience lecturing in classrooms and conference halls, teaching qigong and playing in a band. I might be nervous beforehand, but when I spoke my first word or played the first note, I stepped away from my ordinary self, and when it was over, it was almost like I woke from a dream.

Ending a concentrated period of therapy can be hard for many different reasons. We may worry about stopping prematurely, avoiding or leaving necessary work unfinished. But if we stay, is it because we have become unhealthily dependent on the therapist? Are we now unprofitably picking away at the inescapable pains of life, or should we continue on the basis that we can always benefit from insight into our feelings and decisions and will be better able to face life's necessary losses?

In my case, I had a clear measure of my progress. The day finally came when, ushered into the presence of God, I was able to lift my eyes, say "this is me", and allow myself to be seen – nakedly, right into my core. It's not that I was now pure and cured of vices. It was that I was no longer ashamed of who or what I was, despite those faults. I accepted myself at last - indeed I could say that I loved myself, or at least had a warm affection for the complex creature that I am. I was also no longer afraid of what might lie waiting to hijack me if I delved again into the depths.

I should say, at last, that I do not believe in God or Christ (or anyone). Although the God I had to face was the judgmental, Old Testament God – male and bethroned - I never for a moment believed he was real. Like Christ, he was a symbol that my wise unconscious adopted to assist this most interesting of journeys.

Jackie Clements 1933 – 2019

PICKING MY DAD OUT OF MY POCKETS

We're all in the family car. My father's driving and the rest of us sit like smoked bees in the miasma of his pipe tobacco. Next to him my mother gives off her own fug of saccharine Russian perfume. In the back my brother and I slide around on the leather seat, mostly amicable but sometimes bitterly and silently fighting.

We're on our way back from Nan's. She still lives in the tiny terraced house in North London where she raised her five children after her husband died. My father escaped to the leafy suburbs in the South and jumped a whole class in doing so, but Nan and the other four remained amid the bare streets with their rows of houses bookended by corner shops and pubs. My brother and I would wait outside one of these pubs, sipping lemonade and scuffing our shoes, while Dad and my uncles took their Sunday morning drink. Then we all walked back to Nan's for lunch, the men carrying quart bottles of stoppered brown ale.

This time, however, we'd just been for a visit, Christmas maybe, when my uncles tried to outdo each other in how much they could eat and drink, and my aunts loaded the table with sherry trifles and cakes. Tired but not sleeping in the back of the car, I pass the time fantasising about which of the shops we pass I'd like to own. Any toy shops of course but I'm keen to have one of everything – newsagents, furniture shops, stationers – that I can just walk into any time and take whatever I want. And then as we approach home, the moment comes when we have to pass the long dark cemetery and I cannot bear to look at it. I have to turn my head to the other side of the road, away from all the dead people and the dreadful realisation that one day my Mum and Dad are going to die.

*

The phone call comes on a Sunday. Dad has collapsed while taking a shower and is unconscious. The neighbours had to come in and pull his scrawny body out of the bath and now he's in hospital. He's had two strokes already. After the first he was unsteady on his feet and his vision was hazy. I had to hold his hand to cross the street to the doctor's. The second time his eyes got much worse and he could no longer read. I found him in his hospital bed teaching himself Braille – this man who never went to a new country without studying the language for months beforehand. I told him the Jewish joke about the blind Englishman encountering his first matzo cracker, "I don't know who wrote this but it's complete rubbish".

But this time it's obvious, as soon as I see him laid out on a trolley in the hall of the hospital, that it's much more serious. The doctors are saying that the longer he is unconscious the worse the outcome is likely to be, and he's already been like this for hours. He is moved to another hospital and my mother, now eighty-two, visits him every day. She takes the bus for an hour in the morning but is there in time to spoonfeed him breakfast. He is marginally conscious now, waking suddenly from a stupor to speak whole sentences, his brain flickering fitfully. My mother sits with him all day, stroking his hand and ceaselessly repeating that he will be fine and that he just has to get better and come back home where she will take care of him. Each time I visit, I know he will never make it but I cannot tell her. Late in the evening, she takes the long bus journey back to the dark and empty house.

Twice he falls out of bed. The nurses forgot to raise the side rail and he tried to get up to walk. The whole side of his face and one arm are bruised terribly but he doesn't seem to notice. I want to tell them that this is not just some dumb old man but a headmaster and a natural leader, with a keen intelligence that even his enemies respected.

As the days, and then the weeks, go by, his moments of clarity get fewer and fewer. He is no longer there, though he still breathes and eats, pisses and shits. Then the last days come. My brother and I stay all the time, listening to my mother's incessant pleading. "My darling, my darling, you must get better, I need you, what will I do without you, you are my life". Now every breath is a fight, a great physical rasping intake followed by a silence that each time feels as though it will be the final one. But it isn't. Day turns into night and back into day and I sit there willing him to die. I am angry with him, both because he is my father and because he is making me watch him endlessly drown.

Finally my brother and I take my mother outside. "This is torture. If you love him you have to let him die". In a sudden turnaround she accepts this. This short, dumpy Russian woman, brought to England as a young bride, is now holding his hand and weeping and saying "It's alright my darling, you can leave, I will be alright" but still he doesn't die. The measures of morphine increase and it's clear they are moving towards the final dose. Suddenly I just can't bear it any more. I, who have sat for hours in Buddhist meditation contemplating death and impermanence and viewing my own body rotting in the grave, cannot stand this. I have to leave, yet my mother and brother both have the love and strength to stay. It only takes a half hour more. I am back at my mother's house when the phone rings. It's my brother saying that he has just died. At the final moment, black liquid poured from his mouth and his face darkened and collapsed inwards.

*

It's a cold October day at the crematorium, the wind rattling the leaves on the browning trees and gusting along the clipped grass and bare earth. For once at a funeral I am not wearing a mask of forced solemnity. Inside, I stand with my brother and my voice trembles as we read out the mourner's Kaddish, "Blessed and praised, glorified and exalted, extolled and honoured, adored and lauded be the name of the Holy One". Irony of ironies; all of us are rampant atheists. Yet my father was technically a Jew, converting as a soldier in the hated British army in Palestine as a mark of solidarity with Jews in general and my mother's family in particular. And just a year ago, he and my mother were remarried in the local synagogue by the same rabbi who is here today, a wedding to complement the brief army ceremony of fifty-six years ago.

I collect the ashes from the crematorium. They have been there a long time as my mother has been unable to decide what to do with them. I am surprised how heavy they are in their smart maroon box with matching string handles, like a magnum of champagne. I drive my mother to Kelsey park, where my brother and I ran exuberantly as children, safe in the knowledge that our living parents strolled behind. I have tried to tell my mother that you can't just scatter ashes without permission but she is adamant. I am consumed with anxiety that a park keeper (ogre of my childhood) will come along and I look back and forth constantly as I step over the low wire fence onto the flower bed by the lake. I fumble with the box, struggling to rip open the tough plastic bag that holds the ashes, then upend them as quickly as possible. It's another windy day and they blow everywhere, into my mouth, my hair, my shoes. It feels good to be taking my dad home with me. For days afterwards I find bits of him in my pockets.

14. MUSIC

I've described how I was brought up drowning in music and how my father wired up speakers throughout the house and played opera and heavy orchestral music (Mahler was a favourite) from morning till night. At other times we would gather round my mother on the piano to sing Scottish and Communist folk songs ("John Brown's body lies a'mouldering in the grave") or listen to Paul Robeson on 78rpm shellac records on a wind-up gramophone. We loved him as much for his politics as his marrow-vibrating bass. He became a cause célèbre among the left when he was denied a passport by the US government because of his support for civil rights at home and the Soviet Union abroad. After my mother interpreted for his meeting with the Russian Red Army Choir he became even more of a hero in our household.

My mother had abandoned her fledgling piano career (playing for the troops in Palestine), when she married, but all through my childhood would be taken by sudden fits of enthusiasm and practise every day for a few weeks, riven by frustration that she couldn't play Bach and Chopin like she did as a nimble fingered nineteen year old. As the years went by, these fits grew fewer and shorter while her frustration mounted, yet she stubbornly ignored all pleas to pick something simpler and just enjoy herself.

What made it worse was that she was interpreting for some of the greatest musicians in the world. Arriving with the violinist David Oistrakh one day for rehearsals at London's Festival Hall, and seeing the instruments laid out ready for the orchestra, she gave a deep '*oy vey*' sigh. Oistrakh, also Jewish and thus attuned to the depths of sorrow conveyed by that simple sound, asked her why the lament.

"I'm so sad that I gave up the piano," she said.

"I'll tell you what to do," he replied. "Every day when you wake up, thank God you're not a professional musician."

After every evening concert he moved on to the next city, slept, had breakfast, practised for up to five hours, rested then performed. "If I miss one day's practice, I notice," he said. "If I miss two, the critics notice. If I miss three, the audience notices."

I owe him a personal debt. After a concert at London's Royal Albert Hall, famous for its terrible acoustics, he was asked how it sounded. To be honest would be insulting while to praise the hall would be ridiculous, so he simply said, "From where I was standing it was fine." I've used this line often when asked – after a seminar or a workshop – 'how did it go'?

Oistrakh, always measured and sedate, with the shiny, chubby cheeks of a well-fed baby, recorded a Bach concerto one freezing morning in Russia. He drove an unheated car through the hard snowy landscape, washed his hands briefly in warm water, and without any further preparation knocked off one of the seminal Bach recordings. It may be that only a violinist can fully appreciate his *gongfu* (also written kung fu), that lovely Chinese term which means 'the effortless skill that comes from thousands of hours of practice', rather than flying through the air and trying to knock someone's head off.

David Oistrakh

Oistrakh came to our house one time, listened to me play my grade three pieces on the violin and gave us a Hornby Dublo train set which we played with for a few days before forgetting it in the attic (sorry model train enthusiasts).

Over the years my mother worked with most of the top Russian musicians – Mstislav Rostropovich, Shostakovich father and son, Khachaturian (who transcribed on a paper napkin the two notes of a rather dramatic sneeze I came out with and gave it to me), Richter, Gilels and more. I would often be the mute witness to their backstage lives.

My mother with Rostropovich

One, was the unstable conductor Evgeny Svetlanov. I watched fascinated when - relaxing in his dressing room after a concert – he would be visited by obsequious fans and local bigwigs who crept in, bowing apologetically, addressing him as maestro, effusing for as long as his plump and extravagantly perfumed Russian wife allowed, then backed away, still bowing all the time as if in the presence of the Queen. Every strange thing he did was viewed through the lens of his perceived genius. He once conducted the Brighton Festival Chorus in a performance of Carmina Burana after which the local paper went on at length about his unique interpretation and the layers of meaning in his decision to play it at breakneck speed. I was privy to the inside story and knew that he'd become obsessed with snooker and was determined to get back to his London hotel in time to watch the final.

Inspired by my father's valiant attempts at the violin, I announced that I too wanted to play and, aged seven, I started weekly lessons with kindly nineteenth century Mr Purkiss in his living room full of old dark furniture. I would walk to his house, clutching my violin case, my mood ranging from fear to self-assurance, depending on how much preparation I'd done. My parents never forced me to practise but the expectation was writ large. And sometimes I truly loved it, day-by-day shaping my skill and setting up a habit, an expectation, of daily dedication to learning - something that has stood me in good stead throughout my life and for which I am very grateful.

Children generally want to please their parents, and especially boys their fathers. My love of the violin, of boxing (we listened on the radio, beamed from America in the middle of the night), and of watching live athletics, all began in order to please him, this man who was in London's White City Stadium at the Olympic games when, to the amusement of the crowd, the tannoy called him to go home because his wife was giving birth (to me).

I did fall for the violin though, and relished the annual trip to Guivier's violin shop in London for its annual service – shiny new strings, newly haired bow, a fresh block of rosin smelling of pine forests, and a thorough clean and polish. I was less keen on the nervous journey by train and bus to the Albert Hall where the Royal College of Music held their exams. In an echoing room that smelled of floor polish and history, I would stand – a tiny figure – in front of three unsmiling examiners and tremble through my scales and my set pieces.

In later years, when I lived in Brighton and played in The Matzos band, I'd get my violin serviced by Peter Ratcliffe – a local luthier. His main work is dating old violins. The wood that makes up the back of every instrument shows a unique signature of tree rings that can reveal when and where the tree was cut down.

By measuring the rings and comparing them with his ever-growing database, he can tell if a violin is a genuine Stradivarius (worth several million dollars), a fake, or a mistaken ID. He's much in demand.

Once I had to play the violin in front of the whole school and there wasn't a single thing about it that I enjoyed. A few years later, the school orchestra was due to give a performance to parents and invited guests. The music teacher decided that as I was 'especially advanced' I probably didn't need to come to rehearsals, so I didn't. Indeed he set the tone for my whole casual approach to the affair which is why, the night before, it dawned on me that I'd barely looked at the pieces and was completely incapable of playing them. I should have called in sick but one thing reassured me. On stage, amidst the other violins and far from the audience, I could fake the hard bits.

But when I arrived I found that we'd gone all modern and were to sit right in the middle of the crowd, who were so close to me I could elbow one of them with my bowing arm.

He was an elderly man who kept giving me enthusiastic smiles, clearly excited to hear such a talented neighbour perform.

There was only one thing for it. Pretending to make a minute adjustment to the bridge (it holds the strings up from the violin body) I gave it a secret push and collapsed it. There's no way back from that during a performance and I spent the next half hour exchanging commiserating glances with my friend, trying to convey how devastated I was to lose the opportunity to entertain him, whilst also subtly indicating that life is full of the unexpected and we can only be philosophical about it.

When I hit sixteen and seemingly overnight lost my puppy fat - sprouting lengthways and shrinking widthways - I was in a hurry to make up for lost time, particularly in the exciting, terrifying and confusing world of girls that I'd been locked out of for some time. It seemed obvious to me that a violin was unlikely to add to my sex appeal, any more than a chess board would (plus I finally admitted to myself that I'd had a belly full of classical music and never wanted to listen to it again), so I just stopped playing. And when, just a few years later, I joined a band with my brother and friends and picked up the violin again, I realised that without a sheet of music in front of me, I had no idea what to play. Seven or eight years of taking one exam after another and never an invitation to learn a tune by ear or, god forbid, make my own music.

When I was twenty-one, David Bowie (on the cusp of fame) and his girlfriend Mary Finnigan opened the Beckenham Arts Lab in the Three Tuns pub. It was the nearest thing to my local since I'd spent many hours there, mingling with my anarchist and CND friends. And somehow, Mick (guitar), Bob (drums), my brother Alan (harmonica) and I became the Art Club's house band (going under the dreadful name of Oswald K. Aldehyde). Lacking a trace of self-doubt, we'd launch into blues or jazz covers – Miles Davis's So What was a favourite – which rapidly degenerated into long and self-indulgent noodlings.

I didn't take to David Bowie in those early days. Always a chameleon, this particular incarnation was full of a luvvie campness that couldn't have been further from the worthy authenticity of my black and white politics. As soon as he'd announced us he would disappear into a back room. I had no complaints there – I wouldn't have stayed to listen to us either – but when he swanned back at the end of our set saying how absolutely faaaabulous we were darlings, I choked on the insincerity.

When he died in 2019 I spoke to my brother about those times and he told me something I have no memory of.

"We were at Brian Eno's house," he said, "and you had a row with David about how he shouldn't be charging people money to get into the Arts lab. You kept calling him a 'bread head, man' " [bread head = money-obsessed in hippie talk).

The summer of that Arts Lab year, 1969, Bowie organised Britain's first Free Festival in our local park. Beckenham Recreation Ground represented everything I'd loathed about growing up in this bland London suburb. Grass cropped to within an inch of its life, dogshit, mean little flower displays, thorny, clipped bushes spaced out along bare and barren beds, a sour and officious park keeper and bored kids hanging out by the swings, smoking, and wondering what terrible fate had condemned them to live in Beckenham. This was the park where I'd walked our dog Rex as a kid, wondering when the hell my life was going to begin.

But this day it was transformed. A crowd of hippies lounged on the grass and the smells of weed and patchouli wafted through the park. We'd put together a scratch band with a guest drummer, managed a quick soundcheck, and halfway through the afternoon launched into our first number. Within seconds Mick – our front man and the only real musician in the band - started turning his head and looking back at us with an agonised expression. It wasn't till the end of the song we saw he'd busted two strings. We soldiered on with our next tune but had to abort the gig halfway through when the park-keeper – in full uniform and shiny peaked cap – wrestled our drummer to the ground, kicking the drums away and screaming "You're not playing that bloody loud in my park".

On the 50th birthday of the festival, after Bowie had recently died, the bandstand was given Grade 2 listing as a historical monument and a photo appeared in most newspapers and TV channels. There I was with my violin, somewhere to the rear of a supremely cool-looking Bowie, while Mick sat plucking at his guitar strings.

When I started travelling I took my violin with me. I don't know how many trains, buses and hitched rides I carried it on, how many fires I sat around on dark nights with this delicate, fine-boned instrument lying naked by my sometimes drunken or stoned feet, yet somehow it never got damaged or lost. When I'd get off a bus in some Moroccan village and the street kids or the men drinking tea beneath a shaded tree saw it, they'd always ask me to play. I only knew one Arabic tune which they never seemed to recognise but they nodded and grinned along and honour was satisfied.

The violin was my passport. It's not that I played particularly well, but I did have a connection to the instrument and was always willing. And in most places that travellers gathered – isolated beaches or mountain villages – there wasn't much other entertainment. In Morocco I lived for almost two months without money - generous friends paying my way and encouraging me.

"Mick Jagger is in Fez", they said, "you should go and look him up". Or else it was Jimi Hendrix in Tangier. I was flattered but also embarrassed for them since I knew I wasn't good enough, even if they didn't.

There was a longish period in my life when I struggled to get, or hold on to, money. It's true that however much they might grumble, my parents were a safety net, but they weren't that well off and anyway their disapproval meant that I tried not to ask – even when I was really up against it. I travelled on a pittance, always alert to any way of saving pennies, and there were times – both abroad and in the UK – when I had no money for food.

I was also pretty self-centred, but despite that I met with untold and undeserved generosity from so many people on the road. My youth helped but often it was the violin that sealed the deal, and of course the kindness of strangers.

Later, when I found my purpose and threw my energies into Infinity Foods, I worked for years with scant thought of money, earning next to nothing, but committed to the ideal of feeding people as cheaply and healthily as possible. It wasn't conscious then, but looking back I can see how driven I was to pay back the debt I owed the world, or rather I was 'paying it forward' – passing some of the generosity I'd received on to others. Those years also fundamentally changed my relationship with money, for after I quit the food business, I never really lacked it again.

My first adult adventure back into music was joining a samba band. I played the surdo, the big drum that lays down the core bass beat and is the most physical of the samba drums. It was thrilling – parading through the streets, the tremendous noise of the band thundering and echoing off the buildings. We played street gigs, celebrations and demonstrations, often accompanied by brilliantly costumed samba dancers, and I loved my humble but vital role in this powerful tribe. But after a while I wanted something more musical, and to be honest, less anonymous.

For many years the violin had slumbered in its case. I'd take it out once in a while and play some half-remembered tunes, and it was one of those things that I always expected to go back to. I hadn't lost the yearning to be in a rock and roll band and I realised that's what happens in life – we all have things we've let go of and think we'll go back to, but then without us noticing it, the years pass and it's too late.

I was in my early fifties and it was now or never. I was looking for some kind of music that excited me and when I came across a book of old klezmer tunes I realised I'd found it. Klezmer was the dance and celebration music of European Jews. Passing freely as they did from Western to Eastern Europe they integrated many musical influences, but probably the most important were Jewish devotional music, Romani (gypsy) music, and, when they travelled to the USA in the early 20th century, jazz. The klezmorim were jobbing musicians, playing at weddings and parties, and sometimes for gentile (non-Jewish) audiences. By all accounts they were a disreputable lot, with warnings to 'lock up your daughters when the klezmorim' are in town. It might have been my Jewish genes but the music catches most people in the same way. The melancholic minor keys ("D minor – to you it's just a key, to me it's my livelihood" as one old klezmorim put it) go straight to the heart, while the driving polka and bulgar beats make dancing irresistible. Then, in most tunes, there will be the sudden lurch into a major key and an upbeat Germanic oompah arms-in-the-air passage (for the klezmorim were wandering musicians and had to please the Gentiles too) before the inevitable return to the minor to remind us that joy is fleeting.

I played a couple of tunes to my friend Nigel Broderick, a talented jazz and Latin keyboard player, who, it so happened, had been thinking about taking up the accordion. Soon we had a band – The Matzos (originally the Matzo Boys - matzo balls – get it? – maybe it's a Jewish thing). Dave Lacey on drums and percussion, Paul Smith on double bass, Mark Pointing on guitar and frontman Nigel on accordion. None of them were Jewish and all were better musicians than me, but I had a driving energy and was happy to take on the role of manager. The others were jobbing musicians, playing in various bands and combos – often for beer money – and that's how we began too, but after a while we started to get better-paid gigs. We played clubs, festivals, weddings and bar mitzvahs all over the country – anything to bring in a bit of money (Q: What do you call a musician without a girlfriend? A: Homeless). Personally, I was settled financially at the time so I did it for fun, for the music, for the company and the adventure.

Sometimes we played to heaving crowds in sweaty basement clubs and sometimes at weddings where the only dancers were one little girl and her granny (then when our set finished the wedding DJ would put on Abba and the floor would fill with dancing queens).

Sometimes we were treated like we were famous, sometimes like the hired help. I remember flying back from a teaching trip in Denmark where I'd been feted, if not as a god, then at least an archangel, and going straight to play a wedding where the band were ordered to keep out of the way at the back of the kitchen while the guests dined (on gleaming china, silver and glass). The kitchen staff would bring us a sandwich, they said, if they had time. And in truth I didn't mind at all. I was with my buddies, having fun and looking forward to the show.

I was always nervous before a gig and would get more and more keyed up as the evening approached. Would I be able to hear myself and the others on stage, would I even remember the notes? But then - sound check done, in-

struments ready on stage, the five of us standing in a dark and crowded little backstage corridor, hearing "Please give a big hand to The Matzos", stepping out into the lights and the applause, picking up the violin, the drummer checking we're all ready and counting us in – one, two, three, four - and we all hit the first note on the nail – that was a thrill indeed. And that first note was special. It carried the full fate of the gig. If it sounded great it meant that the stage sound was good and we could hear each other and play to our best. But if it was uncertain and muddied to our ears, whatever it was like out front, the gig would be a struggle. When that first note sounded right, we were ready to rock and roll.

Unlike a lot of modern klezmer musicians – often classically trained - who treated their Jewish musical heritage with reverence and even piety, we were rough and ready, loud and fast, and liked nothing more than sending our audience into a vodka-fuelled frenzy, always trying, and sometimes forgetting, to remember Dave the drummer's rule of "follow your audience into oblivion, don't lead them there".

We played Glastonbury Festival – the UK's biggest – on its fifth biggest stage (Avalon) at ten thirty on a Sunday morning - possibly the worst possible slot, as anyone with a heartbeat was asleep after partying all night. But the scanty and mostly horizontal audience couldn't detract from the buzz of playing on a stage so wide we could barely see each other. Dave, hungover and excited, set a fearsome tempo and like a runaway train we just kept getting faster.

Dance of Delight (https://www.youtube.com/watch?v=QcT8QtvtL04) is a recording of our first number (still fairly moderate in pace). The sound is a bit rough (taken from the mixing desk) but it conveys the spirit of the gig.

Later that day and into the night we waded through thick mud all over the site, Paul dwarfed by his double bass, and played for drinks in any of the cafes, bars and saunas that would have us.

Three years running we organised New Year or Christmas gigs with magicians, dancers and guest bands. For one year's finale we filled the stage with musicians. It opens with a solo doina (improvised, slow introduction) by the wonderful Rohan Kriwaczek playing a chalumeaux (https://www.youtube.com/watch?v=THWeTdU9T80).

One year we wore pink tutus for our encore of the Sugar Plum Fairy - my idea despite heated (and valid) objections from the rest of the band. But we were united on our plan for the following year.

It started when we were heading back in the early morning from a distant gig, monotonous miles of motorway rolling beneath the van tyres. I was driving while they slept, turning tunes over in my head, and it hit me that the klezmer standard *Hava Nagila* wasn't so different from Offenbach's *Galop Infernal* – the cancan tune that everybody knows. I woke Nigel and we hatched the plan.

In Komedia's basement club in Brighton, at the end of a cracking New Year gig, we kicked off with *Hava Nagila* as six figures appeared dressed in black cloaks, hats and sidelocks. They performed a tasteful circle dance, then at a signal, ripped off their velcroed costumes to be revealed in full cancan dress as we segued into Offenbach. The high kicks and knicker flashing triggered furious emails after the gig. I was even called a 'self-hating Jew' (not for the first time) for disrespecting precious traditions and I guess that's exactly what we did.

I loved the camaraderie and even the fraught arguments in rehearsals when we worked on a new number. I recognised how similar this was to my lecturing career. Sometimes I'd spend weeks preparing an hour's presentation but I could then travel and repeat it all over the world. It's the same with bands. I don't know how much blood and sweat the Rolling Stones put into Satisfaction but it definitely paid off.

Most bands, like all things, have an arc, and The Matzos were no different. Interpersonal problems began to get in the way and it felt like we'd reached the top of the hill and were starting to slip down the other side. So a few years after we began, we disbanded.

I'd fulfilled my desire to be in a band and there was a part of me that was relieved to stop. The music we played was fast and difficult and sometimes at the very edge of my skill set. They say that it's impossible to improve basic violin technique after the age of twenty. I didn't believe that and thought that if I practised hard enough I could get better and better. But I discovered that it's largely true. For every increment of improvement gained, I had to put in endless work, and from the day I joined the band I practised every day.

Imagine (if you don't play the violin that is) that you're standing on a dark stage, floodlights blinding your eyes, surrounded by so much noise you can barely hear yourself play, and that you have to throw your hand up the short, slim neck of the instrument, with no frets or landmarks to guide you, and hit a spot with pinpoint accuracy (or be woefully out of tune). That's just one of the skills that has to become embedded as a child, or at least in one's teens, and I'd never put in the spadework.

When the band folded, I stopped playing the violin. A bit like my mother, I'd ended up more frustrated that I couldn't reach the level I wanted, than joyful about the music I was able to make.

Now, I just listen to music - from Amy Winehouse to Fats Waller, Miles Davis to Missy Elliott, Jazzmataz Guru to Jackie Mittoo – and every few days I jack up thespeakers and dance around like a fool[4 5]

I have always marvelled at the power of words to move us in so many different ways - simply because the writer chose this word and not that one, joined to this word and not another, in this order, this rhythm, this cadence. Music does this even more directly with just a few basic notes and a limited number of rhythms, and can transport us into happiness, desire, melancholy, sensuality, excitement and transcendence. And, if we allow it to, music will move our bodies like puppets responding to a puppet master.

Combine music with words and its power is doubled, which is exactly why

---

I practise qigong most days but sometimes I'm not in the mood and don't force it. Instead, I'll put on some music and dance around, letting the sound move my body whichever way it wants. It often seems there's no great difference between qigong and dance. I've created several playlists on Spotify including a five and a half hour dance playlist: peterdeadman/Pete's music to dance to.

I adore Bob Dylan so much (though not to dance to). I have been endlessly inspired by him, he has been a constant companion through the years and I feel blessed to have been alive at the same time.

15. CAMPS

I first heard about the Natural Trust from my eldest daughter. Their plan was to sell memberships and when there was enough money, to buy a piece of land to protect and manage on permaculture lines*. I paid up, not really expecting anything to happen. These people were young, naïve and very idealistic, and I knew how expensive land was. But then I heard that they'd negotiated a deal to buy a piece in Kent, an hour's drive away, and were going to christen it with a month-long 'Natty Gathering'. I was curious, so Jenny and I packed a tent and set off to spend a weekend there.

What I found amazed me. This seemed to be a whole new generation, practised in ways of communicating that were strange to me and I watched in fascination. Every one spoke their piece quietly and was listened to. There was no apparent conflict. Sometimes discussions about the simplest practical decisions went on for hours and I bridled with impatience, but things did get done - eventually. A primitive grey water system was installed, young fruit and nut trees planted, supplies brought in, and everyone was fed from a tiny kitchen hut. A friend of my daughter made banoffee pie for 150 people in a smoky wood-fired oven and received 147 thank yous and three marriage proposals.

In the evenings a great fire was lit, there was music and singing, and I had such a good time I stayed on. Though the deal to buy the land fell through, I was keen enough to go on my own to the second, unhappier, Natty Gathering the following year in Wales. [see short story *Clearfell* in part two].

The original Natty Gathering in Kent was the first time I'd been in a tent for years, and inspired by the experience, I signed up for a ten-day qigong camp on the edge of Dartmoor in England's South-West. I pitched my little nylon tent in the long, damp grass in a matter of minutes, and was sitting waiting for the kettle to boil when a woman drew up in an estate car. Its roof was piled high with bundles of sticks, and the inside was packed to the roof. Apart from a quick hello I didn't pay much attention, and after I'd drunk my tea I went for a wander round the camp. A couple of hours

---

* Permaculture is a set of design principles based on a whole systems approach, taking its inspiration from how natural ecosystems operate.

later I trudged back. Although it was August, a chill wind blew rain into my face and my clothes were soaked. As I neared my cold, damp tent, I stopped. My new neighbour had erected a palace. It even had a front door – open now, and I could see inside to where she lay at ease on a pile of sheepskins, basking in the warmth of a brightly burning woodstove. Whatever this thing was, I decided on the spot I was never going camping again without one.

Once I'd learned it was a yurt I set about trying to find one, but without success. The answer seemed to be that I'd have to make it myself. I got hold of a brief instruction sheet and set to work.

A few miles outside Brighton lies Stanmer Park. It holds a tiny village, a church, a manor house and miles of woodland. Decades ago, the woods were managed for coppicing, a practice that goes back thousands of years. When the trunk of a young tree (usually ash, chestnut or hazel) is cut close to the ground, it sprouts side shoots which over the next few years grow long and slim. These can be harvested for furniture, fencing, tool handles, charcoal burning and, in this case, yurt making. Since the cutting can be repeated over and over, the tree never dies, and sunlit spaces are created in otherwise dense and dark woods for a variety of plant species to flourish.

The woods at Stanmer were full of abandoned ash coppice and I spent days roaming through tangled scrub, seeking the best, the straightest and the most knot-free poles, cutting them close to the ground (on a slant so the rain would run off the stumps to prevent them rotting), and peeling the bark to reveal the creamy-pale, sweet-smelling wood beneath. When I had coppiced enough poles, I was ready to start constructing my yurt, and three months later it was done [for maybe too much detail, see *How to Make a Yurt* in part two]

At first, I was so excited I put the yurt up every opportunity I got, even for a single night. But it's hard work and I soon saved it for when I knew I would be camping for at least a few days. It takes several hours to load and unload the car and raise the yurt, and that's before fitting out the inside with carpets, bed, woodstove, gas cooker, kitchen, bookshelves, lights, incense, fruit bowl, bar and decorations.

But once it's done. I lie on my bed of sheepskins, looking up through the open crown at clouds scudding across the sky. Then my eyes start to wander over each individual pole that I coppiced, stripped, carved, bent and sealed. I inhale the smells of linseed oil, turpentine, canvas and maybe a whiff of

woodsmoke from the stove, and feel a deep and primitive joy.

The second time I went to qigong camp I took my yurt with me, and as the years passed (I went for twenty annual camps), Holybrook field slowly filled up with more and more yurts, bell tents and benders. In early mornings as wisps of smoke from banked up wood stoves drifted and mingled with the mist, it began to look like a Mongolian horse fair.

This closed camp of around 130 adults and children (roughly the size of a traditional hunter-gatherer tribe) was the inspiration of Daverick Leggett and Brad Richecouer Everyone arrived on the first day and stayed until the end, allowing the community to build and bond.

Mid-mornings we'd gather in the giant yurt for pow-wow – babies, children, youths, adults and elders sitting in a circle. There was a formality to the opening and closing of these meetings – a poem, a reading, a song, sometimes a game. In-between we'd discuss which work group would cook lunch or supper or maintain the site, what was planned for the different qigong and children's groups, and what entertainment plans we had for the evening. Birthdays were always celebrated and the lucky boy or girl would stand in the centre of the circle as the whole camp bathed them in song.

The work groups maintained the site, chopped wood and cooked lunch or supper. In the early years we catered outdoors on open fires, turning out meals for the entire camp as rain beat down on our heads and fire singed our ankles.

Holybrook field is fringed by mature trees – mostly ash, oak and alder – and the Holy Brook itself runs along one edge. The stream arises deep in the hills of Dartmoor and is bitingly cold. Most mornings I would dip in one of its shallow pools, taking stoic pride in not grimacing or uttering a sound as I ducked beneath the surface. [see short story *Alex* in part two]

This part of Dartmoor has a microclimate of its own, which often meant rain, sometimes for days on end. But we were tough, and camp life carried on in good spirits and laughter. For myself, bad weather added a selfish frisson as I settled into my yurt at night, snuggled up next to the stove on my bed of sheepskins.

I'm a social creature and I loved the constant connection. Wandering from my yurt at the edge of the field towards the central fire at any time of day or night, I'd be waylaid by friends for chats, laughs and hugs.

But being in a large group like this (indeed any group) can also be challenging. Like others, I found myself flipping between feeling secure in the throbbing, loving heart of this little community, and - at other times - standing isolated at its edges, shipwrecked, lonely and stranded as the loving tide passed me by. Being there without my family (they preferred beach and diving holidays to camping in a damp field) made these feelings more intense, but also offered a greater opportunity to confront them. I knew they were of my own making and that the remedy was to give out more love, not wait to receive it. But that knowledge didn't necessarily make it easier to bear.

Qigong camp was the first time I sat in a men's circle. I'd never been a macho kind of male, and like a surprising number of men often felt more comfortable among women. So I experienced an initial flush of nervousness which quickly dissipated in the warm embrace of brotherhood. Whatever differences we might have, we shared much in common, and I was taken aback by how relieved I felt that - for the moment - there were no women to try to please, attract, seek solace from or misunderstand. Nowadays, I jump at the chance of sitting with other men in safe surroundings like this and feel a deep sense of comfort in doing so.

The men's circle observed a couple of simple rules. There was a talking stick and whoever needed to speak would take it. Nobody could interrupt – whether to offer words of support, interpretation or advice – and the speaker had the floor until they replaced the stick. It is very moving when men speak from their hearts like this, sharing their fears, worries and embarrassments, creating an atmosphere that allows all this without judgment, and offering each other their silent encouragement and support.

As the days passed, there was a growing confusion of offerings – botanical walks, storytelling, fire-making classes, raku pottery, dancing, wood-fired saunas, football or frisbee games, massage exchanges and more. On top of three qigong sessions, meetings, work tasks and endless conversations round the fire, the days were full to bursting.

One year I laboured to build an oven to bake bread and pizzas, digging and hauling heavy and obstinate clay, mixing it with straw and packing it round a hazel wood frame, then firing it for hours before baking the first loaf. I did it for the challenge (and it was), because I'd always wanted to build a clay oven, and because I wanted to offer something to this pop-up tribe I was such a willing part of. Sadly, it was only used for a few days before I had to ceremoniously destroy it because the farmer who owned the field wanted it gone.

Inspired by my creative writing course, I also organised a regular microfiction night. Microfiction is the art of telling a story in as few words as possible – anything from a thousand down to a hundred or even fewer. Ernest Hemingway is reputed to have started the trend. He was challenged to write a story in six words and came up with the haunting, "For sale; baby shoes; never worn."

We offered prompts to those who needed them – for example an opening or last line, or a character, place and emotion - which had to be woven into the story, but the only strict rule was the word count. I can get tearful when I remember the joy of sitting in a circle around the giant yurt, listening to so many funny, imaginative and moving stories – often written by the most unexpected people. [see examples of my own microfiction in part two]

The closing night cabaret was joyous proof of what had been built in these ten days of community. From a day or two beforehand, little clusters of people would be tucked away in corners of the field, practising their acts. On the night itself, the great yurt was hung with lights and decorations, the compere would step forth, and from tiny children to elders, up to half the camp would take to the stage and perform songs, playlets, stand-up comedy, poetry and music, usually ending with wild drumming and dancing.

Qigong camp was often the highlight of my year. It was a chance to be in my beloved yurt, to be in nature, to play, to explore and let loose my creativity, to engage in direct and honest communication, to open my sometimes chilly heart and to be my best self. I made some of my closest and best friends there and it has been a treasure in my life.

16. CREATIVE WRITING

In 2010 I enrolled on a two-year creative writing course at Sussex University. That meant going back to the place I'd been thrown out of so ignominiously 43 years before as a bored and rebellious teenager. This time, however, I felt enriched by the opportunity, and walking into this citadel of learning was a treat. Sometimes education is wasted on the young.

I'd done quite a bit of academic writing in the past, and like many people I'd written a few poems, but I'd never tackled fiction and had no idea if I could pull it off. Our first assignment was to go out to one of the University cafes, choose someone and observe them – what they were wearing, how they sat, how they talked, and then weave a story about them. I found it easier than I expected [see my first short story *Three Dreams* in part two] and would recommend it as a great starting point for anyone who wants to write.

I once heard a series of radio interviews with well-known authors. They were asked whether they enjoyed the act of writing. Most either liked the initial creative process but hated the necessary editing that followed, or else they sweated over the creativity but loved shaping it into its finished form. There were two exceptions. The winner of a recent literary prize confessed that he hated every single part of the business of writing, while Will Self owned up to loving it all. I'm with Will.

In the creative phase, I sometimes feel that I'm taken over by another self (no pun intended). Ideas and words seem to appear from nowhere – as long as I allow them to – and I often look back on stories I've written with no idea where they came from. But then comes the editing process – cutting away and refining to let the essentials shine forth, much like revealing a figure from a block of wood or stone. Cutting is one of the hardest and most ruthless of tasks. As one of my favourite writers, Truman Capote, said, "I believe more in the scissors than I do in the pencil." [Over the years I've collected some of my favourite quotes about writing and added them to the end of this chapter].

One important component of a creative writing course is receiving feedback on a piece of work from the tutor and the other students. Most try to observe the 'critical sandwich' principle – start with praise, then constructive criticism, and end with more praise, though sometimes the bread is wafer thin and the filling spills out all over the place. Whatever the case, we had to learn to listen with an open mind, weigh up the feedback even if we didn't like it, and then decide whether to accept it or not.

I'd seen this modelled wonderfully in a different setting, during group sessions with my therapist Jackie. If someone accused her of favouritism, or avoidance, or any other failing, she'd say, "Wait. Let me think," and then, after a long silence, she'd come back with something like, "Yes, you're right, I realise you remind me of my daughter and I'm not seeing you as you really are," or else, "No, I'm not having that. Let's try and find out what's going on with you that you feel that way." It was one of the many impressive things about her and it prepared me for writing class.

I also think this approach can spill over into the rest of our life. We are receiving feedback from others all the time, and if we want to grow and develop, we have to try to be open to it. As the English proverb says, "Write down the advice of those who love you, though you like it not at present."

The year after I finished my creative writing course, I wrote a young adult (YA) novel called *Juice*. The idea came to me when I started to imagine what life would be like without electricity (juice).
The preface set the scene,

He'd had the talk from Mrs. Wilkins - the big one they gave you when you turned eleven. It was in the schoolroom one day in late August as the wind swirled the last of the brown leaves from the trees.

"We had warnings," Mrs. Wilkins said. "Lots of them - so many we hardly noticed anymore. It all seemed too far away, too difficult to grasp. It was easier not to think about it. But then in a few short years, they all came true and everything fell apart."

Weather changes started it - slow at first, then rapid, runaway, unstoppable. Here, where they lived, winters became bitterly cold for months on end. In summer the crops rotted in the fields and whole towns and villages flooded under weeks of pounding rain. Far away, mountain glaciers disappeared, drying up the great rivers of Asia, and searing heat sucked the moisture from the land.

Plants withered and were ravaged by disease. Cattle, sheep, pigs and humans died of thirst and hunger - their bodies strewn unburied across the landscape. Millions migrated in search of water, food and safety but were beaten back by those desperate to hold on to what they had. Wars broke out everywhere.

Weakened by years of turmoil and starvation, the people of the world were scythed down by successive epidemics, like fields of grain.

As untold numbers died, everything fell apart. Without electricity, oil, gas, hospitals, supermarkets, telephones, computers, law or government, small communities of survivors struggled to rebuild their lives.

It took me a year to write it - following the adventures of my young hero Will as he navigated the post-apocalyptic world he was born into, and I thought I was onto a winner. But deep down I knew something wasn't right. I asked various friends to read it, but in the end it was a professional critic who told me the truth. He said that he liked the writing, the idea, the characters and more, but the plotline was just too weak.

I immediately knew he was right. Since a gripping plot is probably the single most important feature of YA books, that was a real problem. I realised that in my two-year creative writing course, storyline was never discussed – as though it was beneath the dignity of writers with literary aspirations. That may be why I find so many literary prize-winning novels wonderful for the first fifty pages ("what gorgeous language, what sentences") then lose interest because I'm just not absorbed in the story.

I'd written some successful short pieces during my course. My story *A Comrade Summer* was shortlisted for the inaugural £10,000 Manchester Fiction prize. When I got the phone call inviting me to Manchester along with five others for the ceremony announcing the winner (not me), I went into a kind of shock. It so disturbed me that I felt unsafe. I dropped things, tripped on the stairs, and generally risked life and limb until I did some qigong to settle myself.

With several short stories under my belt, I'd approached writing a novel in the same way - assuming that my rather vague initial idea would unfold naturally. But it hadn't worked and now I faced having to do a major rewrite.

I started by reading books about plot, particularly those written by Hollywood scriptwriters – the world's foremost story experts. That's when I realised how hard it is to come up with a good and original story. Tens of thousands of plots are pitched to movie producers and most are rejected within minutes. The hundreds that are considered promising are then sent to script doctors to work them into viable screenplays. Finally, of these, only around three hundred make it to production every year - and as we all know, many turn out to be turkeys.

I discovered something else too about writing in the modern age. It's common to hear the terms 'first or second draft' applied to novels. It comes from the days when an author would write out the first version of their novel by hand, with limited opportunity to chop and change. Then they would look at the whole thing, identify the sometimes major changes that were needed, and produce the next draft. Working on a computer can change all that. Whenever I felt uninspired or uncertain where the story was going, I'd close-edit and polish what I'd already written, maybe many times over, so that it became embedded or carved in stone, in a way that was difficult and painful to change.

When it really dawned on me that the plot of *Juice* - the spinal column of the novel - had to be ripped out and everything rearranged round a new one, I didn't have the heart. I put it away in a metaphorical drawer (where it still languishes) and wrote *Live Well Live Long: Teachings from the Chinese Nourishment of Life Tradition* instead.

Writing quotations

There are three rules for writing the novel. Unfortunately, no one knows what they are.
W. Somerset Maugham

The secret of being a bore is to tell everything.
Voltaire

You have to know how to accept rejection and reject acceptance.
Ray Bradbury

You can't wait for inspiration. You have to go after it with a club.
Jack London

It was a book to kill time for those who like it better dead.
Dame Rose Macaulay

The covers of this book are too far apart.
Ambrose Bierce
I was working on the proof of one of my poems all the morning, and took

out a comma. In the afternoon I put it back again.
Oscar Wilde

Read over your compositions, and wherever you meet with a passage which you think is particularly fine, strike it out.
Samuel Johnson

This is not a novel to be tossed aside lightly. It should be thrown with great force.
Dorothy Parker

People who like this sort of thing will find this the sort of thing they like.
Abraham Lincoln

I have read your book and much like it.
Moses Hadas

A good many young writers make the mistake of enclosing a stamped, self-addressed envelope, big enough for the manuscript to come back in. This is too much of a temptation to the editor.
Ring Lardner

It took me fifteen years to discover that I had no talent for writing, but I couldn't give it up because by that time I was too famous.
Robert Benchley

Your manuscript is both good and original, but the part that is good is not original and the part that is original is not good.
Samuel Johnson

When in doubt have a man come through the door with a gun in his hand.
Raymond Chandler

17. LIVE WELL LIVE LONG

"There exist no miraculous methods in the world, only plain ones, and the perfection of the plain is miraculous."
Fei Boxiong 1863

After contracting hepatitis in Morocco, I'd turned to a macrobiotic diet to heal myself, and more broadly to turn my life around. And from there, the inspiration for Infinity Foods arose.

Infinity was as much an educational and political project as a business, and during my time there I used to give talks and write leaflets on diet, as well as co-writing *Nature's Foods*. Studying Chinese medicine and dealing with another post-travelling illness on my return from India, then deepened my understanding of health and disease.

The two thousand year old *Yellow Emperor's Inner Classic*, probably the most important Chinese medical classic, taught that disease was not caused by gods, demons or other malign influences but by objective factors, of which lifestyle was the most important. Its opening page is a discussion between the mythical Yellow Emperor and his advisor Qi Bo (Chee Bo). The Emperor asks why in ancient times (and remember when this was written) people stayed strong and healthy until the age of a hundred, whereas 'nowadays' they are decrepit at fifty.

"It's their lifestyle", Qi Bo replies. "They don't know how to live. They drink too much alcohol; their diet and sleeping habits are chaotic; they give in to their desires all the time."

When we study Chinese medicine we are taught to ask, "where did this disease come from?". Is it from excessive or disruptive emotions, poor diet, lack of sleep, infection, overwork, too much or too little exercise and so on?

This aspect of Chinese medicine really captured my enthusiasm, and chapter two of the *Yellow Emperor's Inner Classic* hit home. It taught that the wisest doctors intervene early, before a disease has arisen. Waiting until it has settled in is like only starting to dig a well when you are thirsty, or forging weapons when the battle is already raging all around you.

I realised after I'd been practising for a few years that many chronic diseases can never be cured by medicine, only helped, and the only way to 'cure' them is to prevent them arising in the first place, through adopting a lifestyle that supports mental and physical health and wellbeing.

For me, this is one of the treasures of Chinese medicine. It has a deep and rich understanding of human life, health and disease, deriving from its philosophy of inter-connectedness and its unbroken history of over two thousand years of careful observation. Its unique pattern-based approach to diagnosis means that it also has the tools to home in on what is likely to have contributed to an individual patient's disease. One of the doctor's roles is then to reflect this back to the patient so that they can understand, and work on, what may need to change in order to get well, and to inform the patient about ways they can help prevent future illness.

A Chinese saying goes, 'the last creature to discover water is the fish', i.e. the sea we swim in is so familiar to us that we are unable to see it. We may receive clues, though. Our family or friends might constantly comment on how we gobble our food, stay up too late, never take exercise or worry too much, but we are adept at tuning out their words. Coming from an empathetic doctor, however, the patient may really hear this information for the first time.

The subject of how to live to maximise our chances of living a long and healthy life is called *yangsheng* (nourishment of life) in Chinese. It is at least two and a half thousand years old and draws from Daoist and Confucian philosophy, from the wisdom of generations of doctors, and from the internal cultivation tradition (qigong, the internal martial arts, meditation etc.) and folk medicine.

There were two things I especially valued about yangsheng. The first is that it is comprehensive and deals with every aspect of human life from birth through to ageing and dying. However, four are key and in my book I used the image of a chair. whose four legs represent the emotions, diet, exercise/ rest, and sleep. Like a chair, we need all four to be stable and strong. The 3rd century alchemist Ge Hong, warned "one must be on guard against the tendency of specialists to tout the one thing they are good at". For example, there are plenty of people who teach or follow a healthy diet, or are passionate about exercise, but suffer from a chaotic and destructive emotional life or never get enough sleep.

Secondly yangsheng has a history going back two and a half thousand years so it tends to be immune to passing fads and fashions in favour of what has been shown over many centuries to work. It is time-tested.

I started to read everything I could on the subject and began to teach seminars - three hours at first, then a whole day, then two days. And as a displacement activity for my inability to tackle a rewrite of my novel *Juice*, I decided to turn it into a book *Live Well Live Long: Teachings from the Chinese Nourishment of Life Tradition.* I already had five decades of thinking about health and disease behind me, but I knew I had to do some serious research. I wanted to delve deeper into the history and teachings of yangsheng, and I also wanted to see how the past fifty or so years of lifestyle research did or did not bear out the traditional teachings.

I spent a delicious year visiting the British Library. It holds, or can acquire, virtually every book ever written in English. In possession of a precious reader's card, you can reserve up to a dozen books online and turn up at the library a couple of days later in the knowledge that they will be waiting for you in one of the famous reading rooms where Charles Darwin, Charles Dickens, Karl Marx and Lenin sat and wrote books or hatched plots that changed the world. I felt intense gratitude for this wonderful and (still) free gift - being allowed to sit amidst hundreds of writers, researchers, teachers and students, heads down, quietly poring over their work.

Writing *Live Well Live Long* allowed me to integrate my love of the Chinese health tradition with my respect for scientific research. That has sometimes felt like a narrow and precarious path. On one side my love of qigong and Chinese medicine places me as a fantasist (or worse) in the eyes of orthodox science. On the other, my scepticism around much magical new-age thinking defines me as a hard-edged materialist with little understanding of what is often called 'spiritual'.

Second hand

My first hand speaks the truth,
Straight from the horse's mouth.
When open, all is revealed.
An empty hand,
Nothing up the sleeve.
When closed, direct,
A manly right hook.
What you see is what you get.
This meaty fist will get you out of a jam,
Unscrew a jar of pickles,
Sign with a flourish,
In unblinking daylight.

My second hand,
On the distaff side,
Cannot sign, but it can sing
Cats out of trees.
While the frank charm of the right hand
Diverts the gaze,
Its sister hand draws patterns in the sacred ash,
Strokes deep roots,
Scoops dark water
Beneath a clouded moon
Summoning secret desires.

There are a number of videos of my talks on different aspects of health cultivation on my YouTube channel.

18. QIGONG

"There is a joy in repetition and the more you repeat it the stronger it grows"
Ethnomusicologist Michael Veal
on the funk rhythms of Fela Kuti – father of Afrobeat

I have practised qigong most days for almost thirty years. It is an inseparable part of who I am, re-shapes my body-mind every time I practise it, and I'd even say that I wouldn't be alive today without it. I feel very lucky that I discovered it.

Over the years I've learned from a number of teachers and books. I had a few lessons in China in 1981 on the back of an inspiring meeting with a retired maths professor. He'd been diagnosed with terminal lung cancer and given only months to live. A qigong teacher showed him an anti-cancer practice and told him to mentally focus on something pleasant while he did it. This gentle mathematician told us that he loved peony flowers. He had gone to the park at four o'clock every morning and practised for five hours, visualising peony flowers all the while. Now, several years later, he was free of cancer.

During that same trip to China I used to visit the local park in the early morning to do my tai chi practice and watch others doing theirs. One freezing morning I passed a very old woman, bundled up in numerous layers of clothing. She was standing in front of a tree, both hands holding on to the trunk, gently swinging one leg to and fro. When I'd finished my own practice an hour or so later, I returned the way I'd come. As I passed the tree, there she was, swinging the other leg.

In the UK I studied with Michael Tse (wild goose qigong), Shen Hongxun (buqi healing) and Bruce Frantzis among others. I did learn valuable lessons from every one of them, but I can't say I took to them as human beings, however great their skills were

Some fifteen years ago I was introduced to Roy Jenzen (internalintent.com). While there have also been times I haven't seen eye to eye with him, I have learnt as much from him as I have from any person I've ever met, and owe him an immense debt of gratitude. His qigong and *neigong* are rooted in the Chinese internal martial arts tradition (especially *xingyiquan* and *baguazhang*). He trained for several years in China, roughly at the same time as I was first there studying acupuncture. Over the years, I've been to numerous classes and workshops with him and each time my understanding of *neigong* - the internal skill that underlies practices like qigong and taichi and without which they may only be 'empty form' – has deepened. With Roy I have learned five animal qigong (crane, tiger, bear, deer and monkey) whose origins lie in ancient shamanistic practices; the centuries-old eight silken movements *baduanjin*, *baguazhang* – a martial art that develops agile footwork, balance, speed, and sinewy twisting through the whole body; a little *xingyiquan* (another of the internal martial arts); and bone marrow washing.

In recent years I have taken what I've learned from him, integrated it with my other qigong inputs (for example *taichi qigong*) and my by now quite long experience, and transformed it into my own approach to this phenomenal self-development practice. I have posted several videos about qigong on my website *qigong.works*

When I teach qigong and try and explain it, I say it is the equal cultivation of three skills (*gong*) - body, breath and mind. When these three are absorbed into each other, like water into a sponge, we experience the transformative power of qigong.

Body skill draws on the internal martial arts tradition since body awareness, balance, stability, strength, integrated movement, softness, rooting to the earth and much more are essential parts of these fighting arts.

Breath skill (deep, slow, lower abdominal and integrated with movement) resets the autonomic nervous system to a calm, centred, parasympathetic-dominant state that can heal and nourish our body-mind.

Mind skill maximises awareness of the present moment and of the body and breath. Over time, it changes the physical structure of the brain, allows us greater command over unhelpful emotions, and enables us to develop compassion, empathy, knowledge, inspiration and wisdom.

But there's more. I am not religious and I hold as few beliefs as possible, but that doesn't mean that I don't seek transcendence. The Chinese talk of the 'three powers' – the trilogy of heaven, earth and human. One wa sy of understanding this comes from recognising that we are rare among creatures in that we stand upright, our feet planted firmly on the earth and the crown of our head reaching into heaven (the cosmos)..

On a physical level, by sinking and connecting to earth - our root – we increase stability, leg strength and balance, and by softly rising towards to heaven we hold ourselves erect and create more space through the spine and the lengthened body.

On a mental and emotional level, holding a rooted, upright and aligned posture while breathing slowly into our core, helps us feel calm, strong, positive, assertive and integrated. It is hard to hold on to confidence, emotional stability and resilience if our chest and back slump or our legs and feet are weak and unanchored.

And for me, this heaven-earth-human trilogy also has transcendent implications. The Daoist and other ancient traditions teach us that yin earth corresponds to the unconscious, darkness, deep wisdom, nourishment, fertility and birth. By contrast yang heaven connects us to the infinite universe (so easy to forget about), and to brightness, clear discriminative wisdom and the emptiness from which all phenomena (the ten thousand things) arise and disappear.

By integrating earth and heaven, yin and yang, we can draw inspiration from both and become more fully human. And finally, transcending even yin and yang, we may have moments when we can leave behind our discriminating consciousness altogether and become one with everything that is - the Dao. [see short story *The Black Pearl and the White Pearl* in part two]

I used the word transcendence earlier as I have problems with 'spiritual', which has its origins in the separation of mind and body found in some religions whose aim is to transcend, subjugate or discard the tainted physical body and escape into the pure light of spirit. I wrote about this in more detail in my book *Live Well Live Long: Teachings from the Chinese Nourishment of Life Tradition*.

19. THE CHINESE MEDICINE FORESTRY TRUST

The Chinese Medicine Forestry Trust promotes planetary, human and species health and wellbeing by planting trees and protecting forests throughout the world

The profit from the sale of this book will go to the Chinese Medicine Forestry Trust (https://tcmft.ctdonate.org) which I helped set up last year under the umbrella of the UK's Charities Trust. Please also consider making a regular donation.

The aim is simple – to appeal for funds (especially from the global Chinese medicine community) and direct them to organisations which plant and protect forests throughout the world.

It came about because myself and three acupuncture colleagues were feeling overwhelmed with sorrow, anger and hopelessness in the face of biodiversity loss and environmental destruction.

The threats seemed too many to respond to – warming oceans full of plastic, forests burning, the collapse of insect and bird populations and what has been called the fifth major mass extinction of the earth's species (this time through human agency). In the face of these threats it is easy to retreat into denial or despair, feeling that our own individual efforts are futile. Yet the decision to engage in even one action on behalf of the planet and its inhabitants can add another drop to a growing river of change. It can also support our mental health and liberate our determination and energy.

In Praise of Trees, an article called that I wrote , is available for download at https://peterdeadman.co.uk/about/chinese-medicine-forestry-trust/

CONCLUSION

I began writing these memoirs during the UK's first COVID-19 lockdown and am finishing them during the second. Autumn is drifting into winter and the Norwegian maple tree outside the window where I write has decorated the pavement with its beautiful golden-red leaves.

It has been an interesting process. As Socrates says, "The unexamined life is not worth living."

Why do we make the choices we do, take this path not that one? I can see that my iconoclastic streak – powerful in my younger years and not quite burnt out yet - was driven in part by the choices my parents made. They injected me with their left-wing, anti-establishment politics and I am immensely grateful that they did. But an unexpected result for them was that I also turned this education in rebellion onto the socially conservative, suburban milieu they brought me up in.

I can understand why they did it. My father's generation was flung around the world during the second world war and many experienced extreme hardship and trauma, as did their relatives back home when the bombs fell. Once the war was over they yearned for peace, stability and an uncomplicated life. And for my father, the comfortable three-bedroomed house and garden he and my mother settled and lived in until his death fifty years later, was several steps up the ladder from the cramped and cold house he was brought up in.

My mother was happy to follow him to England and even to Beckenham, but she made sure to fill the house with her colourful international friends, and regularly escaped into the glamorous world of musicians, dancers, circus artists and gymnasts.

It was this family background and the winds of change which began to blow in the 1960s that taught me to be open to different ways of doing things and led me first into the path of travelling, and then, after getting sick in Morocco and India, to natural foods, Chinese medicine, qigong and *yangsheng*.

One fear I've had is that writing about myself like this is a narcissistic project. If it sounds that way to the reader, then *mea culpa*. But I do remember back to my very first job – in Beckenham Public Library – and how many people came in asking for a biography or autobiography. We are fascinated by the lives of others which are both so different and yet – in many ways – so similar to our own. We all have our adventures, our successes and failures, our joys and sorrows. We all make mistakes and hopefully learn from them and in all these we share the remarkable fact that we are born, we live rich and complex human lives, and then we disappear into the mystery.

Looking back, especially to my teenage years and early twenties, a lot seemed be happening all the time. Maybe it was because I invited it all in, but whatever the reason, life is quieter now. I practise and teach qigong, grow my vegetable garden and shiitake mushrooms, cook, write, listen to music, dance, get out in nature and spend as much time with family and friends as COVID currently allows.

But at the age of 72, I hope – and expect – that the journey is not yet over and that it will still have some interesting twists and turns. I have no idea what I will do now these memoirs are finished. Every day a new idea pops up but nowadays I'm less inclined to jump on every one. Some days I am reminded of Lady Astor (second ever British female Member of Parliament) who said, "I used to dread getting older because I thought I would not be able to do all the things I wanted to do, but now that I am older I find that I don't want to do them."

I like to take inspiration from Bob Dylan, with his commitment to constant change and development. As a twenty-five year old he sang, "He not busy being born is busy dying". His latest album, *Rough and Rowdy Ways* walks that talk and is the masterwork of a nearly eighty year old, ever-evolving creative genius.

PART TWO - SHORT STORIES

THE COMRADE SUMMER

Unlike much of my childhood, the summer I was eleven stands out clear in my memory. It seemed to be hot for months on end. The tarmac oozed as the roses wilted and the cropped grass turned brown. It was the summer I lived on my bike, like a cowboy in the saddle.

Something had happened to me in the spring of that year. Close to the old brick wall at the end of our back garden grew an apple tree. One morning I climbed it and sat on the wall with my head right among the blossom, just as the sun rose over the roofs of our suburban cul-de-sac. I'd never really noticed apple blossom before, with its fragile pinks and whites and secret reds. The sun glowed through the fresh leaves and warmed my face and I was suddenly overwhelmed with a feeling of beauty and peace, an absolute sense of my place in the world and of my life stretching thrillingly before me.

The excitement stayed with me as the long summer holidays began. I would wake before my parents, jump into shorts, t-shirt and sandals, and go out into the cool garden to eat my bowl of cereal. Then I would hurry to leave the house before my parents appeared and made everything ordinary again.

Most mornings I would cycle to the swimming pool and wait for the doors to open. I loved racing through the empty roads and diving and somersaulting in the echoing pool, and I loved the memory of chlorine that hung on my skin all through the day. I would be back home, with my mother frying eggs, when my father was still in his pyjamas.

"Here he is at last, my fish of a son," my mother would say. "Come and eat," but all I wanted was to drop my wet things and rush back into the sun, to ride up and down the road until Malcolm had finished his chores and would come out the front door of number eight on the other side of the road.

I am in the saddle, one foot on the kerb, the other stretching to the road, rolling back and forth, watching the front tyre score patterns in the black silt of the gutter. It edges closer and closer to the giant stag beetle lying on its back, legs waving feebly. The tyre nudges the beetle, biting at its crisp body.

"Go on then," says Malcolm and gives me a push, and the tyre rolls over the beetle and crushes its shiny, ribbed shell. An orange mess squeezes out.

Malcolm laughs. "That's just what the insides of sea urchins look like," he says. "We saw them in Lloret del Mar last year. They pull out the spines and eat the guts with a spoon while they're still alive. I bet you can eat stag beetles like that."

I shudder. Next to death and nuclear bombs, stag beetles scare me the most, with their great barbed horns and the way they suddenly take off and clatter unpredictably through the air.

"Beat you," I say, and standing on the pedals I race to the green, the oval patch of grass that forms the bulb end of the cul-de-sac. The green is small and the turns are tight; take them too fast and you skid. Our bare knees are always scabbed from grating on the gravelled road.

When we get tired of racing we go down the alley, an unpaved track that winds round the back gardens of the houses, past the wooden fences and gates that smell of creosote in the hot sun. Nobody else ever seems to come down here and it's heavy with the scent of greenery, and hot and still but for the buzzing of insects and the distant grumble of a lawn mower. On the side of the track opposite the gardens is a crumbling brick wall. Here there are wild patches with clumps of hot stinging nettles full of caterpillars, and dark corners piled with bottles and rags and rusting cans.

We throw our bikes down and start picking caterpillars off the nettles and putting them in a dirty glass jar.

"Hey look," I hear Malcolm say.

It's a dead thrush. When I turn it over with a stick I can see the crawling maggots and a sweet, rotten smell pours off it.

"That's what happens when you die," says Malcolm. "Your eyeballs burst and the maggots and worms crawl in and out of the sockets. They try and make the coffins so thick the worms can't get in, but it never works."

"It's much better if they burn you," I say, half-remembering something I've heard.

There's a silence then Malcolm says, "How can you be resurrected if you're just a pile of ash?"

"I don't know," I say, suddenly on shaky ground.

There's a lot I don't know. Not long before school broke up, Mrs Bailey asked our class to tell her what was special about next Saturday. Everyone but me thrust their hands to the ceiling.

"Don't you know what day it is Daniel?" she said.

I felt my face getting red.

"Tell him Amanda," and Amanda Eggerton, sitting next to me, said, "It's the Queen's official birthday miss," and everyone turned and stared.

I'm always denying things too, like when Savidge came up to me in the playground and said, "You're a jewboy aren't you."

"Your dad's a Communist," says Malcolm.

"No he isn't," I say.

Malcolm is a year older than me and goes to the grammar school where my dad teaches maths.

"He's a Commie," says Malcolm, "Everybody knows. I don't care though. I don't even know what it means. My father says they should all be shot."

"It means everyone should be equal," I say quickly. "The working class are the best because they make things. And Russians. And black people in America are good. There shouldn't be rich people or poor people, everything should be shared out the same."

Malcolm looks at me. "So can we share your bike then?" he says.

I try to laugh but my face won't move. I look down at my red bike lying on its side, shining in the sun, the bike I waited for so long and finally got for my birthday two months ago, the bike I still polish and oil and grease nearly every day.

"Only joking," he says. "Let's make a fire."

Malcolm always has matches and caps and cap guns and bangers, even when it's nowhere near November.

We tear the labels off old tin cans and scrunch them up and pile twigs on top. Then we light it and squat either side watching it burn. Once we made a fire close to the wooden fence and you can still see the scorch mark.

"The school I was at before," says Malcolm, "There was this boy Dimmock who blew two of his fingers off playing with fireworks."

We're back in the road, doing nothing, sitting on the kerb in the sun when I hear my mother calling.

"Daniel, Daniel, it is eating time."

I wish she wouldn't do that but I can't stop her; she sounds so foreign and stupid with her Russian accent and everyone in the road can hear her.

"Sorry," I say to Malcolm.

My mother is always trying to feed Malcolm but he's not allowed to eat with us. He has to make his own lunch and wash everything up afterwards. His mother doesn't go out to work but she lies down a lot during the day.

I park my bike, the tyre tight against the kerb, and run inside our cool house that all this summer has smelled of paint as my father, wearing his old army shorts, has whistled his way round the windows and doors.

"Can I take it outside?" I say.

"No. Go and wash your hands, top to bottom," my mother says.

"Please," I say, and I'm already out the door with the triangles of sandwich and a dill pickle. I ride down the road, as far as the green, then sit and eat them in the saddle.

My parents don't allow guns or television. At four o'clock Malcolm and I go to his house, which is full of dark wood and smells of polish.

Malcolm's house has fitted carpets. When he opens the front door with the key that hangs on a woven leather strap clipped to his belt, his mother is already standing in the hall.

"Shoes," she says, and Malcolm has to change into his slippers. As I take my shoes off I see that my socks have holes in them.

"Please may we watch television?" Malcolm says to his mother.

We can watch children's television in the sitting room but only Malcolm's mother can open the shiny doors of the wooden cabinet and switch it on. We sit on the carpet with Malcolm's guns and shoot the Indians who leap out on the Lone Ranger and Tonto as they ride through rocky passes.

My dad was an athlete and a boxer at university. Malcolm's father is big and fat. His head is shiny and he has a ginger moustache and a red face. His stomach pokes out of the khaki cardigan with leather buttons he always wears at home. On weekdays he wears a suit and spends ages fussing with his Morris Traveller before squeezing himself into it and driving off. Malcolm says he's in insurance.

"It was eight years before he would so much as nod his head to us," my mother often complains. "He would never have opened his mouth if he hadn't had to eat his humble pie and talk to your father about Malcolm at Parents' evening."

Malcolm's father builds miniature steam engines in his shed and when he's in a good mood we can go and watch them working, the brass pistons pumping away, red-painted wheels spinning. The rest of the time the shed is padlocked.

He comes in when the pistol shots are ricocheting through the valley and says, "Turn that thing down." Then he sits in his armchair and reads the *Daily Express*.

"Bloody trouble makers," he says, "Ought to be rounded up," and Malcolm's mother who is passing in the hall says, "Gordon, shush."

We are Communists and we read the *Daily Worker*. Some Saturdays I go out with my dad, delivering it to party members. We walk up front paths that look just the same as everyone else's but I know the people in these houses are Comrades and are different. Some of them are foreign, with thick accents like my mother's. Others, usually in smaller houses on the estate, are what are called the proletariat like Dick, one of my dad's best friends. He's a bus driver and always lets us off at the end of our road, even though there's no bus stop there. Anyway, we never just push the paper through the letter boxes of these houses but have to ring the bell and then my father stands on the doorstep and talks for ages and ages.

They meet in our house in the evenings. Sometimes I sit at the top of the stairs in my pyjamas. Mostly they all talk at once, but the one voice I hear clearly is my dad's. When he talks everyone goes quiet, maybe because he's a teacher, and even when there's long pauses and I know he's filling his pipe, they wait to hear what he has to say about people like Krushchev and Stalin, and the Labour party. The smell of his pipe tobacco fills the house and gets right into my bedroom.

Other evenings we sit together in the living room. Sometimes my mother, who used to be a concert pianist, plays the piano and we stand around and sing Scottish songs like Over the Sea to Skye. Or we listen to records. All of us like Paul Robeson because he's black and a Communist and is treated badly by the Americans, but my dad likes opera best. In fact he likes opera so much that he's wired up speakers all round the house so he can hear it even when he's in the toilet. He plays it so loud that Mrs Bouvier from next door keeps complaining.

"I really must draw your attention once again to your music," she says. "It's far too loud. I've asked you before. Especially on Sunday mornings."

When she's gone, I prance round the room with my chest puffed up and my nose in the air, and say, "It's far too loud, I must complain," and my parents laugh.

Just there, next to the broken paving stone, is where Malcolm hit the kerb, face first.

We were racing round the green and he'd got in front. Whenever I tried to get past, he'd block me. I know I clipped the back of his wheel but I didn't mean to. There was blood and bits of white tooth coming out of his mouth and he lay there without moving and with his left arm twisted. A builder who was working on the roof of number seventeen came down the ladder really fast. He got Malcolm up and kept saying, "You're all right lad, you're all right," and Malcolm started crying so loudly I was scared. Mrs Stokes came out with a tea towel and the builder held it to Malcolm's mouth as he helped him over to number eight and rang the bell. Malcolm was cradling his arm. I saw Malcolm's mother white faced at the open door.

There was a small crowd of people now and someone said they'd called an ambulance. Mrs Stokes, who is old and smells sour, like she doesn't wash much, came up to me as I was standing to the side.

"It was you," she said. "You knocked into him."

"No I didn't," I said. "He skidded."

"You brought him down," said Mrs Stokes. "I know your sort."

I felt my face grow hot and I ran home, leaving my bike lying in the road. My mother was in the kitchen holding on to the washing machine that always juddered across the floor when it was on spin. I told her what had happened, with my face pressed into her apron. I didn't tell her it was my fault, though, as she stroked my hair and called me 'bubeleh'.

I didn't see Malcolm for several days. I kept to the house and the back garden. I was terrified that Mrs Stokes would say something to Malcolm's parents.

A few days later my mother and I were walking down the front path on our way shopping for new school clothes. She was behind me as usual, thumping my shoulders with her hand to get rid of the dandruff and stray hairs. I saw Malcolm's father walking over, his face redder than ever.

"You kids need to be a bit more careful on those bikes of yours," he said, and then to my mother, "You want to keep an eye on him."

The next time I saw Malcolm he had stitches on his forehead, a bruise right down one side of his face and his left arm in plaster up to the elbow.

"You can still see my blood on the pavement," he said and grinned. There was a gap where one of his front teeth was missing.

"Do you want to play down the alley?" I said.

"I can't," he said.

The holidays seemed to last forever and then suddenly they were over. I had brand new everything - blazer, cap, coat, pencil case, satchel, all smelling fresh from the shop. I wished I was going to the school that Malcolm went to; we could have gone on our bikes. But because my dad taught there I had to go to a different one that was two bus rides away and where I didn't know anyone.

When I got home that first day I dropped my bag and blazer in the hall and went into the kitchen to make a cheese and honey sandwich. It was one of my mother's weird mixtures that I always pretended I didn't really like.
I could hear my parents talking in the sitting room with the door closed, which was strange as my father always got home much later than me. I went in. My father was sitting in the armchair and my mother was on the arm of the chair with her hand on his head. I'd never seen him cry before. I stood there furiously concentrating on twisting and turning the sandwich to stop the honey dropping on the floor till my mother told me to go out into the garden.

My father had been suspended. They said he'd been using his maths classes to spread Communism.

Dick came round the next day when we were having breakfast with a copy of the *Wickham Advertiser* folded to the letters page.

"You've got to bloody hear this," he said. "'Dear Sir. Most right-minded people will be shocked to hear that Communism is rife in our local schools. Our children are being indoctrinated by the very people who are supposed to teach them right and wrong.' Then he says we should all write to our MPs - that's a joke - and it's signed Gordon Simmonds. Isn't he that neighbour of yours?"

Though the letter didn't mention my father, there was a short piece on the front page saying how he'd been suspended and anyone could work it out.

The Comrades rallied round. They came to share their outrage and the cakes and pots of food they'd made. I got my hair ruffled and my cheek pinched more than ever. Some of the neighbours were all right too; people he'd lent his lawnmower to or whose kids he'd helped with maths. But others, like Mrs Stokes, crossed to the other side of the road whenever they saw us. Mrs Bouvier next door turned her head and went back into the house and shut the door if any of us went out into the back garden. If Mr Bouvier didn't follow her, she'd stand at the kitchen door calling him in with her shrill voice.

I know my father tried hard to appear normal but he'd stopped whistling and he didn't play opera any more. A reporter from the paper came to the house to interview him, "so you can put your case," but my father wouldn't speak to him. When the reporter rang for the third time my mother took the call and said, "He doesn't want to talk to anyone; he would rather pull his leg off," and slammed the phone down.

The day before his hearing with the school board he went out for a long walk.

"Your father is very worried," my mother said.

"What happens if he doesn't get his job back?"

"It will kill him," she said.

I went out and sat on the wall at the end of the garden. There were only a few apples and most of them were wrinkled and small.

"I think it's going to be all right," my father told us when he came back from the hearing. "They've done the whole thing properly. They spoke to all my kids with their parents present, and none of them said they'd heard me talk about anything except maths and opera. It was Malcolm's father who made the complaint. The Head told me after the hearing that he'd turned up on the first day of term demanding that Malcolm be dragged out of his lesson and they sat in the Head's study and Malcolm's father kept saying, 'tell him Malcolm,' and Malcolm didn't look up once and just mumbled into the carpet that I was always going on about how the people would rise up and overthrow capitalism."

"I never say things like that even in my own house," said my father, though I was pretty sure he did. "Anyway I'm sure it's all going to be OK."

But it wasn't. The letter came two days after the hearing. They had the highest opinion of his teaching, the governors said, but the school had come under a lot of pressure and their responsibility was to be seen to do whatever was necessary to restore its reputation. Reluctantly they had decided they weren't able to give him his job back. They would, however, provide excellent references and they were sure he would be made welcome at another school.

It didn't kill my father, of course, but he wasn't ever quite the same. He was very proud and he'd never really failed at anything before. But it was my mother who seemed to take it the worst. I remember sitting upstairs in my bedroom, doing my homework, hearing her shouting at my father that she should never have come to this horrible country and why had he brought her to a place filled with such cold stuck-up people. She was yelling so loud I was sure the Bouviers must have heard. Six months later we moved house when my father got a job as head of maths in a big north London comprehensive school.

I only remember seeing Malcolm once after that, though I must have done. I suppose he just became somebody I didn't know any more.

I was cleaning my bike on the pavement outside our house. I'd turned it upside down and taken the chain off and laid it in a white enamel pan that I'd filled with pink paraffin. I was scrubbing the black grease off with an old toothbrush when I saw Malcolm come out of his house and hang about his gate. Then I heard him walk over.

I didn't look up though I could see his legs. He shuffled from foot to foot and kicked at a few bits of gravel.

"What are you doing?" he said.

I didn't say anything.

"Shall I get my bike for a bit? My parents are out."

I stood up.

"That time you smashed your face on the kerb and broke your arm," I said.

"That's all right," he said quickly.

"It was my fault," I said.

"I know," he said. "But you didn't mean to."

"I did mean to," I said. "I did it on purpose and I'm glad you got smashed up," and I lifted my bike and carried it through into the back garden. Then I came back for the pan and emptied the paraffin, black now, into the gutter where it flowed through the dark silt and down the drain grating, down amongst the gum wrappers and cigarette ends and wooden ice lolly sticks.

The Comrade Summer was shortlisted for the inaugural £10,000 Manchester Fiction Prize

EMILE IN THE CIRCUS

"He looks sad ..." says Lily, "thin and forlorn ...".

"Yes, thin, forlorn, and sick, and he smells ..." says Looby.

"Yes, smells, worse than before, of something rotten," says Lily, "and to be left just ...".

"Just abandoned like this," says Looby, and they stand in the cold wind, circles of skin puckering and blueing like love bites where their tights have sprung holes.

Emile's small eyes are red and weeping a thick ooze. They look like they have seen everything and no longer care. He slumps against the post to which he is chained, his collar eating into the matted fur around his neck, his coat shredded and patchy like a toy bear that has been used too long. He no longer wears a muzzle, all fight and bite long gone.

Lily arches into a backbend, palms in the cold mud, and Looby somersaults over her, but Emile does not look up.

The same wind that nips at the twins' legs now flaps and shreds the canvas of the big tent. Inside the circus ring, the straw and sawdust have been reclaimed by damp earth. The trapeze bars are cold and slippery as they begin to practise.

This morning Lily and Looby woke entwined in each other's arms, as they do most days. Some nights though, one of them climbs to the narrow bunk above the stove while the other takes a companion into the big bed; to be deceived, perhaps, by the intimacy of the embrace he wakes to.

But there are no lovers now. The troupe has dwindled. The Ferruti brothers no longer bounce and tumble through the twins' bed, nor do village lads come peeking through the canvas, full of vague yearnings.

"We should ..." says Looby.

"Practise the double ..." says Lily.

"After we warm up ..." says Looby.

Just a year before, in white satin spangled with gold and amber, the twins had flown and twisted high above the heads of the nobility. But the twice daily shows have faded to one a week, and, like Lazar's pawned gold teeth, more red painted seats gape empty than are filled. And where there was silver there are now only a few coppers, barely enough to buy food. Yet each morning the twins ignore their empty stomachs, put on their practice costumes, from which the spangles and sequins have been torn and ripped, dip their hands in the resin box and climb the ladder to the apex of the tent where the crows roost.

It is Pavel, the strongman, who volunteers to cross the field each day in search of food. Bullet-headed, slabmeat Pavel, with his hairless body and delicate feet and slow smile and tattoos of writhing girls, carries the old carpet bag to market.

Times are hard. Women in bright headscarves offer embroidered cloths dredged from the bottom of dowry chests, but nobody is buying. Old men cough in front of worn hoe handles, a bunch of onions, an egg or two. But as Lazar says, no matter how thin the milk, some cream will always rise to the top, and here and there are merchants with fat sacks of grain and well-stocked tables.

Everyone loves a strongman. The men stand slack-faced as he lifts two, three, four sacks at once, and like to feel the muscles of his arms, and sometimes, finding for a moment a way to grow bigger themselves, press coppers into his palm. And the women imagine being embraced by a man who could snap them like a twig, and wonder if he is big all over or whether it is true what they say about small feet.

Yet despite his smile and his impromptu performances and his popularity, most days the carpet bag comes back filled only with sprouting potatoes and barley.

Lazar collects news and gossip from the Roma who flit through the camp at night. "There is nowhere else to go," he says. "It's the same shit everywhere," and he spits through the gaps in his teeth.

"Perhaps a town ..." says Looby.

"Where there are more people ...".

"Anything must be ...".

"Better than here ...".

There is a sharp crack as Lazar slaps his hand flat on the table. Pavel blinks.

"Every damned where it is the same. Hunger. They only care for bread, not circuses. In the town there are just more wretches fighting over the scraps."

"And anyway we are stuck in this bog," he says after a pause.

They are sitting in Lazar's swaying caravan, smoke belching from the stove when the wind changes direction. Only Emile is not there. Igor, pale and grey like a shadow, is fingering a quiet waltz on the accordion. Out front the gold-painted wagon shafts slope empty into the mud; the horses were sold long ago.

"You must do something ...".

"For Emile, he is ...".

"Not well," says Lily.

"Not well," says Looby.

Lazar the Ursari passes his hand over his eyes. Emile is the son of Valentina, his father's bear, snatched from the wild when young, defanged and declawed, trained to dance over hot coals. But Emile needed none of that. As youths, Lazar and Emile rolled and wrestled, the bear's rank breath and drool hot in Lazar's face. When Lazar's father died and Valentina was no more use, Lazar took her round the back of the tent and cut her throat. They ate bear stew for days. And the new act, man and bear wrestling in a roped ring with a referee, drew long applause from crowds who had only ever seen the pitiful shufflings of mutilated animals. But now Lazar stays in his caravan and Emile sits alone in the cold wind.

Lily and Looby lean towards Lazar.

"Maybe some better food ...".

"Or an animal doctor ...".

Lazar glances down at the four quivering half moons nestling in their corseted costumes, but Lily and Looby see that his eyes do not change and that they now have the same dead look as Emile's.

"I would give my right arm for a drink," he says.

The following night the crowd is smaller than ever. There is hardly a soul for miles around who has not yet seen the circus and nobody comes twice. It is not a good performance. Lazar's whip and voice have lost their snap, the twins play safe with single twists and Pavel drops the iron ball. There is faint laughter from the crowd. They sit again in Lazar's caravan.

"It is finished my friends," says Lazar. "Everything has turned to shit, we're just too stupid to realise it. I will close the circus."

There is a long silence, then Pavel speaks.

"I have been thinking that way too. My father used to say that everything has its end; we only need to recognise the moment and accept it. We must go our separate ways. I will find work in the docks, or on a farm - I have done it before. Igor can wander the villages - everyone needs music in their lives. The twins will be all right; they are young and pretty and they have each other. And Lazar has Emile and a silver tongue if he ever finds it again. We will fly away and leave the tent for the birds to nest in."

It is Igor the musician who suggests the farewell performance. "To make a proper ending," he says.

"We must invite everyone ..." says Lily.

"And show them what we can really do ..." says Looby.

"Our best ...".

"So that they never forget."

Lazar says nothing.

The next day, Pavel and Lily and Looby and Igor cross the field to market. Igor plays the accordion as the twins cartwheel through the square. People gather, wrapped in scarves, their breath smoking in the frosted air. Children run to call parents, brothers, sisters. Pavel, dressed in tiger skins, his meaty arms and legs red with cold, strides to the centre of the square banging a drum.

"Ladies and Gentlemen. Friends. You are invited to the very last, the final, the terminal performance of the world famous Circus Lazarus one week from tonight. Everybody is welcome. Free entry to all."

They rehearse as they have not done for months. Pavel lifts and grunts all day and pulls caravans with his teeth. Igor practises tunes in strange time signatures, his right hand flashing over the keys, his left making occult shapes on the buttons. He polishes the silver and black of his accordion till it flashes even in the dim winter light. Lily and Looby ban everyone from the tent while they work. Only Lazar sits morose in his wagon, and Emile slumps against his post - weaker now and leaving even his meagre meals untouched.

"We are worried ..." says Lily.

"About Lazar ...".

"And Emile ...".

"We need a ringmaster and ...".

"A bear, or it's ...".

"No good," says Looby.

Then Pavel shows them the bottle of peach schnapps he has hidden in a wooden chest, under his tiger skins.

The circus once again is full of people and noise. Children flock in the aisles when the seats can take no more. Lazar, flushed and febrile, has been drinking for the last hour. He stands backstage, peering through the curtains at the crowd, dressed in a gold waistcoat and top hat.

The torches are lit. Igor sets a frenzied tune while Lily and Looby turn cartwheels and Lazar cracks his whip. Pavel invites members of the audience to strike him in the belly with a club and lifts a chair with his teeth. He throws the iron ball high and catches it on the back of his neck, then lifts a bar hung with weights while Lily and Looby pose at either end and are raised into the air. Igor glides a sword down his throat and then a long metal flute that he plays by contracting the muscles of his stomach.

Lazar slips backstage. He has kept back some of the schnapps and now grasps Emile's jaw and pours it down his throat. Emile chokes and coughs and the alcohol drips off his muzzle hair but he has swallowed enough. The transformation is rapid. Though he can barely see through his inflamed eyes, when Lazar leads him into the ring Emile remembers the shouts of the crowd and he and Lazar wrestle and dance to the accordion. Lazar leaps in the air, slapping his shiny black knee boots and bellowing Romany cries while Emile shuffles and bangs a tambourine.

Then the ring is cleared. To the slow beat of the drum, Lily and Looby, perfect in white satin, hair pinned up to show their pale necks, climb the ladder barefoot to the crow's nest high above the crowd.

Looby sets the first trapeze swinging a lazy arc across the tent. As it returns to where she stands it seems she just steps off the platform to drop like a stone - and the crowd gasp - but now they see that in passing, she has caught the bar with one hand, as though it is the most casual thing in the world. Two more sweeps and she pulls herself up to sit on the bar, then suddenly - again as if to plummet to the ground - she drops and is swinging upside down, hanging by her legs from the trapeze.

Now it is Lily's turn to swoop above the crowd, higher and higher, like a child on a swing, and then she lets go. For a moment she seems to hang motionless, then she turns ... and turns ... and turns - a triple backward somersault - and is caught in Looby's resin-tight grip. And all this while Emile is looking upward, blinking, an expression of total concentration on his face, as though what he sees thrills and amazes him. And when the twins have slid down the plaited ropes, back to the dull ground, Lily skips over and plants a kiss on his bedraggled muzzle and the bear hangs his head in seeming foolish delight.

Afterwards Lazar wants to celebrate, the alcohol still flowing in his blood.

"That was a show," he says. "Dammit, we're a great circus. The triple somersault - I never thought I'd see it again," and he stands and makes a formal little bow to Lily and Looby and clicks his boot heels. They sit a while longer in his caravan. Lazar wants to talk of past glories, but it is late, they are tired and there is nothing more to drink, and slowly they drift away.

Out in the cold air, Lily and Looby go to see Emile. They find him lying on the ground, racked by spasms of shivering.

"We must ...".

"Take him to our wagon ...".

"And warm him up ...".

"Somehow ...".

With Pavel's help they drag the bear, stumbling half upright, across the cold ground and up the three steps of the caravan.

That night, with the curtains pulled across the window, Emile lies on the bed, and all around him, from cupboards and ceiling, hang satin costumes, tights, and lengths of braided rope, smelling of perfume and female sweat. And Lily and Looby do what they have never done for another male; they lie either side of him under the great eiderdown, warming his body with their embrace, enveloped in his great bear stink.

But in the morning, when they wake, Emile's body is cold and stiff, and they close his poor eyes and weep a little.

Emile in the Circus won Plymouth University's Short Fiction New Writer's Competition

READING TOLSTOY IN BARCELONA

We clattered down the gangplank, over the black waters slapping between the wharf and the ship, and into the hot Barcelona night. It had rained earlier and I followed Louis, Hank and Emilio as they clomped through puddles iridescent with diesel slick, past rusty stacked containers and warehouses lit by dim bulkhead lights.

Showered, talced and aftershaved, pockets full of wages, loud and cocky for the night, they swept along the inner docks road towards the city, only slowing, shuffling into silence as we neared the gates where the Guardia Civil loitered smoking Ducados.

It was my maiden voyage - on a jobbing merchant ship seven weeks out from Southampton. We'd hugged the French and Portuguese coasts, passed the Punta de Tarifa where you can almost reach out and touch Africa, and turned back up the East coast of Spain, dropping off and loading containers along the way. I'd survived sea sickness and home sickness, the throb of engines and men, the banter and the threats and this was my first real shore leave.

They didn't venture far from the port gates - just along a couple of streets to a dark bar full of barrels and lacquered hams hanging from brown oak beams. Louis slammed a whiskey down in front of me and they crowded round and jostled me till I drank it and then another.

"Leave him, el pobre," the girl behind the bar said, looking at me with dark eyes. She was the first female I'd seen for weeks and I blushed.

"Look, he's in love now," said Louis.

Finally they lost interest in me and turned, business-like, to their own drinking.

When they set off for the brothel they dragged me with them. But though I was seventeen and had never been with a woman, that wasn't how I wanted the first time to be. And I was afraid of these grown men with their barely contained violence. I slipped down an alley, saying I had to take a slash, calling that I'd catch them up, and stood in the dark amidst the dustbins - swaying a bit from the whiskey - as their footsteps and laughter faded into the distance. Then I found my way back to the bar.

It was still early and I settled at a quiet table and plunged back into my book. I was in the middle of *Anna Karenina* amidst the drawing rooms and balls, perfumed countesses, leather harnesses and horse sweat. I'd got to where the pull between Anna and Alexei Kirillovich Vronsky was unbearable but nothing had yet happened. I was in love with Anna myself and afraid of what would happen to her if she surrendered to the self-obsessed Vronsky.

"Hey kid, what's the book?"

When I was older, I would slide invisibly through strangers' lives like a ghost, but when you're young - boy or girl - it seems everyone wants you for some reason or another.

The man coming towards me wasn't easy to ignore. He was big and wide, with a massive, food-stained belly, long greasy hair and grey stubble. He bore down on me like a train and I held up my book to ward him off.

"Ah, Leo Nikolayevich," he said. "*Anna Karenina*; the only one. War and Peace drags on forever. Resurrection is dull enough to kill you. But *Anna Karenina*," and he smacked his fingers with wet lips. "He was still a man when he wrote that - before he stopped drinking and lived on nuts and God."

"I can read in Russian, Turkish, English and Armenian," he said. "I can speak fifteen languages and fuck in twenty more."

He rocked to and fro on his heels.

"I used to read them all," he said. "Turgenev, Dostoevsky, Kemal, James, Conrad, Cafavy. Then one day I simply stopped. I sold every last book and I've not opened one since. Living is better than reading. And when my own story bores me, I can listen to somebody else's. You can drown in stories if you keep your ears open. They call me the Turk. Let's have a drink," and as he turned to the bar and shouted for a bottle I slipped my book into the side pocket of my pea jacket.

"So come on, tell me your story kid," he said.

"My name's Tom," I started.

He slapped his hand on the table and people looked round.

"That's no name for a boy like you - out to make his fortune. I swear that by the end of tonight you'll be washed clean as a lamb, reborn and renamed."

The girl came over from the bar with a bottle of red wine. He put his arm around her waist and pulled her towards his lap but she was looking at me.

"Lucitta," he said. "Meet my young English friend. You should hear him speak. The language of Milton, Shakespeare, Defoe drips from his tongue.

But he is very much in need of a new name. What do you think?"

"I think you should never listen to a word the Turk speaks," she said and pushed away from him. "He is full of merda."

"You pay her," the Turk said to me and I fumbled in my pocket. When I handed her the money, she smiled.

The Turk had lost interest in my story. I didn't mind; it was full of bad luck and nothing to be proud of. My mother had died long ago and my father and I had suffered in silence punctuated by thunderous rows until he died in his turn last year. I moved in with my uncle who drank even more than my father. I was thrown out of school, I read a lot and I ran away to sea. I was proud of the last bit but the rest was all other people's stories. Mine didn't seem to have begun yet.

The Turk didn't need me anyway - he talked enough for both of us.

He'd worked in the gold and diamond trades, been a tour guide in Istanbul and Madrid, run a bar in Antwerp. He was Turkish-Armenian-Jewish, "a mongrel; an outsider; a citizen of the world."

"And now? I said. "What do you do now?"

"Ah, now I'm retired. I eat, I drink, I shit, I talk shit. What else is there?"

A pack of Greek sailors in crisp whites came in and suddenly the bar was full and hot and noisy. A woman appeared behind the Turk and whispered something in his ear. She wore a red dress and red lipstick and hair pulled back tight from a lined face. She stood like a dancer with one hand resting on her hip, her dress pulled taut against her haunch, the other foot tapping restlessly on the floor.

The Turk took her hand and turned to me.

"This is Almunda, the most beautiful whore in Barcelona. And this," and he flourished his hand towards me in an elegant gesture, "this ... ah I forgot, we still have not found your name."

"Your new friend?" Almunda said to the Turk. "He won't be needing me then."

There was a lot of drink going round the table now, tequila, rum and red wine. I stuck to the wine but I was getting hot and everything was taking on a dreamy, slippery quality.

A woman flopped down next to me. She looked like she'd been weeping. Her dress was cut so low that one breast fell out when she leant towards me, the nipple hanging over the top, and she sat like that trying to make me understand something until Almunda slapped her arm and fired a torrent of Spanish at her.

The woman pulled up the top of her dress and tried to drag me to dance with her but when I wouldn't she started shouting and calling me *bastardo* until Almunda told her to get lost. I saw her later with one of the Greeks. He was hoisting her back up as she slid down his belly towards the floor.

The Turk was dancing in tight circles with his hands in the air. His shirt had come loose from his trousers which hung half unbuttoned. His hairy belly ground and wobbled.

I grabbed Lucitta's hand as she passed with a tray.

"Maybe later ... mas tarde ... I can see you?"

"See me? You see me now," and she laughed.

"Meet," I said. "I mean meet, just you and me somewhere."

She looked around.

"My father," she said as the Turk threw himself down next to me, hot and rank. She slipped away.

"You like her?" he said. "She will go out back with you if you pay her."

"That's a lie," I said.

"Don't be naive, kid," he said. "It's how the world works. Get used to it."

I wouldn't talk to him any more and decided to leave. I went out back to the bathroom - a flat pan flooded with waste and a cracked basin with a cold water tap. When I came out, Lucitta was coming up the wooden steps from the cellar with a case of wine.

"It's not true," I said. "What the Turk said. That you go with men ... for money?"

"Hijo de puta," she said. "You believe that?

"No, I don't believe it. No, Lucitta, please," and then - with no warning - my whole body began to shake.

Lucitta looked puzzled. She put down the wine, reached out and stroked down my cheek with a rough thumb.

"Strange boy," she said and her expression softened. I could smell her breath, sweet like aniseed, and I kissed her.

There was a noise behind me, an arm round my neck pulling me away and a man's voice, hot and loud in my ear. He dragged me backwards through the crowded bar. I heard laughter and shouts then I was out of the front door and on the street. He kicked me in the back of the knees and I fell onto the pavement.

"No fucking good," he said and went back into the bar.

"So you met Lucitta's father," the Turk said as I examined my scraped palms under the streetlight. "This is a Catholic country you know."

I turned my back on him.

"It's a shitty bar anyway," he said. "Let's walk. Where are you staying kid?"

"I don't know," I said. "I guess I'll have to go back on board," but he could hear the hesitation in my voice.

"Stay with me," he said. "Come on; it was just a joke. It's not far."

We walked through dark streets of looming stone buildings with blank shuttered fronts. The Turk was silent now. After a while we stopped outside a weathered wooden door which the Turk opened and I followed him across a cobbled courtyard, then up a flight of stairs. He fumbled a long time at another door, muttering and breathing heavily. Inside it smelt of damp, stale feet and rotting food. He flicked a switch and the bare bulb on the ceiling threw a harsh bright light onto the one room. There was a double bed, strewn with grubby sheets, a sink full of dishes and scummy water, a plain wooden table with a couple of chairs.

I sat down as the Turk rummaged in a cupboard above the sink and came back with a bottle of Bell's whiskey, a blue mug and a smeared glass. He gave me the glass and poured a large shot with a shaking hand. The smell of the whiskey combined with the foulness of the room suddenly made me nauseous.

"Air," I said, and moved towards the window. I was struggling to open it when he came and stood behind me. He reached over and opened it and I leaned out. He didn't move away and I felt his hand on my buttock, stroking and kneading, then both his arms around me and his hand moving down onto my crotch. My heart thudded and I twisted away.

"Hey, no," I said. "Not for me."

"Come on kid," he said, "it's only a bit of fun. What else is there to do?"

"Fuck off!" I shouted. "Why won't people ever fucking leave me alone."

"Suit yourself," he said. "That woman was right; you're a little bastard."

He swallowed down the whiskey in the mug and threw himself on the bed.

"Your new name - Bastardo," he mumbled and fell asleep, his mouth hanging slack. He suddenly looked like an old man.

I slammed the door behind me as I left. Downstairs, I stumbled around the courtyard in the dark, pushing on locked doors till I found the way out onto the street.

My anger soon passed. I began to feel good; reckless, heroic, full of yearning for Lucitta or for any girl who might have me. I walked wherever my eyes and feet led me - as if by keeping on walking I would find what I needed. Some kind of message, truth, love.

I stopped to play with a cat, mangy and thin, on a stone window ledge. It wound itself round my arm, restless and aroused, purring and butting me with its head whenever I stopped the stroking.

"You and me cat," I said.

I sat in a great, empty square on the marble steps of a stone fountain. I looked in the dark windows of bookshops and at cheeses piled high in an ornately gilded delicatessen. I tried to get into a church but it was locked.

Occasionally I heard footsteps, singing, shouted conversations but I never saw anyone. I walked all through the night until dawn lightened the sky and the city woke up around me. Men with briefcases hurried past, women clacked over the stone slabs of the squares, the racket of pneumatic drills started up. Though it was chill in the shade, the sun was already warm and friendly and I stood with my eyes closed in a pool of sunshine while life hurried around me.

I went into a bar where men stood at the counter amidst a haze of cigarette smoke. I ordered breakfast and sat at a table at the back by a pinball machine, dunking my doughnut in a bowl of milky coffee. I thought of the books I'd read as I lay long days in bed at my uncle's house after I stopped going to school - Hemingway in Pamplona, Orwell in Catalonia, Laurie Lee with his donkey, treading the mountains from one end of Spain to the other, sleeping under the starry skies.

Then I reached my hand to the pocket of my pea jacket and found that *Anna Karenina* was gone. I must have dropped it in the night - at the bar maybe, or on the pavement when I fell, or in the Turk's room, or just somewhere in the streets of Barcelona.

Bookless, I returned to the ship. The gulls wheeled around the boats unloading the night's catch and the air was filled with the smells of fish and diesel, coiled rope, fresh paint and warming tarmac. The ship's cook waved to me as I climbed the gangplank.

I never got to finish *Anna Karenina*. I picked up a faded copy the following year in a bookshop in Athens, but it wasn't the same. The magic had gone and I left it on a stone bench in Zappeio park.

IN RAHANI

We made it to the eight o'clock bus - the only one that would get us to Rahani the same day. Regine had laughed the night before and said it would be a miracle, but I'd woken when the first call to prayer came coughing from the mosque and had lain close to her, watching her sleep, smelling her night breath. It was the first chance I'd had to look at her without interruption, without her saying, "Mais quoi? Why do you look at me like that?"

She'd had her hair cropped the day before and it was shorter now than mine. My eyes followed the long Roman nose that took two kinks before the tip, the eye lashes - luxuriant like a camel's - fluttering on her cheeks, the slender neck - bleached by the white scar around the throat - falling to the tender points of her collar bones.

When I nudged her awake she opened her eyes wide and looked at me like I was nobody she'd ever seen before.

Though she twice packed and unpacked her travelling bag, shifting books and face creams and contact lenses to and from the rucksack that made everyone say 'Ouf' when they tried to lift it, we got to the bus station with half an hour to spare. We bought tickets and sat over milky coffee and warm bread on the edge of a sea of shouting and sleeve tugging, seed spitting and ticket touting. The buses revved clouds of diesel smoke which mixed with the tang of roasting lamb and oranges.

We'd met in the tiled courtyard of the Hotel d'Afrique in Imdrah just two days before. I'd watched her talking to Jim, the American. Then he pointed at me and she came over to where I sat by the fountain.

"I'm looking for someone to go south with," she said. "I have to get to Arifa to meet my sister."

Her long arms and legs were smooth and brown against her white dress. She wore slim sandals that had a little coil of leather for the big toe to go through and her naked feet stretched to the longest second toes I had ever seen - encircled in silver rings.

"My friend she has had enough. She wants to go home but I have to get across the border. I need someone to travel with, to share expenses. And for safety."

I was young and following my nose. I was happy going south with her, or just about anywhere she wanted.

"But, you know, just as friends," she said.

We climbed on the bus as the sweet and cigarette boys jumped off, and sat near the back, our thighs touching on the narrow seat. As the bus swung onto the road out of town, it was already bouncing and bumping on worn springs.

"Mais qu'est ce qu'il veut?" Regine cried. The shepherd in the seat in front had turned to look at us the moment we got on, his eyes passing from Regine to me and back again as though magnetised. A felt skullcap, once white, now stained dark at the edges, perched on his walnut scalp. His mouth hung slack over brown teeth and his hands hugged a sour-smelling bundle wrapped in muslin and string.

"Why do they have to stare like that?" Regine said.

"Maybe he likes us," I said and leant forward in my seat.

"Salaam ale-kum," I said.

"Walekum assalam," he replied, and turned away.

I found the hash, bit it in two and handed her a piece.

"Suck it," I said. "It's what I always do on long bus rides. It gets to be like a film. You just turn into a giant pair of eyes and watch everything flow by."

After a while the journey slowed right down. Music surged from the radio above the driver's head. People got on in the middle of nowhere and others got off - whole families - and were swallowed up by the flat stony plain.

We watched the landscape rolling by. Villages came and went; dusty main streets with butchers swatting flies from piles of meat and sheep's heads dangling from hooks, porters lounging against bicycle carts, and everywhere men sitting drinking tea and smoking. Then there would be a few collapsed buildings, or half-built houses sprouting wooden scaffolding, a tethered camel, a dog barking at the bus, and again the scrubby desert with the long low hills in the distance. Regine fell asleep, nodding against my shoulder, and I rested the back of my hand on her thigh. I wanted to put my arm around her, to kiss the scar on her throat.

The driver finally took a break in one of the villages. We bought bread, tomatoes and a can of sardines and sat on a low wall by a dirt football pitch. Boys gathered round us like flies, saying, "Donne moi quelque-chose." Regine wrapped her shawl more tightly around her bare shoulders and turned her back to them.

"Why won't you sleep with me?" I said. "Don't you like me? It's so hard ...

with you lying there in the same bed."

"I told you. That's not what I want. It never works out for me. I'm always the one who ends up getting burned."

It was late evening when we got to Rahani, a couple of kilometres from the border. We found a room over a harshly lit cafe and went out to find something to eat.

The wind had got up and the lanterns hissed and sputtered on the few stalls still open. We'd walked almost to the end of the one street before we found somewhere. Through a dim doorway I could see blackened pots cooking over a charcoal fire.

"This is it," I said.

We sat at a plastic-sheeted table. It was late and we were the only customers. The cook, in a dirty brown jallabah, was chopping meat on a worn block of wood. He barely nodded at us as a boy, no more than ten, slapped down a basket of bread and some paper napkins.

Regine wiped the bench with her shawl before she sat down.

"Do you think it's clean?" she said. "You know, for eating."

"People eat here every day, Regine. Just because it's cheap doesn't mean it's poison."

The boy put down two plates of chopped salad.

"I know they made this right next to that meat," she said. "Why do they do that?"

"You shouldn't think that way all the time. What's the point of travelling if you worry about everything. You might as well stay at home."

"We got ill," said Regine. "My friend and I. Just after we got here. We were stuck in the hotel for three days. It wasn't fun."

"That's travelling for you," I said. "You've got to take the bad stuff with the good. If you want insurance, book a package tour."

The soup came then, fiery hot with shreds of meat floating on its oily surface.

Again there was only a double bed. Regine let me hold her this time, curled against her back.

"Why are you travelling then?" I said.

"I've never really done anything. I've never been away from home on my own before. My sister got this job in Arifa and said why didn't I come and visit. My friend and I, we just decided one night to go overland. Our big adventure. What about you?"

"I was bored. I wanted something real, exciting."

"And your family?"

"My father's mad at me - he doesn't understand anything. He wouldn't even say goodbye. He told me I was spoilt. And selfish and lazy and irresponsible and lots of other things I forget. And that I was breaking my mother's heart."

"And your mother?"

"She made a big drama out of it. She even came running down the road after me, holding me back."

"Have you written to her?"

"A couple of times."

After breakfast we walked to the border. I carried Regine's rucksack.

"What have you really got in here?" I said, as I put it down to rest every few hundred metres.

It was a joke we had going. Every time I asked she said something different - a set of encyclopaedias, a bidet, drugs.

"I bought some tiles," she said. "For my sister. She's rebuilding the Alhambra in Arifa."

Within sight of the border post we stopped. I took out a ten dollar bill and folded it into my passport next to the photo.

"What are you doing?" said Regine.

"I don't have a visa."

"Are you crazy? How do you expect to get through?"

"It's OK," I said. "American Jim told me. You just give them ten dollars and they wave you through."

The customs officer was black, an African not an Arab. He swelled out of his green uniform as though someone had blown him up with a bicycle pump.

"What is this?" he said when he found the bill.

I shrugged.

"You do not have a visa," he said.

"Is that a problem?"

"Yes, of course," he said.

"But someone told me I could ... buy one here."

"Not today," he said. "Maybe when the chief is here."

"And when will the chief be here?"

"He has gone to a wedding."

"So when will he be back?"

"Tomorrow maybe," he said, pocketing the ten dollars.

Regine and I sat in the shade of an outbuilding.

"Stupid, stupid boy," she said.

I didn't reply.

"I have to go on," she said. "My sister is expecting me."

But in the end, when I turned to go back to Rahani, she came with me. The room above the cafe was still free.

There was nothing to do. The wind was blowing hard now, buffeting waves of sand and grit into the streets, sand that stung the legs and face and clogged the eyes and gathered in the corners of our room though the windows were tight shut. We lay on the bed and tried to read. After a while I put my book down and began to stroke her arm, then her face. My throat felt constricted.

I leant over her and put my lips to the scar on her neck. She lay very still.

"What's this?" I said.

"I was ill once," she said, then gripped my head tight and kissed me.

We made love but it wasn't like I'd imagined it. Afterwards we lay listening to the wind.

"Why didn't you get the visa? My God, you're a fool," she said.

"It was too much hassle. You wait a whole day in line then they tell you to come back again tomorrow. Jim said he'd been through loads of times without a visa; just the ten dollars."

"We can go back and get you one," she said. "I'll come with you. I can get a message to my sister. Then we can go together to Arifa. After I see my sister - if you wait for me, just for a week or two - we can travel on together. Where shall we go?"

"That's mad. All the way back to Imdrah and then another two days to the embassy. It'll work out here, I'm sure. Anyway, I don't really know my plans yet."

We made love again, then I felt terribly tired.

"I've got to get some sleep," I said.

The next day there was a storm over the hills. We could see lightning muffled through the heavy dark clouds. Soon the rain began to clatter against the windows. In the afternoon we went down for tea. They said the road was cut off in both directions. When the rain eased up, we went out to look. Just outside Rahani a flash flood had cut right through the road. A few cars were backed up either side of the crevice while a gang of men with shovels swarmed in the brown mud.

We spent four more days in Rahani. Each morning we walked to the border.

"Is he here?" I would say, and the customs officer, barely looking up, would shake his head.

By the fourth day Regine and I seemed to have run out of things to say to each other. In the evening she told me she had met a couple of German guys when she was buying bread.

"They are going through the border tomorrow and on to Arifa. They said I could travel with them."

"If that's what you want," I said.

"You know what I want," she said. "I don't know what's wrong with you. I can't wait here forever while you make up your mind."

She said she hoped I would be all right; that she would worry about me. She wrote down her sister's address in Arifa.

In the morning I stayed in bed, watching her pack. Then I pulled the sheet over my head, pretending I was asleep. When she pulled it away to say goodbye I kept my eyes shut.

I made friends with a hyperactive little Berber called Yousef. He tried to sell me a carpet but the tenth time I told him I didn't have any money he nodded and said, "Never mind. Let's drink tea." I sat in his shop for hours while he played cards with his friends. I decided I'd give it a couple more days and then - if the chief hadn't turned up - I'd head back the way I'd come.

The next day I went for a walk, towards the low hills. After a while I came to a cleft in the ground that you couldn't see until you were right upon it. It was a gorge cut deep into the soft rock. At the bottom was a river bed, dry now but littered with broken branches tangled with vegetation from the flash flood. I heard a shout and saw someone standing on a ledge halfway down the side of the gorge. I scrambled down to him.

He wore a dirty jallaba over jeans. His grey hair was long and matted, with beads and silver rings woven into it.

"Do you have something to smoke?" he asked. He was French.

He started rolling my cigarettes and my hash.

"What are you doing here?" I asked.

"I live here."

"Where?"

He pointed and I saw a low cave entrance beneath an overhanging rock?

"You live in a cave?"

He nodded.

"You live out here, in the middle of nowhere? Alone?"

"Yes," he said. "Here, alone."

"Why?"

"Why not?"

"But ..." and I didn't know what to ask first.

"And you," he said. "Where are you going?"

"I'm trying to go south. Over the border."

"Why?" he said, and I didn't really have an answer.

"Exactly," he said.

The joint was strong and I lay in the shade, loath to move. He sat cross-legged on a blanket despite the heat, very straight and upright. The sun moved across the sky. He made tea, building a fire from the scrub plants that dotted the landscape.

I started to ask some of the questions I had turning in my mind but he interrupted me.

"You know, before you open your mouth you should make sure you have something worth saying."

After that we sat in silence.

When the sun had cooled and was starting to get low, he stood up - direct from cross-legged.

"This is the time I do my yoga," he said.

I got up too.

"Maybe I'll see you tomorrow," I said.

"If you do, bring water. And food. And tobacco."

I asked Yousef about him.

"Ah, the marabout."

"What is a marabout?"

"A marabout, my friend, is a holy man. Or perhaps a crazy one. Maybe he wasn't so crazy when he came but he is now. He was on his way over the border. Someone stole his bag; another traveller, not anyone from Rahani. So then he had no money and no passport. We thought he would go back to his embassy but he moved into the cave. He said he had lived in a cave in India and this one was better. He comes into town for food and water. He is good at fixing things - TVs, refrigerators, car engines."

I went out to see him several days running. Mostly we just sat. Sometimes - out of nowhere - he'd make little pronouncements.

"Wherever you are, whatever you're doing, however difficult things get, remember - when you get up in the morning, first thing is you have to wash."

"But how do you wash out here?" I said.

"I can wash my whole body with two cups of water."

Another time he said, "You have to use your head when you choose a mate. A woman needs to be strong if she's going to bear you children and fetch water and do the house work. Look for big hips. And a good mind. Look at their mothers," he said. "Don't mess with the skinny, nervous ones."

"I'm not planning for kids just yet," I said.

"You don't know the first thing about women; you just follow your prick."

"What else?" I said.

"In the end it will make you unhappy, and the woman you're with. You just want a woman to make you feel good. To add to your list. You're young and cocky, you don't care anything about women."

"How the hell do you know?" I said, standing up.

"I saw you," he said. "With that woman in Rahani. What happened to her? I could see how miserable she was hanging around with you."

Suddenly I couldn't speak. What was I thinking when I let Regine go like that? Most of the time I didn't have the first idea what I was doing.

"That's it," he said. "Now you're asking the right questions."

"I didn't say anything," I said.

"You've got to still the mind. Stop the endless chatter. Then you can connect; the world only becomes real when you can do that," and he closed his eyes and sat without moving for the rest of the afternoon.

The next day I woke up feeling different. I couldn't bear the smell of old grease in the cafe, the charcoal smoke and roasting lamb in the street, the bustle, the faces, the hot sun.

I walked out to the cave, heavy legged. He wasn't there when I arrived and

I lay down in the shade. I woke to feel his hand on my forehead.

"You have a fever," he said.

I shuffled a few steps to the side to urinate. It came out a deep brown. I felt sick and a bitter fluid rose to my mouth, burning my throat and scorching its way down to my lungs and for long moments I struggled to breathe. Then he was clapping me on the back and saying, "OK, OK."

When I woke again, I was lying in the cave. I felt too weak to move. His face loomed over me.

"You're eyes are yellow," he said. "You have hepatitis. We have to get you to town. I don't want you dying out here."

He carried me most of the way to Rahani, my face lying in his thick hair which smelt of body grease and woodsmoke. When we reached the edge of the town he dropped me down against a tree and disappeared. After a long while he came back with Yousef and between them they dragged me to my room above the cafe.

I don't know how long I lay there. There was no pattern to day and night. Sometimes I woke to noises from the street, shouting, the radio from the cafe, the sun burning through the dusty glass. Then it was suddenly night, my room lit by a single bare bulb. When I had to I would drag myself along the corridor to the foul toilet. In the broken mirror I saw that my skin and the whites of my eyes had turned a deep yellow.

And all this time I was consumed with disgust – at myself and at everything around me. Whatever I looked at or could imagine was soiled and corrupt. I had water, and food - bread and dates, brought up from the cafe by Yousef, but I had no appetite. I could feel my stomach caving in towards my spine. Sometimes I felt so weak I couldn't lift my arms. Yousef stood at the end of the bed and shook his head.

I became overwhelmed with the need to save myself, to escape from this village, from this terrible country. When I slept I would lose myself in feverish dreams that seemed more real than my waking state. Once I woke to find the marabout sitting on a chair by the window.

"I'm scared," I said.

"When we overcome our fear of death, there are no more fears," he said. "It is time you grew up."

After he left I wept.

I dreamt of my father, stern like he was when I last saw him. He looked at me a long time and said, "And what have you learned in your foolishness?"

The sun had risen again and I was dozing when I heard the door open. I found it enormously difficult to open my eyes, as though they were weighed down with stones. Then I felt a cool hand on my face and a voice, "Oh look at you."

She was wearing the same white dress she had on the first day I saw her.

"I heard news of an English boy lying sick in Rahani. I knew straight away it was you and that you needed me."

I was overcome with joy but as I reached my arms out to embrace her I woke. It was night and the bare bulb, flecked with the corpses of flies and mosquitos, swung to and fro - blown by the wind gathering in the street outside and finding its way through the gaps in the window.

ON CADAIR IDRIS

I had to get out of the city in a hurry; there didn't seem to be anywhere that wasn't hers - her place, her streets, her friends.

I packed the basics, some outdoor gear and a few books and walked through the early morning streets to the bus station. I didn't know where I was going, just away.

When I was young I'd stayed with friends in a cottage in Snowdonia and one day I trekked up Cadair Idris. They say that whoever sleeps on the mountain will wake up either a poet or mad. It had been a difficult time then too, and though I didn't stay the night, something of a transformation had occurred. Climbing to the top and sitting in the giant's chair looking down on the world had seemed to sort me out. I thought it might help again, so I took a bus to Wales.

The thing about buses is that you can't read, or at least I can't, not without getting sick. I spent a long time staring out of the rain flecked window and thinking. People say all kinds of cruel things when they're trying to get rid of you.

I bought a guide book in Dolgellau and picked a little hotel near the mountain. The cab driver wanted to talk. "It's late in the year for visitors," and "would you be travelling on our own?" but after a while my silence wore him down. I checked into the hotel and found I was the only guest. In the empty dining room, with hunting prints on every wall, I ate a watery lamb stew with boiled potatoes and peas and went to bed.

When I woke, it took me a while to remember where I was. The rain had stopped, though a thick mist hung in the hollows. After a rancid fried breakfast, I packed a bag with hotel sandwiches, a bottle of water and a book and set off for the mountain. My boots rang hard on the tarmac lane before I turned through a stile onto a muddy path that snaked up to the first ridge and then onto the Fox's path that led to the summit at Pen y Gadair.

There were many things that she hadn't liked doing. Walking was one of them and it must have been at least a year since I was last away from houses and roads. I pushed on fast through the bare hills and lowering sky, building up a sweat, letting the body take over. I knew if I walked long enough, the thinking would start to die down. Apart from a couple of water breaks I didn't stop till I got to the summit. I'd imagined that I'd sit up there and everything would just fall into place, but in the end I didn't stay long. The sky had been getting heavier and a bitter wind cut through my jacket. I hadn't thought about it but it must have been summer the last time I was here. I remember lazing in the sunshine as I looked at the world laid out below, suddenly rich and full of possibility.

I'd been descending for about half an hour when the weather set in. First a cold sleet, then snow, then a real blizzard. It was getting darker all the time and before long I knew I was in trouble. I hadn't told the hotel where I was going and I'd brought no survival gear, not even my phone. I was out in the open, with no shelter. I had no choice but to go on and I focused all my attention on my feet as the wind buffeted me and the driving snow seared my face. I knew that I mustn't lose the path though it became harder and harder to see as the snow settled. Several times I had to retrace my steps. I must have been getting tired because twice I thought I saw a dark shape in the swirling snow and once I called out, though a moment later the snow swirled again and there was nothing.

By the time I found the hut, I had begun to lose hope. I almost walked past without seeing it. It was low and stone built and almost indiscernible from the rocks it seemed to grow out of. It was clearly abandoned but it would give me shelter and get me through the night.

I pushed on the weathered door and entered. It took me a few moments to get used to the dimness; there was just one window and that was curtained. Then as my eyes adjusted I realised that someone must have been living here until recently, perhaps a warden or a ranger. In one corner lay a mattress, neatly made up with blankets and a patterned bedspread. A blackened pot stood on a trivet in the fireplace amidst cold ashes and a single shelf held a plate or two, a mug and several books. An oil lamp sat on a wooden table with some matches alongside it. I lit the lamp and carried it over to examine the books. There were several on British wildlife, especially beetles, rodents and birds, some classics - Dickens, Conan Doyle and Robert Louis Stevenson, and a batch of books on transgender studies. I was just taking one of these off the shelf when I heard the front door open and wheeled round.

He almost growled when he saw me and I found myself stumbling through an explanation.

"I was lost, sorry. I didn't mean to come in. Well I did but I didn't know anyone lived here. I had to get out of the blizzard."

And then I told him about my walk and being caught out by the change in the weather. All the while he just stood there, the snow slowly melting on his coat and thick black hair. He really was extraordinarily hairy, his narrow forehead, long sideburns and beard leaving little of his face uncovered. As I spoke he fixed me with a hostile glare. His eyes had a look that I almost recognised but it hovered just outside my awareness.

Finally I stuttered to a halt and there was a long silence.

"You can't stay here" he said quietly. "It's out of the question".

The thought of going out into what was now almost night, in the middle of a blizzard, was so threatening that I became desperate.

"I'll pay, whatever you like. And I won't interfere. I can just sit in a corner. I won't even speak. I'll die out there".

His face changed and an expression of what looked like sadness came over it.

"Yes you wouldn't survive out there", he said in a low voice. "You can have my bed. I'll sleep outside".

"That's ridiculous, nobody could survive on a night like this. You'll freeze to death. Why on earth can't we both sleep in here"?

I guessed that he was desperately embarrassed about something. Perhaps he didn't want to undress in front of me, but surely he could sleep in his clothes. I tried my hardest to persuade him, but he was adamant. Finally when I had nothing more to say, he turned to leave.

"Bolt the door as soon as I'm outside and don't open it until the morning. Do you understand".

It was a command not a question.

Did I not guess, even then? I can only think that I was stupefied with tiredness. And also, absurdly, hurt. He was the second person in the past week who'd said they didn't want to sleep anywhere near me.

I built a fire with paper and wood from a basket by the hearth, and sat on the floor in front of it to eat my sandwiches. As steam began to rise from my soaked trousers, I was overcome by sleepiness. I just managed to get my boots off and fell on the mattress fully dressed. I hadn't meant to get inside the bed but when I woke some time in the night I found that I had burrowed under the blankets in my sleep.

At first I thought it was the wind that had woken me, a low intermittent grumbling, gathering in intensity and then dying down. I settled back to sleep but was jerked awake again by the most awful sound I had ever heard. It was a howl of such pain and desperation that a spasm of shivering, like an electric shock, rippled through my body. I rushed to the window. It was starkly bright outside as the moonlight reflected off the snow but I saw no movement, just snowflakes hitting the glass and melting. Then it came again, even louder, from somewhere behind the hut amidst the rocks.

It must have lasted an hour or more. I sat on the bed, under the blankets, weeping uncontrollably as each fresh outburst of howling tore through me.

When I woke, sunshine streamed through the window. I repacked my knapsack, unbolted the door and pushed it hard to break through the snow that had piled against it in the night. A covering of the purest white lay as far as I could see, yesterday's sharp rocks and hollows smoothed into soft contours in the still, cold air.

I saw him lying close to the wall of the hut, beneath the window. The snow had almost covered him and at first I thought he was dead. But when I shook him, he moved a little. He groaned as I managed to pull him half upright and with great effort dragged him into the hut. I got him as far as the bed, and rolled and wrestled him to get off his sodden coat. He gave off an overpowering animal reek. When I covered him with the blankets he curled into a ball with his face to the wall.

I watched him for a long while but he didn't move. Then, closing the door of the hut, I set my face towards the sun and walked back down the valley.

A SIMPLE MAN

In church this morning I pushed aside the hassock and knelt on stones I had collected from the road. Their sharp edges cut into me like knives as I prayed, carving the lesson I knew I must learn - unless we are ever watchful and strict in small things, we will end up lamenting what has crept up on us through our own weakness.

I thought this my secret penance, but when I opened my eyes Madeleine was watching me without expression.

The abbé took his text from Matthew 18, 'If thine eye offend thee pluck it out.' He spoke of hell fire but the stone floor throbbed with cold. I could not concentrate on his words and my eyes drifted to our stained glass window that pours blood red shadows onto the plain walls of the church. There in the corner, the Good Samaritan tends the stranger, bathing his wounds with oil and wine. But then, the Bible tells us, the Samaritan loaded the Jew onto his donkey, carried him to an inn and left him there. He did not invite him into his house and allow him to swallow up his very life.

As we left the church the abbé took my sleeve.

"Is there any news, my friend?" he asked.

"No, abbé," I managed to reply, the communion wafer still laying like glue on my tongue. "Perhaps he remembered his past all of a sudden and ran to it."

"Maybe it is better this way," said the abbé, and smiled with his raisin eyes. And then the smile crept towards his lips and I knew he was building up to the one joke he permits himself with me; the one that always used to please me and make me feel important in my work and linked to something solemn and true.

"We share the calling you and I. Helping transmute modest flour and water into the stuff of life ... yours temporal and mine eternal of course," and as he chuckled his black hat dipped up and down like a crow pecking for crumbs.

"It is nevertheless a mystery, abbé, just to disappear like that." I heard Madeleine's voice from behind my left ear and turned. She was standing there, placidly smoothing down her Sunday apron.

There is nothing wrong with having simple tastes. Our Lord did not spend his years amongst us chasing after luxury. When I bake, it is with plain, honest flour, for as my father used to say, bread is humble and needs no flattery.

And just like my father, I am made plain. Our bulbous noses and mounds of cheek and chin could have been fashioned from soft dough. Indeed on a kind day, my father, in instructing me, would say "too dry", or "too wet", then lift my fingers to his fleshy earlobe, and say, "just like this." But in another mood he might knead my own lobe fiercely and tug down so that my cheek was pressed against his fat knee and with his other hand clap my head so hard that my ears rang and my face was numbed.

I do not remember my mother; Madeleine is the only woman I have known. I did not set my sights above my station, and looked for a woman whose modesty matched my own. There were girls who were more beautiful, or who showed a greater sparkle of wit or mischief, or whose petticoats flashed beneath their dresses as they danced, but I needed a wife who would carry heavy trays of bread without chatter or complaint, and serve long hours in the bakery.

She worked right until the day of her confinement. I remember her standing in the shop, a trail of flour across her forehead where she had wiped the sweat with the back of her wrist, for it is well known that women heat up as the baby proves and swells in their womb. She was back at work within a week, nursing Astrid upstairs between rings of the shop bell.

*

This dull, dusty man with whom she has lived for eleven years and whose daughter she has borne is not Madeleine's true love. Her true love is Jean-Luc, her almond-eyed cousin. As children they had hidden and whispered under tables at family feasts, down amidst the shoes and long skirts and lounging dogs, or sat in stiff clothes at funerals and weddings, trying not to catch each other's eye lest they explode with laughter. Once, after they had made themselves sick on stolen wine, Madeleine shivered as she watched Jean-Luc beaten with the strap and then again, knowing his eyes were on her, as she received her punishment.

When she was fourteen and he fifteen, his face thinned out and grew finer as his voice fell. He was full of excitements that would spill out of him as they walked by the lake. She would lie in the ruined boat, eyes half closed against the glinting sun, as he sat and read to her from books and then from his own poems, his leg warm against her thigh.

"No-one here understands me," he would tell her.

"Except me," she would say.

"Yes, you are different, you understand me," and her heart swelled with adoration and pride.

Then he was sent away to school. He wrote her long letters and poems, aching with loneliness, and in the long summer holidays they spent every spare moment together.

But when he left for the University at Rheims the letters became less and less frequent and then finally ceased. She did not see him again until the day he appeared in church with his wife and child. The pews creaked as her neighbours turned to catch the expression on Madeleine's face.

Not long after, when her father came to her with the baker's proposal of marriage, she offered no resistance.

*

It is God's blessing to rise early, before anyone else is about, and walk the silent roads to the bakery. In summer, the stars still hang in the lightening sky. I hear the first birds calling from the birch woods and smell the wheat ripening in the fields. In the autumn, mist hangs over the lake and the dew is so heavy it seems as though the trees are weeping. But it is the harsh, black mornings of winter that I like best. My boots ring out on the empty road and the glitter of stars is mirrored in the sparkling frost. A faint wisp of wood smoke from the ovens scents the air and my walk is just far enough for the cold to bite my ears and nose and that makes the bakery a welcoming place. The great oven still holds live embers and I stack it with olive and apple wood and work the bellows until the flame catches. Then I mix and knead for an hour or two in warm silence before anyone else is abroad to disturb my solitude with their chatter.

It was on just such a bitter morning that I found the stranger, almost naked, curled up by the bakery wall. I did my Christian duty and dragged him into the lingering warmth of the ovens and sat him down with the proving sheet as a blanket. His skin was blue from cold and his shock of black hair and wild eyes were stark against the floury cloth. Before long he began to shiver uncontrollably. I could not smell drink on him and began to think he must have been waylaid and robbed.

"You will soon be yourself again," I said as I lit the oven and started folding back the mix that had been fermenting in the trough overnight.

"I am Bernard," I said when I could spare a moment, and I offered him my hand. There was a long fumbling beneath the sheet, as though he was hunting for something, and finally his own hand emerged, skeletal and filthy with dirt.

"I am ..." he started, then gave a little shake of his head. He tried again. "I am ..."

It was then that he wept.

"I do not know who I am," he said at last.

I had my work to do and was at a loss until Madeleine arrived and took charge of him. She led him upstairs to the rough bed where I snatch an hour of sleep on long nights of baking before the holy days at Christmas and Easter.

We forgot him as the day's work began in earnest. I loaded and unloaded the ovens with baguettes and flutes and boules de campagne and the heat built up steadily.

*

She thinks he looks like a wild animal, or like the birds with broken wings she would take in as a child. She has never seen a creature look so lost. She feels his presence, there right above her head, but she does not have a moment to go to him.

It is late in the morning when he suddenly appears. She is wrapping a baguette for Valérie from the pharmacy when she hears her gasp, and turns to see him reaching out to the bread racked behind the counter. His white, hairless skin is stretched tight across his ribs and the sheet he is wrapped in threatens to fall from his narrow hips. She asks Valérie to watch the shop and hurries him back upstairs.

"I will bring you something," she says, and he lies back with closed eyes. When she returns with warm bread and milk he has not moved. She has to lift him to eat and for a moment, as his gaunt head, pale as marble, rests on her bosom, she feels a tugging in her breasts. She feeds him pieces torn off the loaf and dipped in milk and even when the bell rings in the shop she does not leave him.

*

The stranger did nothing but sleep and eat our food. I watched Madeleine climb the wooden stairs with pots that she brought from home and warmed in the bakery oven. I heard them murmuring over my head. She said she had read to him from the book of names she borrowed from the abbé. Though he told her he could not remember, she thought his expression had changed when she arrived at Joseph and that was what we called him.

I expected that when he had rested he would move on. The authorities must have a place for people such as him. But Madeleine said that because he was found by the bakery wall it was our duty to care for him. Doctor

Lebras told us that he might regain his memory any day or never and sent us his account for five francs.

"How long must we keep him then?" I asked my wife.

"God will decide," she said.

On the third day I found him sitting in the bakery when I came in, his narrow wrists poking out of an old shirt of my father's. He had shaved and Madeleine had cut his wild hair, though his long face was still as pale as milk.

"I would like to help," he said, looking around him.

I asked him if he had baked before.

"I do not know," he said, "But it feels like something I could do."

I lifted a batch of dough onto the kneading table and carved it into pieces with the long knife. Though I must weigh them or risk the indignity of a summons to the magistrate, nine times out of ten my eye will slice the dough to within a few grams of its baking weight. I showed him how to take a piece and roll and fold it into shape for a baguette or flute. He managed well enough for a beginner.

When the first batch of the day came out of the oven I wheeled it into the shop where I found the abbé, passing on his rounds. He took me aside and spoke, his breath warm in my ear.

"And the stranger?"

"It seems we will support him for a while longer," I said, and glanced towards Madeleine.

"Ah, the softness of women," he said.

When I returned to the bakery, Joseph was working at the table, his back to me. I looked over his shoulder.

It was a wheatsheaf made out of dough, perfect in its detail. The wheat stems were gathered in at the middle with a twist of dough and the heavy heads of grain swelled at the top.

"If we bake it before it has risen, then seal it with egg wash, I think it will keep," he said. "Maybe it can stand in the window."

"Are you a baker then?" I asked but he just shook his head.

The wheatsheaf was something all our customers spoke of. Madeleine said that life is dull when everything is eternally the same, day after day, and that people need something to give spice to their lives. I permitted Joseph to add plaited loaves to our daily bake and this kindness sowed the seeds of our fate.

*

Joseph comes to her one morning.

"I cannot ask the baker, your husband," he says, "but I know you will understand. Some memories have returned to me and there are things that I need," and he lifts his long-lashed eyes to hers.

She wonders. She has given him razor and soap and clothes enough.

"What can you need?"

"Sugar and fine flour," he says. "Vanilla and cinnamon and cream. Butter and chocolate. Nutmeg, mace, eggs, cocoa butter, sultanas, strawberry conserve. Here, I have made a list."

Madeleine smiles. She has not heard such poetry for a long time.

*

Pâtisserie - the very word sounds feminine. It was a weakness but I indulged Madeleine when she pleaded for him. Just one day a week, on Saturdays.

Next to the old counter, engrained with flour, there was now a shining glass cabinet. I would lean by the bakery door and watch the women. They stood in line as Madeleine's tongs plucked raspberry and strawberry tartes, mille-feuilles, kougelhopfs, macaroons, galettes, gateaux, meringues and chocolate eclairs, and laid them down in white card boxes tied with golden ribbon. And rather than showing impatience at the slow progress of the queue, their faces were intent and absorbed with desire. Women's appetite for their husbands soon fades, but it seems sugar and cream will always seduce them. Madeleine, who now had a habit of constantly licking her lips, was forever sprinkling her conversations with references to 'our master pâtissier.'

How could it be that such a fount of recipes poured from the ruined mind of a man who could not even remember his name, or where he was from, or whether he had a wife or children of his own?

Yet at close of business on Saturdays, when the tin box was emptied of twice, three times what it held before, there was nothing I could say. Perhaps the world has changed. In my father's day, profit was found in simplicity and restraint, not in always chasing after pleasure.

*

She loves to watch him, so precise and quick, as he whisks eclair batter, pipes Chantilly cream, slices immaculate trays of torte. For these moments her life has colour, fragrance, hope. When the shop is quiet she helps him and learns.

Sometimes, though, his face darkens and she is moved to say, "This is your home. Joseph is your name. You have work here." When she has the courage, she might add, "And there are those who care for you."

He wears a Sunday suit now, bought with money she took from the tin box. As the four of them walk to church, they are stopped by women who catch his arm and say, “What delights you bring us,” and Madeleine, given now to wearing brightly coloured headscarves, smiles and steps a little closer to her pâtissier.

He dines with them most evenings. “He has nowhere to go,” Astrid says. “We cannot leave him to sit alone in that horrid dark room.”

Afterwards, the baker rises and stretches and says, “Perhaps a beer,” which he never used to, and though once or twice Joseph accompanies him to the bar, more often he remains close to the fire with Astrid and Madeleine. Bernard begins to return later and later, waking Madeleine as he fumbles with the door catches. When he rolls on top of her, she now imagines a crisper body wrapped in her soft arms.

*

I am not stupid and I know how this village works. When I went to the bar they would ask, “So how is business at the bakery?” and their gaze lingered a little too long, as though with a different question.

I would say, “Business is good now I have that clever little pâtissier working for me”. And it was true; I could not argue with the tin box.

The pâtisserie was now open every day. Instead of warm crust and wood smoke, I had to endure the scents of chocolate and vanilla. Joseph’s station along the back wall had taken over half the bakery and whenever I looked up from my work, it was to see his narrow backside pointed at me.

Madeleine urged me to make Joseph an offer; a regular wage or even a share of profits to tie him to us. I promised I would talk to him.

Two Sundays ago I invited him to walk with me after church. I said we both needed fresh air after a long week at the ovens. We took the North road out of the village then cut down through the birches towards the lake. It was a brilliant day with the low midwinter sun picking out every detail in the frosted landscape. I was reminded how beautiful God’s creation can be. It is only human lust which spoils it.

We talked for a while of practical matters - which products were selling well and which not, the ordering of new stock and so on.

I had prepared a little speech. I would say that we had come to value his contribution to our bakery. That we - Madeleine in particular - were delighted with the way things had turned out. That we hoped he might consider making his home among us - at least until he regained some greater memory of his former life.

But as I opened my mouth to speak, what came out was, “Why did you come here, and why, for God’s sake, don’t you leave?”

“I do not know where to go,” he said. “It drives a man mad to have no memory of his life and no home and family of his own.”

“So you take mine. Our life was good before you came; the same as it had always been.”

I was shouting now.

“You have stolen everything from me.”

A look of terrible hurt came over his face, and seeing this, a rage descended on me and I struck him - hard across the mouth. He simply stood there, neither trying to get away nor to fight back, and my fury grew. I picked up a rock from beside the path. He turned away from me when he saw that and I struck out again. The back of his head began to bleed fast, red drops falling onto the white grass. He collapsed to the ground, then rolled onto his back, his arms outstretched, his pale face looking up at me.

“You can kill me if you must,” he said.

I did kneel by him then and raised the bloody rock high over his head, but the heat left me as suddenly as it had come and my arm did not descend. I stood up, and throwing the rock into the undergrowth I turned and stumbled back towards the bakery.

I was almost at the road when I realised what I had done. I laboured back as fast as I could, but when I got to the spot where he had fallen, there was only the imprint of his body in the grass and a dark patch where his blood had soaked into the ground.

CALLIE AND THE GURU

"You just can't imagine what you're missing Tom. It's like I've just been born, like I wasn't ever alive before."

Callie does look different. She went off in tight jeans and a skinny vest and now she's draped in loose white things. And she's put on weight; I can feel how much bigger she is as we hug. Her face looks different too. Her puppyfat cheeks are more rounded and shiny than ever and her wide blue eyes are languid with inner delights, as though she's sipping at a secret pot of cream.

She's been away for a month and I've been missing her. My hands start roaming and then I make for her mouth but she's still talking.

"It's the best thing, Tom. It's what I've been looking for all this time."

I'm pressing myself against her now but she doesn't seem to notice.

"He's only here for another week. You've got to stop being cynical for once; this is the chance of a lifetime. He just touches you and then everything's different," and she stretches out a finger to my forehead, right between my eyes, and looks at me intently as though she expects something to happen.

Callie and I have been together nearly two years but the thread between us is stretched to breaking point. She says I'm selfish and won't commit and that she's always offering her love while I'm always holding back, and that I run her down all the time. I know she's right, but it's suffocating when someone's always so available. Then a couple of times when she said she'd had enough and was going to leave, I found myself begging her to stay.

We have sex the first night she's back but she's still hardly there. And right after, while I'm still inside her, she starts up again.

"You can't get it from sex, you know Tom. Or money, or drugs or food. You can only get it from the Divine. The guru opens up the channels in your soul so the Divine can stream in."

Callie's always been burrowing away, with her yoga and brown rice diets and Buddhist retreats. This time it's different though. Her sermons get worse as the days go by and we haven't managed a conversation that doesn't get round to the guru within three sentences. And she's sleeping in the spare room now because she's getting up at five in the morning to meditate and that means going to bed early and she says that if we sleep in the same room we'll only disturb each other.

In the end I give in. It's a hot and humid day and on the London train, as

I sit opposite her in her filmy cheesecloth whites, I know that this time she really is leaving me and I feel sadness and a thud of fear. Callie is happy with me for the moment though. I'm the show-and-tell she's taking into school and on the tube she stands very close with her hand clutching my sleeve and allows herself to bump up against me.

We walk from Southfields tube station, Callie's sandals slapping on the pavement. Away from the high street, the roads get quieter and the car exhaust gives way to the scents of suburban flowers and mown grass.

It's a big detached house in a street lined with garden gates and front paths. The door bell chimes like a church and we are greeted by a grey-haired woman in white who presses her palms together, smiling beatifically. Inside, the house smells of feet and incense. There are bowls of sweets and cream carpets everywhere and piles of shoes by the door.

I go into a room with the other aspirants but Callie remains outside with those who have already received the divine touch, all of them still awash in an ocean of bliss.

There are about twenty of us. Mostly we seem a bit nervous, checking each other out and trying to get comfortable on the carpet, but there are a few - in saffron drawstring trousers and tanned feet and khadi waistcoats - who sit frustratingly still with their eyes closed.

Nothing happens for a long long time. Then the door opens and three lean young men with shaved heads and thick socks pad in. I know none of these is the guru as there are pictures of him everywhere - mounted on a throne festooned with flowers, plumply bursting out of his white suit and only twelve years old.

One of them speaks.

"The guru is leaving us in a few hours," he says in a dry American accent. "The Knowledge he offers is the greatest gift you will ever receive in your lifetime. The guru is ready to offer you this gift but you have to want it with all your heart. If you don't, he will know," and his eyes pass slowly round the room. "Please think about it carefully."

They leave and a lot more time passes.

When they return, the same one speaks.

"The guru says that there is one of you in here who is not sincere. That person knows who they are. They can either find their sincerity or they can leave, but nobody receives the Knowledge until every person in this room is ready," and they go out again.

Is it me? Do I really want this enough? How can I know how much I want it until I've got it? What about the others - are they so different from me? And the fact is I've come all this way and I've been sitting here for hours and I don't want to be left out. There's no way I'm leaving now.

We sit there for another aeon. Then they come in again. The guru has gone, the same one says - to catch a plane to India. He won't be back in the country for at least another two months. It's your own fault he says.

Callie doesn't come home with me and I don't see her again for a long time.

It must be two or three years later when I'm leafing through a magazine in a health food cafe. There's a big piece about the guru. He's abandoned India and moved to the United States. It seems he's very big over there, with ashrams all over the place. There's a picture of him - a teenager now with a downy black moustache - still in a white suit and still sitting on his throne. And there, next to the lean shaved-headed men, standing just to the side of the throne, her hand resting protectively on its carved back, is Callie, frowning into the camera.

It was years before I saw her again. She phoned one evening when I was watching football and said she was in the country for a few days and that she'd like to visit. She had something important to tell me.

Callie had moved to California. She wasn't wearing white any more and all her plumpness had gone. Her skin seemed to have drawn in round her bones and in her tight face her eyes looked unnaturally large.

We didn't talk about the guru. I'd read the stories. He'd been disowned by his family in India and his brother appointed guru instead; bitter disputes had broken out among the disciples, with different factions setting up their own centres; the organisation was being investigated by the tax authorities and then was declared bankrupt. Finally the guru disappeared and all the devotees were left stranded - high and dry.

I'd cooked her a meal but she wouldn't eat any of it. She got out her own bottled water and a battery of pills and green powders.

"I've come to share with you the gift of Immortality," she said. "Everyone needs to know - we don't have to grow old and die, none of us, that's just an idea."

"Come on Callie, everyone dies in the end. They always have done."

"You think you know that," she said, "but it's not true."

"What are you saying? That some people are immortal? Have you met any?"

“They keep themselves hidden,” she said. “But the clues are there if you look. And the information.”

“What information?”

“The secret of Immortality.”

“Do tell,” I said.

“You have to stop eating,” she said. “Or as little as possible. Most food is poison and we don’t even need it. You can keep yourself alive on water and a few raw superfoods, and take all the energy you need from your breath. If you do that, you’ll never age and you can live forever.”

I looked at her. I saw the fine network of wrinkles round her eyes and in the skin above her upper lip, the painful tautness of her skin. For a moment I felt moved with tenderness and regret, but then she started up again and I tuned out, smiling and nodding and waiting for her to leave.

SPUNK

Graphic content

Me and Amir and Solly and Nadia swept along Shoreditch High Street, taking up the whole pavement, all talking at once, past the kebab shops and the bars and the money changing shacks, into Rivington Street and up to the Honeyclub just as Matt was placing his meaty hand on some punter's chest and saying, "It's nothing personal mate but I don't like your face," and slowly pushing him down the steps one by one. He seemed almost to bow as he saw us and said, "Good Evening Mr Solly sir," and we sailed through the dim redlit hallway into the club, still mostly empty, just a couple of girls jigging in the lights swirling across the floor and a fat bloke at the bar, buttocks hanging off a red leather stool, slowly fingering peanuts one by one into his mouth. Giorgio was over taking our order almost before we'd sat ourselves down in our favourite alcove, Solly and Nadia on the banquette and me and Amir in the red leather armchairs that always made me think of money. Solly ordered Krug and a lemonade for Amir and when our drinks came he made us do a proper toast.

"To spunk" he said and we all drank to that.

*

It was Nadia, Solly's girlfriend, who'd started us off. She'd slipped into England on a tourist visa six months before.

"Anything better than being doctor in godforgotten Siberia, sewing up vodka sodding coal miners," she'd said. And seeing as how she was pale and blonde and stunning, she'd caught Solly's eye when she ended up behind the bar in the Honeyclub.

Solly was an odd looking guy. Even his mum wouldn't call him pretty. With his fat lips, round belly and short little legs, he looked like a toad and walked like a barrel on stilts. But I've never known anyone have so many girls falling over him as Solly. I'd never have guessed it till the first night me and Amir went out with him. They couldn't leave him alone. And all he seemed to do was sit there with his eyes hooded, soaking it up but also looking like he couldn't care less.

Though it wasn't exactly my territory, I had to ask.

"I hope you don't mind, Sol. No offence but you're not exactly George Clooney. How d'you do it?"

Solly's face lit up, like he'd been waiting forever for someone to ask exactly this question.

"It's just something I've got, Paul, a little je ne sais quoi. I don't know what it is but I've always had it. Maybe it's my smell. Did you know the smell of a man's armpit relaxes a woman. And I listen to them – not many blokes do. Anyway, they just seem to feel good around me. They forget their troubles and keep coming back for more."

Me and Amir hadn't known Solly long. We'd gone into the Honeyclub with this scheme we had going. We got some girls, dressed them up in short skirts and skimpy tops and bought them strap-on trays, like the cigarette girls you see in old movies. But these weren't for cigarettes, they were for shorts, vodka or tequila, two pounds a pop. On busy nights, when the clubs were rammed, people often couldn't get to the bar, or even be bothered, but the blokes would fork out a couple of quid for a drink and a flirt, and women nowadays just want to get caned. The club got half.

It was going pretty well, and we had three pairs of girls working different clubs. Anyway Solly was in the Honeyclub that night and when we'd asked at the bar could we talk to the boss, the barman had just pointed a thumb at this funny looking guy.

Solly was friendly enough, very easy-going, but sharp. He heard us out and said, "It's a nice idea, lads. But tell me why we'd want to give you a cut for selling drinks in our own bar? And anyway if we took you on and it worked, then we'd start doing it ourselves, wouldn't we?"

He was right of course. But he bought us a drink and we stayed for a chat. As soon as he heard Amir's name he clocked him as a Muslim. Well you couldn't not really, what with the name, the colour of his skin, and him asking for a lemonade.

"And what's a good Muslim boy like you doing in the alcohol trade," but so friendly that Amir laughed.

And Solly went on about how he was a Jew and how he could never get enough bacon.

"Four thousand years of deprivation to make up for. It's in my genes Amir."

Amir and me had been mates since we were eight. We just hit it off as soon as we met. There was something about Amir's foxy face and sweet nature and the way he did everything so neat and fast that got to me. We've been inseparable since.

Amir's family ran a restaurant in Bethnal Green - starched tablecloths and twangy music and polite waiters like undertakers. His dad used to feed us in the back and I'd make any excuse to eat at Amir's. I loved curry, I couldn't get enough. Mind you, Amir's dad used to laugh at the customers who spent so long choosing their Dansaks and Jalfrezis and Pasandas. There was always one great big pot on the stove - Curry Gravy Number One - Amir's dad called it, but there was never a Number Two. Anyway it was loads better than the frozen pizzas and tinned peas we got in our house.

And Amir and I had been like two peas in a pod when it came to life's little pleasures. We always had a scheme going from the start. Dealing Pokemon cards, flogging the trainers and Walkmans my dad got cheap, selling homeworks to the kids who were too lazy or thick to write their own. We didn't write them ourselves of course, we just introduced the homework-challenged to the boffins and took a cut.

Our friendship got a bit strained for a while when we hit puberty. We got tense and tongue-tied for months but when we finally realised we fancied the pants off each other and did the deed, everything went back to how it was before, better in fact.

So as I was saying, it was Nadia who started us off. She had this idea, and I have to say there was nothing blonde about the way her brain worked. She reckoned there was cartloads of money to be made in fertility clinics.

Seems lots of women can't get pregnant nowadays. They reckon it's something in the water or women leaving it too late, but Nadia said it's really common. These clinics put them through loads of tests at hundreds of quid a time, then the fertilisation itself costs thousands and they often need three or four goes before they get pregnant or give up. Nadia had worked a second job in a fertility clinic back home and she'd figured out that if she could get a license here and Solly would back her, she could make serious money.

"Women cannot get pregnant get desperate," she'd keep saying. "Doesn't matter how much it cost, keep spending, sell house if need to."

Solly spent some time looking into it. He was fond of Nadia and wanted to help, and of course there was the lure of the lucre, but it wasn't to be. He tried all his contacts but there was no way he could get Nadia licensed. They wouldn't accept her Russian qualifications, however much he offered to pay, and it turned out that fertility clinics were pretty tightly regulated. And even if he got past that hurdle, it would have cost more than Solly could lay his mitts on to set up a clinic, what with fancy premises and receptionists and nurses, and labs to do the testing and so on.

We were all in the Honeyclub when Solly broke the news to Nadia. She started crying and even Solly, who had a soft heart underneath, looked a bit blubbery.

"Rubbish life, being Russian," sobbed Nadia. "Crap there and crap here. Sweat fingers to bone to study medicine and get peanuts to work in arse of Russia or come here and work in bar."

Solly always told Nadia she didn't need to work in the bar, or anywhere else for that matter, but she was made like Amir and me - we had to be working.

"Such nice pretty clinic I wanted. Help people have babies, everybody happy, lots of money," said Nadia. "And so good medicine now for fertility, not just test-tube but icksey, good even when man has too few sperms."

"What's icksey?" asked Amir.

"Icksey is get sperm from man, inject into egg, make baby!" said Nadia. "Even if he has no sperm can take from bollocks with needle."

You couldn't have swiped a credit card through my buttocks when I heard that.

"You mean you stick a needle in his balls and suck out the sperm?" said Amir.

"Yes," said Nadia, oblivious. "Man don't have to make sex to woman. Even if he can't, or is in another country or is in coma. Even if he's poof."

Nadia had never quite got the hang of Amir's and my relationship.

"Just take sperm, put on ice, then make baby with woman's egg."

That got the rest of us talking about the wonders of modern science but Amir was unusually quiet. Then, when there was a lull in the conversation, he started back on what Nadia had been saying.

"You mean a man could be out like a light, and you could take his sperm and put it in a woman's egg and she would get pregnant?"

"Yes, I keep saying. Can stimulate him with machine. Or if no good then take with needle," said Nadia.

I was watching Amir; I could see he was onto something. I've got a lot of respect for his thinking abilities. I don't mind admitting that it's Amir who's come up with the best of our little ideas.

"And of course the bloke wouldn't have to be the woman's partner," he said. "In fact she needn't even know him." Amir was talking softly, almost to himself.

And that's how we came to start the most beautiful baby of a business any of us had ever been involved with. What Amir had figured out, with that cunning little brain of his, was that there were thousands of women who were mad for a kid, but didn't have a boyfriend, or else he was shooting blanks. And then there were all the lesbians who wanted babies.

Amir had read that they'd made a law allowing kids to track down sperm donor fathers, and ever since then the supply of sperm had just about dried up. It made us laugh. One thing you could never say was in short supply was spunk, what with blokes from Vauxhall to Vladivostok shagging or doing the five knuckle shuffle from morning to night. But it seemed all these sperm just weren't in the right place at the right time, which I suppose is the secret of life.

We started small. There was a little businessmen's hotel, the Clovis, not far from the Honeyclub. Natalia, one of the receptionists, was another Russian girl and a friend of Nadia's. We got Natalia to look over the men who checked in, and when she saw a likely specimen she'd send them down to the club with a wink that hinted at unfeasible delights. Then she'd text Nadia who to look out for.

Amir and I supplied the girl. It was easy for her. All she had to do was cosy up to the guy when he came in, look into his eyes adoringly and listen to whatever rubbish he was coming out with, then after a few drinks start rubbing up to him and arching like a cat on heat. It's not hard to fool the average bloke like that. Then she'd slip some Rohypnol in his drink when he was off in the bog, and when he started to go whirly she'd drape herself around him and drag him down the road to his room. Usually he'd barely make it and would be out like a light on the bed when Nadia knocked on the door a few minutes later.

I was never too sure what Nadia did in there but I know she had this machine that Solly had bought her, a vibrostimulator. Amir tried to borrow it once, saying something about giving it a road test, but Solly wouldn't hear of it.

"Pull your own, or get someone else to pull it, this thing cost me two grand."

Anyway Nadia would be out in about ten minutes with a mugshot of the victim and enough of his precious sperm in a dry ice canister to impregnate a convent. Our lucky donor would wake in the morning with a sore head and only the haziest memory of the night before. A pair of knickers we'd popped in the bed kept him shtum.

Solly's job had been to sell the goods.

I've learnt in life how, when you scratch under the surface, the most surprising people turn out to be as bent as a three card trick, and the fertility trade was no exception. A certain amount of persuasion was required of course, but having an in to the Russians made everything easy. The Russians can get anything done in London nowadays. They've got the money and the muscle and like the Italians they're very family minded. Natalia had a sister who was married to a chancer called Igor, and Igor worked his way up the food chain till he got to speak to a big fish called Sasha. Solly and Sasha cut a deal and within a week we'd got our first clinic ready and willing to co-operate, though it cost us a cut of everything we made of course.

The thing to understand about women who've reached a certain age and haven't had a baby is how desperate they get. Their biological clock is ticking away like a time bomb and it gets so they can't think about anything else. So when the doctor says, "I'm afraid my hands are tied, we've just got no sperm donors," she might turn to him and say through her tears, "Doctor, isn't there any way? I'd do anything."

And that's when he might say, ever so quietly, "Well there is one possibility, but due to our short-sighted laws it's not strictly legal," and he opens his drawer and pulls out this book that Amir got made up, really professional looking, which is basically our shopping list with photos and prices and everything. I don't know what they made of all these blokes with their eyes closed, but it didn't stop them writing the cheque. And what was so great was that everyone was happy. The doctor got paid, we got paid, and with a bit of luck she got her baby.

Sasha continued to deliver and within a few weeks we had one clinic in London and one each in Manchester, Leeds and Birmingham and we were clearing fifty grand a month.

So there we were in the Honeyclub, me and Amir and Solly and Nadia, champagne glasses raised, bubbles soaring along with our spirits, toasting spunk and the money it was making us. Nadia was trying to do that linking arms and drinking thing with Solly and was looking happier than we'd ever seen her. And then, ever so quietly, Amir started talking, and after a bit we all began to see where he was going and went silent, our jaws dropping in wonder.

"So far we've been working just with regular blokes, but there's women, some of them with husbands or boyfriends even, who'd pay through the nose to have kids from men they fancy like mad but would never stand a chance of getting close to. Footballers, film stars, musicians, even politicians. How much would that be worth to a woman, to have David Beckham's baby?"

I couldn't help it, I just had to, and I kissed Amir smack on the lips in front of everyone. He gave me a quick smile.

Solly didn't give a toss about football, but me and Amir had been Arsenal fans since the days they were famous for being boring, and it seemed disloyal not to stick with the team. Arsenal were going through one of those patches that makes being a fan worthwhile. They were winning all the time and had a team stuffed with great players, two of whom were not only young, good-looking and incredibly rich, but were on the gossip pages nearly every day of the week. Andy Baptiste was one of the best full backs in the business, and Frankie Saville, big-shouldered local boy, was currently top striker in the Premiership.

Solly always says you can't make money without spending money, and in this case most of it was Sasha's. Frankie Saville was patron of the Sunshine Fund, a charity that took sick kids to Disneyland, which personally I thought would be more likely to finish them off. Solly got in touch with Frankie's agent and told him he'd like to make a hefty donation. All he asked in return was that Frankie join him for a private dinner in his suite at the Dorchester and bring Andy along. The formal invite was hand-delivered along with a cheque for forty grand.

Me and Amir wore Oswald Boateng suits, embroidered Paul Smith shirts, white for him and black for me, and black Church's shoes. We looked the real bollocks. There's not much you can do to scrub up Solly, though, but like a lot of squat Danny de Vito types, after a few minutes it's his energy you notice more than his looks.

But the real stunner of the night was Nadia. She'd had her hair cut short and bleached so blonde it was virtually white. She must have had lenses in because her eyes had a red cast that made her look albino. She wore a kind of catsuit, skintight and made from matt black silky stuff. It had long zips down the insides of the arms, and more across the neck and chest. She looked like something out of Blade Runner and Frankie and Andy couldn't keep their eyes off her. Nadia had also brought along two Russian sisters, Lydia and Anya, from the endless supply of beautiful girls that Sasha, our sponsor, kept handy. The overall effect of the crisp white tablecloth and napkins, the gleaming glasses, the uniformed flunkeys, the beautiful women and four fit young men was sexy as hell and we all got intoxicated with it.

Solly, who liked his food, had planned the meal. We started with oysters and champagne, then asparagus with hollandaise. Mains were duck or venison and then there was a whole stack of tiny cakes and creamy things on big white plates, dribbled with red juice and dusted with icing sugar. And of course there were the different wines with every course, and the brandies and liqueurs, and by the end of the meal Andy and Frank had drunk more than they probably intended. As the Rohypnol started to kick in neither of them protested when they were led away by the girls to have a little lie down.

In less than twenty minutes it was all over and Nadia had her two precious canisters. We all scarpered straight away. I can't imagine what Andy and Frankie made of it when they woke up, but the fact that the beds looked like a hurricane had been through and they were stark bollock naked would have given them a clue, misplaced as it happened to be.

Amir and I were to deliver the goods to Sasha. He said he had women willing to pay serious money for the goods, and being fit young lads there was plenty to go round.

We'd not been to Sasha's place before. He had a house over in Kensington where Solly said all the Russian millionaires lived. The door was answered by a shaved headed bruiser in a suit and I don't think he was a butler. He led us along a hall lit with chandeliers to a pair of double doors which opened onto a living room - bigger than the whole of mine and Amir's houses when we were kids. Sasha was sitting on a brown leather sofa watching a screen that took up most of one wall. Chelsea were one down to Barcelona at the Nou Camp and he waved us to sit till the first half was done, though his gorilla did bring us a whisky each. I had Amir's.

At half time Sasha turned down the volume. He was a small guy, dressed rather poncily in a Pringle sweater and jeans, very neat and contained. He had really tiny hands for a man with fingers in so many pies. He wasn't much of a smiler or given to small talk. We gave him the freezer box and that was pretty much it. We'd agreed a one-off payment and Sasha handed over a bag stuffed with a hundred grand in pictures of the Queen there and then. In the taxi back me and Amir couldn't stop laughing, and whenever we calmed down just looking at each other set us off again. We met up with Solly and Nadia and divided the cash. Equal shares in everything was our way.

That was it for the next few months and we went back to our regular routine with the mugs from the Clovis. I spent some of my share on fitting out a gym in the spare room of our flat, and I was working out pretty seriously most mornings. I'd decided to try my hand at a bit of boxing.

One Saturday, as I was sweating on the rowing machine, Amir, who'd been out for some munch, came busting in. He was always a bit hyper but I'd never seen him like this.

"Hold it down Amir," I said, but he couldn't.

"The fucking cunt," he was shouting, over and over, and jabbing at a copy of the Sun.

And there it was, front page, "TWO ARSENAL PLAYERS IN PATERNITY SUITS."

I read on. "In an astonishing coincidence, solicitors yesterday filed simultaneous paternity suits against Andy Baptiste and Frank Saville for two million pounds each. Even more extraordinarily, the two women who say they are carrying the footballers' babies are Russian sisters, Lydia a swimwear model and Anya, a bar hostess. Lydia, who claims she had a long-running affair with Saville, said, 'I love him but now I'm pregnant he doesn't want to know. I just want what's right for me and my child'."

The story covered the next four pages, with photos of Andy and Frankie, a couple of Lydia in a bikini, and one of both blonde sisters standing with their hands over their swelling bellies. A statement from Arsenal's solicitors said both men denied even knowing the women. There was an editorial which, without ever quite saying the lads were guilty, went on about testosterone-fuelled footballers, drunk on fame and wealth, and an accompanying article on famous paternity suits including Boris Becker coughing up three million to another Russian woman after a shag in a broom cupboard at Nobu's. 'The most expensive five seconds of my life,' he'd called it.

We rang Solly and met later that evening at the Honeyclub. I thought Solly would be flaming, but he was pretty philosophical.

"We just got screwed, there's fuck all we can do. I can't see us negotiating with Sasha and his bandits for a cut of the paternity money."

The story rumbled on in the papers. Frankie and Andy had their own solicitors now and they'd obviously told the boys to keep shtum. They put out a joint statement saying that there would be no further comment until the births had taken place, in around three months time, and DNA testing could be carried out.

The weeks passed quietly. I was training for my first bout and was spending most afternoons at Finchley Boxing Club. Amir was ducking and diving as usual. I knew he was helping his dad set up another restaurant but I think he had some other projects on the go as well; he'd tell me when he was ready.

The baby business was bringing in regular money and everything was sweet. I was working the heavy bag at the gym when Gus the trainer called me to the phone. It was Amir.

"Leave the gym right now, Paul. Just get your stuff and scarper. Don't go home. Come to the Rajah as soon as you can," and he wouldn't say any more.

There was so much urgency in his voice that I didn't even shower and caught a cab straight to Amir's dad's new place which was due to open the following week. When I got there, Amir was sitting at a table opposite Solly. I slid in next to Amir. Solly looked at us for a long time. Then, really quietly, he started on us.

"You stupid cunts. You total bell-ends. You knobs. You spanners."

Solly knew a lot of insults and I figured he could keep this up for quite a while.

"What's up Sol?" I managed to get in when he paused for breath.

"Well might you ask, you fucking doughnut," said Solly. "It wasn't exactly hard was it, not rocket science or anything. All you had to do was deliver the canisters to Sasha."

"And we did, Sol, you know that."

"Yes Paul, you did. Two canisters. The one with the red label was Frank's, the blue one was Andy's ..."

"Hang on," I said, "I think you'll find it was the other way round Sol, and we made sure Sasha knew exactly which was which."

"Yes, you fuckwit, I know what you think. It just happens you were wrong. Sasha rang this morning. He is very seriously upset. Lydia's baby was born in the night. And guess what, the baby's only fucking black."

Everyone seems to think it was my and Amir's fault. Solly managed to make some kind of peace by selling his soul and raising the hundred grand to pay back Sasha. He had the Honeyclub and Nadia to think about and we didn't really blame him for putting all the weight on us. He ended up out of pocket big time because Amir and I had spent a fair whack of our share, and we needed what was left to get away for a bit.

Sasha's forgiveness didn't extend to me and Amir, and the word was that his goons were looking all over London for us. We hid out in an empty flat over the Rajah but we knew we had to chip quick. Amir already had a passport from when he'd been to Pakistan as a teenager, and I managed to fast-track one with a story about a dying granny in America. We were on a flight to Ibiza within a week.

I've never been out of the country before. I've always wanted to travel and Solly knows a bloke who runs a club in San Antonio who owes him a favour and will give us work if we need it.

So here we are. It seems a million miles away from London. The season hasn't started yet so there's not much to do, but we've still got a bit of cash to tide us over. The sun shines all the time and the sky is just this perfect blue like you never see in London. Amir seems to be learning Spanish dead quick, though 'buenas dias' and 'cerveza' is about my limit. This is the first real holiday either of us have had. There's a whole long summer stretching ahead and Amir's already started coming up with a few ideas.

TESTAMENT

They don't like to see me writing.

Laticia, who every day seems to swell more extravagantly out of her whites, just put her head round the door - first opening it without knocking.

"Hiding away again Max?"

Her booming voice shrinks me.

"Cooped up by yourself. It's not good for you. All the others are in the day room."

Ah, the day room, vault of the lukewarm dead.

"It's Mr Weldorf," I whisper. "My name to you is Mr Weldorf and I am busy, writing."

She stands by the door in her stout shoes and looks at me; an old, old man hunched over a typewriter, sagging eyelids magnified horribly by pebble thick glasses, one trembling finger pecking at the keyboard.

I, Maximilian Weldorf, eighty nine and three quarters years old, hereby declare that I am of unsound body but in full possession of my marbles. Unfortunately that appears to be the full sum of my possessions. I have not a dime, penny or pfennig to my name, so instead of a Will, there is only this Testament.

Once I lived the life of a millionaire. I exaggerate a little, but I did well for myself before I poured it all away – some down my throat and the rest down the drain. While the cheques dropped onto the doormat it was easy to think the goose would always lay. But now the catalogues say, 'Out of print,' and, 'A minor writer who achieved brief fame in the 1970s,' and the spines fade into blue in the one pound bins outside second-hand bookshops.

So many, many words. I swore I would never write another but now I find it is the only thing I have left. My stamina is not what it was though. With coffee and cigarettes as companions I could sit and write through a whole night and day but now it is like carving stone; a line or two and I am done.

Elmtree Lodge, Room B14; my new and terminal home, where you hand over your very self at Reception when they wheel you in. It seems the Buddhists are wrong though. This loss of self does not appear to usher in Enlightenment.

We monks and nuns in this overheated monastery still count out our miserable plumstones for each other, 'Drinker, sailor, gambler, failure, banker, writer, housewife, thief.' Fingers pluck at sleeves, one milky eye will catch another, a crooked smile ...

"I fought in two wars ... buried three husbands ... made and lost a fortune ...", but in broken voices, for who could believe such things were really done?

Meanwhile the bedpans are emptied and our stubborn bodies shunted aside as our rooms are disinfected and cleaned.

The tracts lie everywhere, light rays streaming out from behind crosses, the good news broadcast in pastel colours.

"You wouldn't be so grouchy if you let the Lord into your life," says Laticia.

Laticia has three children and no husband; her unmarried daughter is pregnant and her son has gone to the bad she says, out on the streets day and night mixing with trash.

"Without my faith," she says, "I could not get out of bed."

I would have thought that to such an ardent supporter the Lord could have been a little more generous.

They have services on Sundays. A vicar comes and hymns are sung round the little oak-clad organ. Afterwards he visits those of us who stayed in our rooms.

"Am I disturbing you, Mr Weldorf?" he asks.

"Ah, it's Mr Wet-Behind-The Ears," I say.

But in truth I look forward to these visits. Not to his casual youth which he does not deserve, nor to my shame as my fabled eloquence is stifled by this rogue tongue, stiff like wood in my throat. But at least he is someone to talk to and he seems to prefer to linger with me than comfort the unconscious along the hall. He is no Arnold Glaister but beggarmen cannot be choosers and he has the grace to smile when I say that either there is no God and life is a bad joke, or else there is a God in which case it is an even worse one.

They have given me a room with a view: the butt end of a wall and a patch of grass. In our first, happy days together I learned to love England, walking with Anne through meadows and villages of worn, glowing brick. But this wall is North-facing and fused with an industrial sheen and the grass is municipal - mown to within an inch of its life and fertilised with weed killer and dog mess. I would prefer to look out onto Elmtree Road where at least there is life, even though it dawdles by over the speed-bumps.

How did I, Maximilian Weldorf, end up in such a place? When I was young and so many bad things happened, I tried to behave as though it all unfolded for a reason. How else to survive? I knew it wasn't true - that would imply a Scheme and a Schemer - but I found I could accept things better that way and in the end even learn something from them.

So what do I learn here? That life begins with a howl and ends with a whimper; that all is vanity; that in the end there is nothing left but endurance.

Unlike many though, I never feared getting old. I considered myself lucky - so many did not get this opportunity - and I thought I was prepared. I used to measure myself against its coming indignities like a funeral suit I must one day wear. But I never expected it to be so mundane and at the same time so painful.

I have two children. One I never see. The other ... my face heats with shame when I remember.

"We can't have you in Scotland, you don't know anyone there. And we can't look after you, we have our own life."

This was my actuarial son Damian, careful and cold, his little wife Poppy wagging up and down next to him.

"She's half his size," I told my friend Arnold Glaister after I first met her. "She wears jeans so tight you can see everything, major and minor. And thigh boots like a musketeer, and one of those brassieres that thrusts her boobies in your face. The poor girl looks like she's got somebody else's jaw stuffed into her mouth. It juts so far ahead of her face that wherever she goes her teeth lead the way, snapping up the world in little bites. He always was an idiot."

"I take it you don't much like her," Arnold said. "Well apart from her boobies perhaps."

Arnold was a writer too. We never read each other's work out of politeness, but how we talked.

Damian lives in Edinburgh. There is no Scottish blood that I know of, unless it's buried on his mother's side, but he was born a sandy-coloured prig with a Protestant soul.

I was always too loud, too rude, too boisterous, too ugly, too Jewish. That's what Anne told me a thousand times before she divorced me. And though I would shrug it off as the delicacies of her pale English soul and give as good as I got, there in the corner would be Damian, aged seven or nine or twelve, looking at me with frozen distaste, like no child should ever look at his father.

"Anyway, all your friends live around here," says Damian's little wife.

What does she know from nothing? I only ever had one friend, Arnold Glaister, whom I met on the kindertransport on the day of my fourteenth birthday, whom I could talk with like nobody else, who last year died on his living room floor as I sat waiting for him in Starbucks in Islington High Street, admiring women young enough to be my grand-daughters.

I said absolutely nothing until another expression eventually crossed Damian's certainty of a face ... puzzlement, guilt, frustration?

They say three strikes and you're out, but I have had my three and I am still here. After the first stroke I limped; a limp I could live with. After the second I couldn't see so well out of my left eye; I still had my right. The third ... ah the third, that was a punishment - as though I had not yet learnt my lesson and the instruction needed to be more harsh. After the third I lost the use of the left side of my body.

But half a body is better than none. There is a passage from Godot that Arnold and I used to declaim to each other. I would say it to him now if I could: Estragon [whispering], "My left lung is very weak, but [booming now] my right lung is as sound as a bell."

Sometimes the arm goes into spasm and lays across my chest, fist clenched, as though I am deeply moved and about to sing the Internationale. Other times, on a good day, I can ease it down so it lies in my lap like a purple claw. I talk to it sometimes, as though if I can only get the words right, it will start to obey me. "You and I," I say, "have to learn our lesson. Perhaps if we are careful there will be no more punishments," but it lies there silent and unmoving.

And, like something fashioned by Dr. Frankenstein, my left leg drags behind me as I shuffle along the corridor clutching my walking frame like a decrepit tea lady.

Blind, lame, incontinent; sans hair, sans teeth, sans everything. The vicar, rude with youthful health, says God does not give us burdens we cannot bear.

Is it not right to expect a son to love and respect his father? And if not love and respect, then duty. And if not duty, then at least common kindness. The whispering voices say it is my fault, however much Anne turned him against me. After all, they say, the father is the gardener, the child the seed. But what can I make of this Damian seed? When he fell and cried and I went to comfort him, he would push me away. He wouldn't allow me to bathe him, to read to him. Eventually I stopped trying.

"How can you bear him?" he would say to Anne, in front of my face, when he was a teenager.

"Tea, Mr Weldorf?" says Laticia. "And a nice biscuit?"

I look at the plate with two plain digestives.

"Once, long ago, I ate Sachertorte to the sound of pianos," I croak. "And to you, my name is Max."

And for a moment Laticia rests her hand on my shoulder and for a moment I let my cheek lie on it.

I often sense them behind me. Sometimes they stand patiently in their old-fashioned clothes; sometimes they urge me onwards. Recently their whispering has become more urgent. They are telling me I have only a short time left before I join them, this horde, these ancestors of mine, a short time left to address the blunders I have made.

So it is time; I have skirted around it too long. It was always my weakness to leave the difficult things to last and Kate is a difficult thing. To lose a son is careless, something that anyone can do. But to lose a daughter, that is a crime beyond measure.

I have always been too proud; what else did I have but my pride? But I know now that every single part of it was my own fault. If I could have said this before, would it have made a difference?

So although I did not realise it when I began, it is for you, my daughter, that I am writing this Testament.

Even after you cried that your father was dead and put the phone down for the last time, I believed that if I could only make you remember you would soften, you would forgive.

When you were small, the sound of my key would bring you hurtling along the hallway. You would throw yourself at me and hug me as if to squeeze me to death. Until the day I came through these doors, if I heard a child shout, "Daddy," in the street, I would turn to look for you.

Every Saturday morning, however late and drunken the night had been, I walked you through Kensington High Street to your ballet class. I tied the pink ribbons on your shoes and stayed to watch you every time. We returned through Holland Park, hand-in-hand past the flamingos, and then to the cafe under the trees where the hot chocolate painted a moustache on your lip.

The worse it became with Anne and Damian, the more I turned to you. Us against them, what had I to fear? When you were fifteen and Anne and I were frozen in bitter silence, it was you I took to my publisher's dinner. The successful writer and his daughter, shining in the blue silk dress we shopped for together.

It is a busy week; you cannot say that Mrs Elphick is not an enthusiastic entertainments manager. On Wednesday a young man with an accordion played as the day room was, 'transformed into a sophisticated Parisian cafe,' with two French flags and croissants with jam for dessert. Tonight - oh my thudding heart - we can sing along to tunes from My Fair Lady, Oklahoma and South Pacific. Ah, to belong or not belong.

Are you sitting comfortably Kate? Then let me tell you a story.

Once upon a time, a man began to drink. First because he could afford to; he had earned it; it helped him forget. It made him feel expansive, though his wife often shouted that there was more than enough of him already, that he took up all the space, all her air. He wasn't an alcoholic then, just a drunk. In his own eyes he was full of bonhomie and Jewish wit, the life and soul of the party, but to his wife he was crude and loud.

"You've driven away all my friends," she would scream.

And then, as the years of drinking and the recriminations and contempt finally brought them to the edge of divorce, his daughter, his jewel, decided to get married.

But this man wasn't good enough for her. He told her to think again. When he was drunk he even shouted, "over my dead body," like in a bad play. And when she wept and told him this was the man she wanted, her father turned his back on her.

As he drove his daughter away the old alliances shifted. She drew closer to his wife as they clustered over the wedding lists and he was alone. His best friend told him he was a fool, that he would lose his daughter forever, but when the heat in the blood of a reckless man pulls him further towards the fire, nothing can drag him away. At the wedding he disgraced himself. He abused her husband in front of the guests until his daughter ran off weeping and the best man and his tight-lipped son dragged him out of the marquee that he had paid for and locked him in a room of his own house.

He made one attempt at reconciliation. She refused to speak to him so he wrote and begged her forgiveness.

"I will come to you on my knees," he said.

He was living alone then, in an apartment in Muswell Hill, the divorce almost complete. He met them for lunch in the Savoy Grill, his daughter and her husband. He had schooled himself; he would apologise, he would not drink. But he was nervous and he was early and he had a couple of glasses to settle himself. As everyone knows, once started, it is hard to stop.

"Please don't," she said, and he replied, "it's only wine, it's not really drinking."

He started to apologise; he was ready to lacerate himself in front of her but not ready for the pent-up fury of her husband. He could not turn the other cheek and once again, from somewhere deep inside, the poison words poured out, each word adding a brick to the wall between himself and his daughter.

After the last phone call he wrote to her twice but the letters came back unopened.

It was Arnold Glaister who cured me of drinking. He was all I had left and one night I turned on him. I can no longer remember what I said, but afterwards he wrote me a little note - very formal. He said he could excuse my behaviour this once, for none of us is perfect, but that if I continued to drink and misbehave so cruelly, he could no longer be my friend.

The vicar was here again yesterday. He must have sensed something and for the first time he asked me if I was in pain and if he could help me. I said I had been reviewing my life and I had much to regret. He said that we are only human but that we are redeemed by the love and sacrifice of Christ. What happened to fire and brimstone when you need it?

Elmtree Lodge, such as it is, will be my last home; one which I shall only leave once - feet first.

The vicar asked me whether I believed in the afterlife.

"Who knows? I have always liked surprises," I said.

But in truth, I no longer care. I am weary now and there is no more toil left in me. When a day goes on too long, whatever its joys or horrors, there comes a moment when we must close our eyes and nothing else will do.

I have one last dream though. Laticia will come to my room. She will stand, filling the doorway so that I cannot see behind her.

"Max," she will say. "You have a visitor."

And as she moves aside I will see you there. You will perhaps be a little frightened for you do not yet know what you will find. But when I see your anxious smile, then my heart will swell and this sterile room will fill and burst with my joy.

CLEARFELL

"Sacred fire, man," says Ash, rearranging the logs minutely. "I learnt this from an old Indian in Arizona. He could make three logs burn all night".

Ash has appointed himself fire tender, a role which places him in the only warm and smoke-free spot and allows him to hold the stage.

This sacred fire is on a bleak hillside in Wales. Though it's August, it's been raining for days and it's cold. Some of us are muttering. We aren't on the dry plains of the American West, with scarce wood and warm nights. This is a clearfell, and the abandoned pine waste is lying around in heaps as far as the eye can see. But arguing with Ash takes untold stamina and commitment.

"The three principles of the sacred fire. Burn as little wood as possible, don't burn anything except wood, respect the fire," and Ash turns away from his audience, places both hands in prayer position and bows towards the smouldering logs.

"Om shanti," he says.

I get up and leave. I arrived late this afternoon, drawn by curiosity, and have yet to set up my camp.

Clearfell is like prolonged cruelty which builds up to a violent rape. You buy land cheap and you plant it with close knit ranks of pine trees, pocketing whatever grants you can get your hands on. The trees grow quickly and soon shut out all light. Nothing flourishes in this bleak underworld. Since the trees are all young, no branches drop and so no swarming ecosystem moves in to digest them - no fungi, no lichen, no beetles. And without such food, no birds hop, no woodland creatures roam, all is dark and silent. Then, when the investment is mature, machines move in and fell and strip the trees in one great swoop, gouging the soil and leaving barren stumps and discarded undersized pine trunks. This is the clearfell. From a distance it looks like a grey scar. At the mercy of erosion, it will struggle to return to any but the most primitive kind of natural habitat.

But now the Natural Trust, a group of permaculture idealists, has moved onto the land in a collection of trucks and vans, yurts, teepees and benders. Smoke curls from the chimneys of the vehicles and the bigger tents, endless kettles boiling on cast iron stoves. The Trust has a few thousand pounds, the small contributions of many members, and unable to afford anything in Southern England where they live, have had a bid accepted on this otherwise useless clearfell. And they have a plan; to repopulate it with native trees so that in a few decades a mixed species wood will flourish. One wall of the kitchen tent is covered with sketched plans and lists of indigenous trees and the native plants that it is hoped will thrive in clearings and dappled areas. When the work is done, the local community will be invited to use the wood for their leisure and enjoyment.

At breakfast the next morning I talk with Jem, tiny and dressed in a multicoloured woollen hat and well worn outdoor clothes. Everyone here knows how to dress for the British weather. They have all lived outside, walked muddy tracks, cooked in the rain, chopped wood with frozen hands. Both men and women sport dun trousers, heavy boots, oiled canvas or hooded jackets. Several of the women wear skirts or slips over their trousers. Jem's trouser pockets are full of ash keys, hazel nuts, beech mast. All day, he tells me, he walks over the clearfell, spreading his seed.

Apart from Jem, everyone else is waiting. The sale will go through any day and then we can start to make plans. But for now we need both a purpose and a toilet, and so we decide to build a long-drop compost privy out of the abandoned pine. A work crew forms late in the morning. Hans has a design which he carefully explains as we hear him out in respectful silence. Then, giving each other space, listening well, taking it in turns to talk, not interrupting, we all start to disagree. We have uniquely different ideas of how this toilet should be built.

The lunch gong - a hammered lorry wheel hanging on a chain - interrupts the negotiations. There's vegetable stew and lots of bread. Ash wants to set some ground rules, and his frowning conviction carries the day. We all have to be sitting with full bowls in our hands before anyone can start. Since people are wandering at their own pace from around the site, it turns out to be a long wait. Then Ash says a blessing, pausing between every few words.

"We are grateful for this food, and for our brothers and sisters who sowed and tended and harvested and transported and cooked it. And to the sun and moon and rain and wind which nourished it. Amazing. Om shanti," and we raise our bowls to eat, but then Ash starts up again. "And to Mother Earth, we feel your pain for this wounded land," and he strikes his chest somewhere in the region of his heart, and bows his head. He remains like that for an interminable silence, while we wait, and fidget, and look around us. Finally, with a big sigh, he straightens up and at last we can eat.

An hour or so later we reconvene at the toilet site. There are fewer of us now. Hans has driven into town to get supplies; Abbie has gone for a sleep;

others have simply given up. Matt, in a ragged tee shirt despite the cutting wind, comes up with a new design and suddenly we're underway, pickaxing deep holes into the stony ground to sink four corner posts, splitting slim pine trunks to make half round planks. We stop often to drink tea, discuss sewage systems, roll cigarettes. By the end of the day, three of the posts are in.

I go back to my yurt. It stands at the end of a long track, forlorn on a patch of rutted gravel close to the entrance to the clearfell. This was the only flat piece of land I could get to in my car. Two of the live-in trucks are parked nearby.

Potholes and dips in the ground have filled with water. One, behind the yurt, is the size of a small pond, and this morning served as my chilly bath.

The potholes are now overflowing and slowly joining up, creating a moat outside my door. The yurt did not go up well and the canvas cover hangs loose and flaps in the wind. I back in through the low doorway, trying to slip off my boots without them falling in the water lapping at the threshold. Inside, despite the whipping of the cover, it is dim and calm. I inhale the familiar smells of canvas, linseed oil and the faintly gamey sheepskins that make up my bed. I flop down for a bit, then sleep.

When I wake I have no sense of time and no clock or watch to find out. I feel agitated at the thought that I am missing something and root quickly around for more clothes as the nights are cold here. I trudge up the track, past the unfinished toilet and over the crest of the hill, then look down on - yes - a blazing, sparking fire. I can see silhouettes moving in front of it.

There has been an argument. That's what I was missing. I hear all about it from Abbie.

"Ash was setting up his sacred fire thing and then Matt turned up with a case of wine. Hans bought it in town with the food kitty. Matt was a bit pissed already. He kept shouting about having a party. Then we all started opening the wine and dancing around saying 'party, party'. Matt dragged up a big load of wood and just threw it on the fire. Ash was going on about how superficial Matt was and Matt was saying 'lighten up, man'. Then Ash called Matt a wanker and went off to his bender".

The party kicks off with a bang. The cooking crew, getting in the mood, decide to fry chips. A cauldron full of oil is set on a blazing fire and when the chips go in, the oil overflows and goes up with a whoomph. Within seconds the blaze is threatening to burn down the cooking tent. We stand around panicking, trying to remember how to deal with oil fires, when Hans, an ex-fireman we now discover, coolly dowses it with a wet blanket.

So, the party. We drink red wine from cracked mugs. Spliffs and pipes are passed around. Laura plays guitar and sings till she is drowned out by the drums. There is dancing and fire leaping. People tell stories and jokes. And then we just sit talking to the people next to us, squinting as the breeze carries the smoke this way and that. Abbie tells me about breaking up with her boyfriend of two years and how anxious and depressed she'd become and how she was only just beginning to come out of it. Jem starts talking about stars, millions of this and billions of that, and pointing out constellations. Looking up, I have to close one eye so as not to see double, and try to fix them in my mind, but I know that the next time this happens, the next time I sit around a fire with a stargazer, I will have forgotten them all.

Matt has been drinking steadily. His partner left him a few weeks ago, taking both their daughters. He laughs and shouts the loudest of anyone, "fucking stars, brilliant" and, "Hey, sheepshaggers," (he's had a couple of run-ins with the Welsh).

It's getting late when I get up abruptly and leave. I do that a lot nowadays. There's a moment in a party when it suddenly goes flat, as though the sound has been switched off. Before, I used to stay till the bitter end, hanging on in case of a late blossoming. Now, and as always it takes me by surprise, I find myself standing up, gathering my things and saying goodnight.

Within seconds I'm over the brow of the hill and all light and sound from the party are suddenly extinguished. For a moment I'm alone in the night, weaving slightly down the track, humming one of Laura's songs, taking great lungfuls of air, windmilling my arms.

I am asleep on my sheepskins when the noise wakes me.

First I make out Matt shouting, or rather screaming wordlessly, louder than before. I hear the door of one of the trucks open and someone says that he's up on the hillside and that we've got to shut him up or one the farmers will call the police. Then I hear another voice shouting. It's Ash, "I fucking love you man, I love you," then the thud of boots running and voices getting closer. I stick my head out of the yurt. In the moonlight I can make out two figures taking swings at each other, then they're wrestling on the ground. As he's pressing Matt's face into the dirt, Ash, through gritted teeth, keeps up his mantra, "I fucking love you, I love you man". And then, slowly, the fight grows deadlocked and the puff goes out of them, and it's easy to move in and pull them apart.

I go straight back to bed.

All through the morning neither Ash nor Matt are to be seen. At breakfast we talk about the night before and about what is and what is not acceptable behaviour. It's agreed that early evening we will have to have a moot - that's what we call a meeting - to process it all.

I go to the toilet site. There's a new mix of people there, only one or two from yesterday. Maybe it's the aftermath of the night before, but we get stuck into the work without any discussion. As the day progresses, a shape emerges, not so much a toilet, more a citadel. The fact is, we have unlimited wood, great lengths of slim pine trunks. We build a platform, two metres above ground level, and put a raised seat on top of that. The view from the seat takes in the whole of the valley and the backdrop of hills. Then we surround the platform with walls of vertical pine, four or five metres high, and build a ladder up to the door - a plastic fertiliser sack nailed on one side and hooked with string on the other. The effect, of a great throne perched in the middle of a fortress, is heightened when Jem climbs the highest spars and hangs pieces of white cloth that flutter in the wind. We feel a ridiculous sense of achievement and pleasure when we've finished. This, we tell each other, is possibly the finest compost toilet to be found anywhere in the world, and then we joke about who's going to christen it.

As evening draws in we gather for the moot, about twenty of us.

Here are the ground rules. If you want to speak, you have to be holding the talking stick. When you finish you put the stick back in the centre of the circle for someone else to pick up. Personal abuse is not allowed.

To start with, the pace is slow. Jem expresses unease about staying at a camp where violence is likely to break out. Several others say they no longer feel safe or supported. Matt is contrite. He has been under strain, he says. He's feeling stressed about his kids. He is sorry. Everyone likes Matt; there's a swell of sympathy and understanding. He's a troubled soul, but in a way we all understand. Attention turns to Ash as he sits cross-legged, silent, looking down at the ground, his face hidden by his long hair and beard. Ash is a different matter. We can feel the violent undertow and are stern and unforgiving. We have to have a guarantee, someone says, that he will control his temper. Others, gaining courage from the prevailing mood, say that he should leave the camp.

"You people have no idea," says Ash. "You haven't got a fucking clue".

"Chill man," says Matt. "We can all see you're hurting."

"You cunt," says Ash.

"Look I've had enough of this," says Abbie. "If Ash doesn't go, I'm leaving."

And that turns out to be the consensus of the moot, Ash has to go.

But in the end Ash just stands up and says, "I've got some serious business with this land. I've seen the spirit of this hillside and it's beautiful," and he walks off.

The moot grinds to a slow halt. Though it's supper time, nobody cooks. People help themselves to whatever they can find in the kitchen, leaving a mess of opened packets and smeared knives. Others go off to their trucks and tents and cook themselves eggs and beans from their larders. Nobody gathers round the fire.

I am up early the next morning. As I strip naked and wash in my mini pond, I remember the straggle-haired American I met who sat all day on a blanket by the river outside the Berber village of Diabat in Morocco. He'd travelled a lot and told me, "Wherever you are in the world, whatever's happening to you, however difficult or strange, when you get up in the morning you should have a good wash." It stuck, and wherever I am, I turn to water and soap in the morning to reassemble myself after the jumble of the night, and to set me up for whatever the day holds in store.

As I finish washing, a Land Rover bumps over the gravel and comes to a halt. A guy in a suit and wellington boots gets out, perhaps in his late thirties.

"Is Hans here?" he asks. I tell him how to find Hans' truck and he walks off up the path.

I mess around in my yurt for a while and after an hour or so see him come back down and drive off.

When I wander up for breakfast, Jem is sitting by the fire, his head in his hands. Abbie, next to him, has her hand on his back, comforting him.

"What's up?" I ask.

"The sale's off," says Abbie. "That was the bloke who owns the land. Says he's been deluged with phone calls from farmers, from the village, from the local paper, even as far away as Aberystwyth. Everyone's been complaining about travellers squatting on the land. They reckon our dogs - what bloody dogs? - will worry their sheep and that we'll be stripping down cars and leaving them all over the place. And of course there's all the full moon raves. What's the matter with them? Don't they understand what we're trying to do here?" and she starts crying.

It turns out that no-one has thought to meet with the neighbours to explain what we're up to. As far as they're concerned we look like the kind of people who wreck land, rather than plant it, who squat awhile and leave mess and destruction behind. We look like the people their newspapers are always warning them against. Every single phone caller has said that on no account should he sell us the land.

And of course that's the irony of it. They are appealing to the very man who has plucked this beautiful Welsh hill for profit, to refuse access to a bunch of dreamers who are hoping to restore it to life.

Mid-morning it starts raining again and the cloud settles low on the hills. It's a nightmare to take big tents down in the wet. The canvas is cold and heavy, and hard to handle, but what's worse is that it can't be stored damp, otherwise blue-black mould flourishes and the canvas rots. So it has to be draped for days in tiny kitchens or living rooms, with all the heaters on, till it's dry, and then, metres and metres of it, somehow folded away.

Nevertheless, as the day wears on, the teepees and yurts come down, and the trucks and cars bump slowly down the track and through the farm gates that mark the exit to the clearfell, and from there onto the B roads and then the A roads and finally the motorways that take people back to Bath and Bristol and Brighton, with perhaps one stop on the way for crisps and chocolate at a gleaming neon service station.

In the end just one bender remains, its torn and stained canvas forlornly hugging its geodesic frame, a rusted cast iron chimney tilting out from a hole in the roof, puffing smoke into the glooming sky. Ash is staying.

ALEX

I woke before dawn trying to catch the shreds of my dream. Then I just lay, listening to the stream, loud after yesterday's rain, and watching the light slowly reveal the roof poles of the yurt. I thought about the day, about which part of the wood I'd visit, about having to go into the village to get supplies, but mostly I was thinking of Alex. How she came yesterday, while I was chopping wood, driving right up to the door of the yurt. There was someone else in the truck with her but he didn't get out. She hadn't left much stuff and it didn't take her long to pack. Neither of us really looked at each other and then we just mumbled goodbyes and she was gone.

Before I came here I'd worried how it would be, living so isolated, without friends, distractions, electricity. The first few weeks I had a lot to do, insulating the yurt for cold weather, sawing and chopping wood, making a compost toilet. When I finally had everything in order I started spending the whole day in the woods. In the evenings I'd write up what I'd seen, work on my thesis and dip into the boxes of books I'd brought. There were the novels I'd always meant to read, books on the stars and clouds, books to teach myself knots and French. And of course my reference books: Sterry's *Complete British Wildlife*, Godden's *Butterflies* and my prize, the *New Atlas of British and Irish Flora*, bought the week before I came. But I was afraid that once the novelty passed I wouldn't be able to stick it out and that I'd want to escape back to town, or at least to the pub in the village every night. Yet the world outside this field and the woods had begun to fall away. I'd started to grow into the silence and into my own company, becoming aware of an inner presence that was new to me. Then Alex turned up.

It was late one afternoon when I'd just got back from the woods. I'd lain my leather bag of samples and notes down near the fire and was filling the kettle for tea when I heard, then saw, a battered green truck rumbling over the field. She jumped down from the cab and walked straight towards me.

"Hi, I'm Alex," she said, thrusting out her hand. "I heard what you're doing here. It's brilliant. I thought I'd come and say hello."

I caught a brown face and eyes and a direct gaze, was briefly aware of how she was a head shorter than me, and then I was watching her mouth and listening to her explain why she'd come.

"I know lots of people record timings of flowers and birds but I hadn't heard of anyone doing it like you till word came around."

Alex was studying permaculture. She was doing a project on forest gardening. She said one of the things they were taught is that you've got to observe a system for a whole cycle of seasons before you act, otherwise you can mess things up.

"So that's why I'm here," she said, "to learn a bit more about how you do it. If that's OK of course."

She parked her truck by the great oak to get the morning shade, with the side door facing the yurt. Now she sat in the doorway in the late afternoon sun, playing her guitar and watching me while I worked around the camp and then made supper. We had rice and vegetables and scrambled egg by the fire and I got out my last bottle of wine. What with the evening chill and trying to find the one place the smoke didn't choke us, we ended up sitting close together on the log, and when Alex fetched a blanket from her truck she draped it round us both. Her dreadlocks smelt of wood smoke over the musty odour of unwashed hair. She did most of the talking that night.

Alex was always animated. She was excited by her course, by the farm and the people on it and by permaculture.

"Dan got us to do this thing on the first day," she told me. "You stand in a big circle and everyone chooses what animal or plant they want to be. I chose Fox. Then you see what connections you have to all the other animals and plants there and you run a piece of string between you. So I was connected to Rabbit and Vole and Worm, because that's what I eat, and Rabbit was connected to Grass. Oh and I didn't say but it's one really long piece of string that weaves between everyone, till you've got a whole web. Then you see what happens when you take just one piece out of the web. One person lets go, even something that doesn't seem important, like Wasp, and the whole web starts to collapse. And the other brilliant thing about permaculture is how it sees that humans are just another part of the web of life. Dan keeps saying that however well a system is designed, if it doesn't take account of the people in it, it won't be sustainable."

Later that night, when I laid the sheepskins out in the yurt and settled down to sleep, my mind was full of her face and her smell.

The next morning I was up early. The long grass was soaked with dew and trails of mist lingered in the hollows. Venus hung bright in the sky, above a low bank of cloud and the hedgerow was vibrant with hawthorn blossoms and red campions. There were a few embers in the fire pit and I fetched dry twigs and quartered birch logs from the box in the yurt. I crouched and blew long and slow so that the embers glowed and flames licked the birch which crackled and spat as it caught. Then I took the tin bucket and my wash things to the dipping pool. The stream, which sprang from the bracken strewn moors, was icy whatever the weather, but I'd come to relish the hard stones beneath my feet as I walked in up to my waist, and the shock of ducking under.

I heard the truck door open and then Alex was by the pool in a thin robe, tousled hair, watching me. I suddenly felt shy and dipped under again and opened my eyes. In the brown water my limbs looked pale and elongated, tiny bubbles winking silver in the hairs of my arms and legs. When I came up and turned back to Alex she was still there. Then she lifted up her robe in one swift movement. I caught a glimpse of a muscular body, small breasts and thatches of dark hair, and with a shriek she was in the water.

Alex was the most unselfconscious person I'd ever met when it came to nudity. Even that first morning she didn't get dressed for ages, drying herself by the fire and squatting to make tea.

She came to the woods with me that first day. I usually find a clearing with a stump or fallen trunk to sit on and note down my first sighting of everything and keep a count of numbers. The bluebells have mostly gone now but the cow parsley and hawthorn are in full blossom. There are butterflies, Clouded Yellows and Red Admirals, and damselflies and dragonflies where the wood meets the stream.

Later, back at the camp, she sat quietly while I talked about what I'd learnt in the time I'd been here.

I was two years into my PhD on the effect of climate change on native woodland and this was the largest piece of ancient forest in the South-West. It had taken months but I'd finally got permission to spend an entire year living here. I was hoping that once they saw that I was harmless I could negotiate a longer stay. That way, as the second year came around, I could compare dates and see how the cycle might be changing.

"My real dream is to blend in, to be a part of the ecosystem rather than just an onlooker. Quiet mind, no ego or desires, that kind of thing," and I laughed, embarrassed.

I ended up talking for a long time. When I fell silent, Alex turned and looked full at me.

"I love hearing you talk about your work. There's something peaceful and calming about it. It really grounds me."

That night she asked if she could sleep in the yurt. I mumbled something foolish like, "Be my guest," and she undressed and slipped like an eel into my bed of sheepskins. I'd never been with anyone like her. She writhed and laughed and squealed and I felt like a log in comparison. But she was so free and generous with her body, so warm, so trusting when she curled up against me to sleep, that when I woke in the morning and saw her there I knew I was lost.

I don't remember ever being as happy as during the next few weeks. I'd usually wake before her and would just lie there, in whatever position the night had thrown us into, listening to her breathe. I'd bring us tea in bed and we would start a conversation that flowed until late into the night when we were finally overtaken by sleep.

Alex was like a kid a lot of the time. She'd suddenly come up behind me and shout, "Catch," and jump so I'd have to grab her in a piggyback. Then she'd ride me around, pulling my ears to make me turn. Or else we'd fall over and wrestle on the ground, with Alex tickling me till I surrendered. She wanted to play tag, or hide and seek, and splash me when we were at the pool. Some days we walked to the River Dart for a swim and she'd duck me, or sneak up and grab me underwater. But just as likely, at the oddest moments, she would come up and give me a sweet kiss.

We also had our quiet times in the yurt. I would read to her by candlelight, or I would write my notes and she would weave things out of leaves and wool and stones that she would hang in the trees. Or she would play her guitar.

One Sunday Alex told me that she had a few things to sort out. "I'll be gone most of the day. I'll bring you back some goodies."

I'd got into the habit of taking Sundays off from my work and I climbed up to Bench Tor in the brilliant sunshine. Some days, when the world is warmed in a particular way and when I've walked hard, I feel as if every molecule of my body is nourished by a special air, full of the essence of wind and sun, heather and rock. And then my eyes see in a different way and everything seems impossibly beautiful.

The granite outcrops of the Tor were full of flowers, and I stood for a long while on the very peak of the moor looking down at the gilded river winding through the valley. Then all of a sudden I felt such a pang of longing for Alex that I turned and retraced my steps rather than going home the long way by the river.

She wasn't there when I got back and as I read, then cooked supper, I listened out for her truck. I fell asleep waiting. When I woke at dawn to find myself alone I thought she hadn't returned, but the truck was there. She must have got back late because she slept well into the morning.

"I missed you. Why didn't you wake me?" I asked when she finally emerged.

"I didn't see the point," she said, yawning. "It was really late. I wanted to make sure we both got a decent night's sleep."

A week or so later she went away again. I was coming back from the woods when I saw her carrying a small bag to the truck. I hurried over and asked her where she was going. She wouldn't catch my eye and turned away, saying that she had to go back to the farm and see some people and would probably be back in a couple of days.

Then she did look at me and said, "I'm not too good with people keeping tabs on me," and drove off.

She was away for three nights. I threw myself into my work, spending most of the daylight hours in the wood. In the evenings I lay in bed and read Thoreau. But for once Walden failed to inspire me. The yurt, the camp, the woods that had begun to feel so vivid, now seemed flat and empty.

The night she came back I cooked pancakes for supper and lit incense in the yurt. She didn't say much about her trip and I didn't ask. I held her all night, not sleeping much.

We soon slipped back into our old routine and Alex seemed loving enough but it wasn't the same. Before, on days when Alex hadn't wanted to come into the woods, I'd been happy to go off on my own for hours. When I got back she'd be by the fire, or in her truck, or in the hammock she'd slung amid the alders by the river, and she'd squeal, "You're back," and throw herself at me. But now, after just a short while alone in the forest, I started to feel restless. Everything - the plants, the insects, the birds and animals - seemed to have a purpose, and none of them cared or even noticed if I was there or not.

I began to slip back to the edge of the field just to check that Alex was there. One day when I went back the camp was empty. I guessed she'd gone into the village. When she hadn't appeared after an hour or so I set off on the two mile walk down the road, hugging the verge when cars hurtled by. There's nothing much in the village. Just a post office, a Tesco, a pub and a church, and Alex wasn't in any of them.

She didn't get back till after dark. She'd been up on the moor. I said she could have left a note and that I was worried about her but she just laughed, saying she could look after herself. That night as I turned to her in bed she put a hand out to stop me.

"Listen, no-one owns me," she said, and curled up away from me, right on the furthest edge of the bed. That's how we stayed all night.

I thought about it all in the woods the next day. I couldn't think about anything else. When I got back I made tea and asked her to come and sit by the fire. I told her that I was crazy about her.

"I want us to be together. I'll give up my PhD if you want. I'll come and live with you on the farm so you can finish your course. We could live in the truck, or put the yurt up somewhere."

She listened quietly and then just said, "I don't think that's what I'm after," and got up and started washing pots and dishes.

It's hard not to keep replaying what happened later in the yurt. I was reading and Alex was sitting cross-legged, making one of her pieces, when she suddenly threw it down.

"I can't take this any longer," she said. "You sit there looking at me with those hurt dog eyes all the time. And you're always following me around. I can't do anything without you tagging along, always trying to touch me," and she jumped up, grabbed her blanket and left the yurt. I heard her truck door opening and closing and then silence.

I didn't get to sleep for hours. When I went out in the morning the truck was gone. I tried to settle down to writing after that but in the end I went up onto the moor and walked for hours. I didn't see anyone else, just sheep huddled against the rain. When I got back I lit the stove, ate some leftovers, drank most of a bottle of wine and went to bed. I didn't see Alex again till yesterday when she came to get her things.

It's going to be easier now she's taken them. She wasn't here long, just a few weeks, and until she turned up yesterday there were times when I wasn't even thinking about her. My brother is coming to stay for a few days soon and I'm sure some friends will visit. And as summer passes into autumn there will be lots to record, sloe berries and hazelnuts, acorns and beech mast, and all kinds of fungi.

In the end it was hunger that got me out of bed and out into the morning. I lit the fire and took the pot I'd left to soak overnight and washed it by the stream. I added water, oatmeal and salt and lifted it onto the trivet. My eyes smarting from the smoke, I stirred it till it thickened and placed it by the side of the fire, then took the bucket and my wash things to the pool. The stream flowed strong and cold after the rain and I stayed in the water till I was numb, then got out and towelled myself till my skin was on fire.

A movement in the corner of my eye made me stop. Just down stream a doe stepped on delicate feet amidst the tracery of young ash. Every sense attuned, it stood for a long while, but its gaze passed over me, and bending its neck it drank. I breathed slowly, frozen in the act of dressing, but either I moved slightly or something startled it and in a flash it was gone.

THREE DREAMS

"I dreamt I was lost and it was dark everywhere. And then it started to get light, but just a dim light, like a winter dawn, and I looked around and I was in the middle of nothing but ice and snow and frozen seas. And then I heard a voice say 'glacial erosion' and I woke up".

What might that might mean to you, Annie?" asks Andrew.

"Well I suppose it's me inside. I feel like I'm in a dark frozen hole. Like glacial erosion, grinding me down".

Annie starts to weep and reaches for a tissue. Her nose is clogged and her eyes are swollen. Damn. All she's done in this room is weep.

Andrew watches Annie suffering. She sits hunched like a bird, dressed in black, and for a moment he looks forward to sitting in the park eating his lunch amidst the tawny oaks and beeches.

"I just don't understand what's going on. I'm at home with Adam, and Howard's at work, and it's what I always wanted and yet I feel dreadful. I'm just exhausted and I feel like crying all the time. Howard's never there and it's me and Adam day after day, all day long. Howard's always working, working late, at conferences, and then when he does get home I find myself moaning at him. It's a complete turnaround because that used to be me. He was always the one complaining about us never having time together".

Annie had loved being pregnant. Smart, beautiful, efficient Annie, sailing to work right until her eighth month. She'd felt special, as though no-one had ever been pregnant in quite that way before. And the glow had stretched into the future. She would devote herself to having a child, just as she had devoted herself to her career, and she would do it the way she did everything else, easily and competently.

"I just never dreamt it would be like this. I love Adam but it's driving me silly spending all my time with him. I hardly see anyone apart from other mothers. My world's shrunk to naps and nappies and Thomas the Tank Engine. And then Howard comes in moaning about product launches and having to take clients out and wants to know where his socks are. It's true he pays for everything now but I'm used to having my own money. More than him in fact. And there's always a sting in the tail when I ask him. And he never seems interested in me or Adam or what we've done and I feel like a fool telling him about how we met a dog or what we had for lunch."

Andrew smiles. He likes Annie. This is her second session and though she's desperately unhappy and fragile, underneath her sense of humour is intact. Deep down he feels she'll be OK but he has to wait for Annie to work it out for herself.

Afterwards Annie meets Ellie at the swings. Adam and Lucy, bundled like Eskimos, are in the sandpit. Lucy, Ellie's three year-old, is carefully making castles and Adam, nearly one and a half, is plopped down next to her knocking them down. Ellie is Annie's one real friend right now. Somehow she just can't face her old ones at the moment. Hardly any of them have kids and they might as well be living in a different universe. In fact she and Howard barely go out any more. He's usually too tired and anyway Annie doesn't believe in baby sitters. And there's something smug and comfortable about most of the young mothers she meets. It's like they're finally doing just what they were designed for, and they make it look so easy and natural, the way Annie expected it to be. Ellie's not like the other mothers though. She's a single mum and there's a streak of stubborn discontent running through her that Annie is drawn to.

*

Annie is in Andrew's room again, staring at the carpet. She's not missed an appointment right through the winter and she knows the stylised birds and camels on the faded kelim well enough to draw from memory. She's just told Andrew about another dream. She was in the kitchen in her parents' home and her mother was angry with her about something but Annie couldn't understand what it was.

"She was just shouting and shouting".

"And how did you feel in your dream" asks Andrew.

"I was really scared and then I woke up. But it's strange because my mother never shouted at me. I can't remember her doing it once".

"Tell me about your mother" says Andrew.

Annie has talked about Adam and Howard and her work and her father who died when she was sixteen but this is the first time she has said anything about her mum.

"She was a great mother. When she was young she went to art school. She was quite talented I think. Anyway she was going to be a painter but then she met my father and got pregnant with me. But she was a good mother. She was always there right through my childhood, cooking and everything, and picking me up from school, and coming to all the school plays and things.

And that's what I want to be like for Adam".

Andrew watches Annie clenching her tissue and doesn't say anything. And now something is building inside Annie, inside her chest and her head, but it gets harder and harder to break the silence. Anyway she doesn't know what to say. Suddenly it all feels wrong.

"I don't think I should come here anymore. It's not doing me any good and it just seems self-indulgent".

"Why is it self-indulgent to try and find out what's making you unhappy?" asks Andrew.

"But that's it. I shouldn't be unhappy. I'm comfortable, I've got everything, I've got an easy life. My mother had it harder and did it for years with me and she was bloody fine".

"You sound angry with her" says Andrew.

"Why should I be angry with my mother, that's ridiculous" says Annie and suddenly the pressure in her chest clutches like a fist and she hunches over.

"What's happening to your chest Annie"?

She can hardly breathe.

"It's like that movie, like there's something in here that's going to burst out".

"And what would it say if it did burst out Annie"?

Suddenly Annie is aware of a ripping feeling and she hears someone screaming over and over "I hate my fucking mother".

*

Once more Annie sits in Andrew's room. The spring sunshine streams in as she tells him of another dream.

"I was riding this horse, a beautiful big white horse. And it was going so fast, like it was flying, and when I looked down I saw I was naked. It was the most wonderful feeling. The horse was so wild and strong but it felt really soft between my legs".

And suddenly Annie stops and blushes. She daren't look at Andrew. When she does, she sees he's looking at her and gently nodding.

Afterwards Annie joins Ellie in the park. This time, though the wind is cold, they sit on a blanket and eat the picnic that Annie bought from M&S. The trees are just beginning to ghost with green. This is the first picnic of the year for either of them. Lucy, dressed in fairy wings, runs circles round them as they sit and Adam chases after her and keeps falling over giggling. A sudden burst of noise turns their heads. A group of teenagers is jostling over by the swings. The long white legs of the girls are blotched with purple and they hug their bare arms across their chests.

“Cleavage or legs, not both, darling” says Ellie and she and Annie laugh till they cry.

THE BLACK PEARL AND THE WHITE PEARL

"Come, children, your grandfather wishes to speak to you".

Kun and her brother Tian followed their mother into Old Li's rooms. They loved their grandfather but there was always something a little intimidating about passing through his red lacquered doors.

Grandfather Li was sitting cross-legged on the raised platform where he now spent most of his daylight hours. When they were younger the children were allowed to jump onto the carpeted platform and marvel at the woven tigers and curl in grandfather's lap. But now they felt a new constraint. It was partly that they were older now, and partly because today there was something different about Old Li. He sat very still and seemed a little stern.

"Sit down, my children," he said, and then spent an age looking down at them and sipping his tea. Finally he nodded to himself. "Yes, you are old enough. I have decided that it is time you learned the legends."

Kun, the eldest by less than the time it took to clean and wrap her, turned towards her twin brother. Her eyes warned him that they were to say nothing and to sit absolutely still. She knew this moment marked a turning point, a step on the path to adulthood.

"You have only known peace, my children," began grandfather, "and so have all of us alive today and for many generations back. But it was not always so. There was a time, long long ago, when all harmony was lost. War broke out between the provinces, and even between villages and families. The love between men and women turned to bitterness, and children were lost and bewildered. Farmers destroyed the irrigation ditches and crops of their neighbours, and soon hunger added to the misery of the people.

"Some appealed to the gods of heaven for mercy and others turned to the older spirits of the earth. Yet even this became grounds for hatred and fury, as the followers of the different religions came to blows and burned each others' temples. It was as though a fiery darkness had fallen on the whole civilised world and many gave up hope".

"Now in those days our own family was blessed with a powerful leader. Because of his courage and great strength he was known as Warrior Li, although he was gentle by nature. You children have kowtowed and burned incense in front of his portrait since you were babies. But until now you have never known why.

"Warrior Li watched with great pain as the conflict raged. He was a strong man and able to intervene physically in most disputes, but now he felt helpless and saw that his strength was like dust in the wind. He could neither eat nor sleep and just lay on his bed in the heaviness of despair. Then one afternoon he finally did fall asleep and a vision came to him in a dream. He was standing by the edge of a wide river when suddenly the waters parted and the Great Dragon, Empress of the Underworld, rose up above him. Her massive head, dripping with weeds from the river bed, swooped down towards Li as if to consume him. But at the last moment, when he was almost choked by the dragon's fishy breath, it slowed and something round and black dropped from the dragon's mouth to fall at Li's feet. In a moment the dragon was gone."

"Before Li could bend down to examine what had been dropped, he became aware of a noise from the sky, and a shadow came between him and the sun. Looking up, Li saw the mightiest of all eagles, the Lord of the Heavens, dropping towards him with its giant talons outstretched as though to pierce and destroy him, but at the last moment with a fierce beating of its wings, the eagle slowed to hover above Li and something white fell from its mouth onto the ground and in a moment the eagle was gone."

"And as Li looked down he saw that the two objects, the black and the white, had fused together into a ball that was neither black nor white and as it began to spin he felt a sense of peace unlike any he had ever known, and a voice came from somewhere deep within him saying, 'You must descend to fetch the black pearl, and you must rise up to find the white pearl. Only by doing this can harmony be restored and all things follow their proper course'."

"When he awoke, Li immediately rose and prepared a small travelling bag. Without saying goodbye, he walked deep into the forest for three days and as the sun was rising on the fourth he came to the Cave of Darkness which was known as the gateway of the Underworld. Without pausing, he plunged into the cave and was not seen again for many months. Those who met Li after he finally emerged said that he looked as though he had undergone a terrible ordeal. His face was lined and his hair and beard had turned entirely white. Warrior Li rarely spoke about his time in the cave, but people understood that in his search for the black pearl he had ventured into the darkest realms. Deep in the bowels of the earth he had witnessed death and decay and terrible loss. He was assailed by visions of hell and taunted by demons. Yet something inside Warrior Li remained unshaken and eventually the visions and the demons faded away. And it was then, in the very womb of the earth, that he saw that it was the decay and dissolution of all things that gave birth to new life and this wisdom he concentrated into his belly in the form of the black pearl."

"When he had rested for seven days, Warrior Li set forth again. This time he walked across the Great Plain to the foot of the Golden Mountains. He was seen to climb beyond the last human habitation and then he disappeared from view. In the vaults of the sky, under the unblinking eye of the sun, Li wandered, and fasted and cried out to heaven. The terrible sun burnt all the moisture out of him and his skin became like old leather and his bones like the bleached branches of a broken tree. Finally at the highest point of the highest peak he resolved to sit without moving until his task was finished. And as he sat, the light of heaven poured onto his head. He took it down through the channels of his body until it concentrated in his belly in the form of a white pearl. Then the black pearl and the white pearl embraced each other and swirled and intermingled and he was flooded with the same feeling of peace and harmony that he had experienced in his vision."

"And what do you think Li did when he came down the mountain, children? Do you think he went round telling everyone what he had learnt and trying to teach them how to be at peace?"

Kun and Tian looked at each other but they knew they were not expected to speak.

"No, my children, he did absolutely nothing. He simply went back to his village and took up his life just as before, cultivating his garden, sipping tea in the evenings, sitting quietly with friends. But something strange began to happen. The village grew peaceful, neighbours forgot why they had been arguing, men and women rediscovered their passion for each other and the children played and laughed again. Soon the provinces made peace, and inside the temples, spontaneously, a new image began to be seen, of a circle made of intertwining black and white hemispheres, each containing a dot of the other colour."

"Warrior Li lived a long life and was buried with honour. He laid claim to nothing and it seemed that whatever had changed had done so of its own accord. Yet somehow the villagers knew that Warrior Li had played a part, and from the day he came back from the mountains, he was renamed Wise Li."

The children rose and bowed before their grandfather and his veined hands stroked their heads. Then they walked out through the red lacquered doors, and feeling tired, they went to lie down and fell asleep in each other's arms.

HOW TO MAKE A YURT

Once I'd cut the coppice, the next stage was steam-bending. A yurt frame is made up of a door and door-frame, trellis walls, roof poles and a crown. Three sections of wall trellis are constructed by criss-crossing lengths of coppice and drilling and tying them at every crossing point so they can be opened like a concertina and lashed together to form a circular wall, or closed shut for transportation. To end up with vertical sides, every piece of coppice has to be steam-bent into a slight curve.

I built a long coffin-like box, stuffed it with stripped coppice, connected it to an adapted calor gas cylinder filled with water, built a fire beneath it and sat ruminating and feeding the fire in the sun-dappled woods while the steam slowly penetrated the wood. After an hour or so, I put on heavy gloves, pulled the now flexible coppice poles out of the box and wove them between three strong poles I'd buried vertically in the soil. As they cooled, they solidified into their new curved shape.

A yurt also needs roof poles. In a Mongolian Ger, these are heavy and straight but in the lighter Turkic yurt that I made, one end of the pole is first shaved flat and then steam-bent.

Every stage of making a yurt has its joys. There is the excitement of finding and cutting the best coppice poles and dragging them back through the undergrowth like a hunter with their prey. Making a fire in a clearing in the woods, then slowly feeding it as the steam softens the wood is an opportunity to slow down, drink tea, and enjoy the sights, sounds and smells of the woodland itself - the wood smoke which triggers atavistic memories of tribal ancestors and the gust of steam, smelling of rich, wet wood, as the box is opened.

The most intense stage is making the circular crown. This is fashioned from two narrow planks of knot-free, kiln-dried wood – much tougher than the green wood used for the poles. The steaming is long and slow – the calm before the storm. Because the wood starts to harden almost immediately, it has to be bent and clamped around the iron rim of an old wagon wheel in seconds. Take even a minute too long and the opportunity is lost, the wood has to be returned to the steamer and the whole process started over.

The final stages of construction is making the door and a dismantlable door frame whose pieces slot in to each other and are secured by wooden pegs.

When all this was done, I sealed everything with several coats of fragrant linseed oil mixed with pure tree-resin turpentine.

The moment of truth comes when the frame is put together for the first time. The three sections of trellis are lashed together together with the door and door frame to form a circle. Hoisting the roof crown is a delicate task. Thirty-two slots have been cut into it to take the narrow squared-off ends of the roof poles. It's possible (but not easy) to raise the crown oneself but it's best done with three people. Each takes a roof pole and slots it at equally spaced intervals round the crown which is carefully raised high ("raise high the roof beam carpenter"). The wider, flattened ends of the roof poles are then tied in to the top of the trellis. As the remainder of the roof poles are tied in place it gets harder to force them in to the top of the trellis and the whole structure would burst outwards if it wasn't for the yurt band – a strong canvas cummerbund that encircles the trellis and holds it firm. The outward pressure of the tensed roof poles is thus transferred downwards and this makes a yurt a marvel of stability. It needs no inside support, you can stand in every part, and it's so strong that two people can hang from the crown high above the ground.

Once my frame was up for the first time, I measured its width, height and girth like a tailor measuring for a suit, and sent them off to the master canvas craftworkers who would make the roof, the wall and a cowl to cover the crown.

A groundsheet with raised sides keeps the floor dry, and the whole yurt is water and rain proof. In fact it's a perfect design, fundamentally unchanged for centuries. It doesn't even need to be tied down as the wind will flow around and over it – anchoring it even more firmly. And for cold and wet weather (such as a typical British summer), a hole cut in the roof cowl allows a long chimney to rise from a woodstove.

EXAMPLES OF MY MICROFICTION

The Lighthouse

Prompted by a character (postman), place (lighthouse), emotion (jealousy)

We have a new postman – Tom Draper – just home from the war. He is fresh-faced still but carries a sadness within him and sometimes his eyes turn away from us towards sights we cannot share.

He delivers to farm and village, and – but only at the lowest of tides – to the lighthouse. He cycles the narrow causeway, the waves lapping beneath his wheels and the sea sucking and slapping over the black rocks on either side.

To the lighthouse keeper's young wife he carries letters from her mother, catalogues from the London stores and, once in a while, a soft parcel of new clothes. But never is there a letter or parcel for the blind and silent lighthouse keeper.

The lighthouse keeper's wife draws Tom into her kitchen and feeds him tea and cake. Sometimes as they talk, her fingers stroke his empty sleeve. Her laughter – unheard for years – now rings through the lighthouse, even as far as the lamp room where her husband sits polishing his lenses and reflectors.

She writes more letters now and orders new dresses, and Tom visits the lighthouse, even when he has nothing to deliver. She learns to count the tides and marks them in a diary that she has no need to hide from her unseeing husband. But when the smell of new baked cake drifts up to the lamp room where he sits polishing and polishing and polishing, his frown cuts deep lines above his dark eyebrows, and he sinks into a deeper and deeper silence.

Then, one day, Tom Draper is gone. The tides are treacherous here and his ruined bicycle is found tangled in the seaweed close to the lighthouse where the lighthouse keeper's wife weeps as the sea slaps and swirls amidst the dark rocks.

Hector

Prompted by a character (an explorer), a place (a café), an emotion (doubt)

Hector, on the eighty-ninth day of his search for Shangri La, has to admit that he, like the fabled city itself, is completely lost. His guides and porters left long ago, turning their noses up and the corners of their mouths down as he promised more and more extravagant riches. And though this morning his heart had lifted as the sun struck the rose-tipped peaks, by noon his world has darkened. The rain runs from his eyes and its chill seeps through his thornproof trousers, his pale freckled skin, his English blood, and makes its home in the deepest marrow of his bones. He sets his jaw and stomps on through streaming gullies and newborn waterfalls, splashes through streams that wash away the poor soil, the stunted bushes and the splendour of his quest. Easing himself onto a rock and letting his rucksack, heavy with books and charts and army rations, slump to the ground, Hector, all six feet four of him, lowers his head and weeps. Later, when he edges along the narrow path and sees the lamplit hut nestled against the sheer rock, he nearly weeps again.

A wave of heat and kerosene fumes hits him as he enters and a brown face turns sleepily.

As the kind heat seeps through his thornproof trousers, his freckled English skin and his cascading blood, into the deepest marrow of his bones, Hector sips at a tin mug of rust-coloured tea.

"This is comforting and delicious tea," he says. "Possibly the best I have ever tasted. Whatever is it?"

And though his host cannot understand his words, he grasps their meaning and smiles again through broken teeth and points at the wooden slats of his hut, stamped everywhere with the trademark of the Shangri La tea company of Kowloon.

Napoleon

Prompted by a character (Napoleon), a place (the Gorbals), and a final sentence "He closed the heavy book and pushed it away"

This is the story of how your great-great-grandmother nearly married the Emperor of France. It is little known, because it was a considerable embarrassment to the authorities at the time, but Napoleon Bonaparte escaped from the island of Elbe much earlier than is generally admitted. He was seeking allies to stir into war against the English and his journey took him to Scotland. Soon after his arrival he was struck down with a fever, and though as Emperor he had commanded great wealth, he was now in straightened circumstances and took lodging in a small guest house for gentlefolk in what is now the Gorbals, to recover his strength.

Your ancestor Adele was then just sixteen and was employed by Mistress Goodhart, the captain's widow who owned the lodging house, to help attend to the needs of her guests.

The Emperor was not the easiest patient. Though feeble, he retained all the arrogance of one used to ordering armies, and everything was a cause of complaint to him, whether the softness of his pillows, the strength of his beef tea, or the quality of the coal that warmed his room.

Now Adele was a spirited lass and she had soon had enough of his manner. It is said that one morning, exasperated by the unceasing litany of complaints and orders issued by the little man from his bed, she answered him back in no uncertain terms. "You may be the Emperor of France", she said, "But this is not France, it is the lodging house of Mistress Goodhart and you are merely one of the guests, and a spoilt bad-tempered one at that. And unless you learn to speak with common politeness, you will be fetching your own hot water and emptying your own chamber pot".

Napoleon was not used to being spoken to in this way, of course, but far from taking against her, he was greatly attracted to her spirit and he apologised for his rudeness, blaming it on his sickness and the disappointments he had suffered. From that point on he was a changed man and he began to treat Adele with all the courtesy that a Frenchman is capable of. They soon became unlikely friends and they used to sit for hours by the fire in his room. It is true that most of the talking came from the Emperor, but she listened sweetly and intelligently as he told her of his hopes for the future and how one day he would rule the whole of Europe as a single nation.

After several weeks of convalescence, Napoleon was sufficiently recovered to travel onwards. He parted from Adele with many promises of how he would summon her when his ambitions were achieved and bestow on her the honour of being the Emperor's companion and mistress, but soon after leaving Scotland he was recaptured and imprisoned again, this time more securely. This final imprisonment was to be his last for he soon died, some said from poison.

But that is not quite the end of the story. After he left, Adele discovered she was with child and gave birth to a son whom she called Napoleon. Though he was born out of wedlock and died in infancy, he is nevertheless recorded in the family archives.

Uncle Rufus took down the old family bible, and turning to the back showed us the spidery family tree that went back to the 1700s. There, in faded ink, was the name of Adele and the first of her children, for she later married and had two daughters, Napoleon b. 1817, died 6m.

And that, said Uncle Rufus, is how your grandmother could have become the Empress of France, and he closed the heavy book and pushed it away.

Saint Paul (unprompted)

It's a week now since he last clattered through Saint Peter's though they say his bony arse has been seen in the alleys of Padua. Finally the tourists can spend again without his dessicated digits wagging over their cleavages.

It was that white smoke fool - Innocente XIV - who started it. Roused from torpor by an empty treasury and the roar of new atheism he announced a great convocation for Saint Paul of Tarsus, thirty years short of his bi-millennium. Arms were twisted all over Christendom and soon reliquaries were being carried to the Holy See by sweating prelates ... clavicles from Catania, a scapula from Sassari, ribs from Perugia, a jawbone and three teeth from Avignon. To the swinging of censers they were laid out on a marble slab in the Basilica. Was it was the storm that raged - the lightning striking the great dome - or simply the yearning of bones, but some time in the night the caskets opened and the relics knitted together into the simulacrum of a skeleton. Most of an arm, a leg and a half, the ghost of a pelvis. But nobody could argue with the jaw, for when the great doors were opened in the morning he started a complaining and sermonising which never stopped. We honoured him for a week but our hosannahs turned to curses as he began to haunt the streets, castigating us all as whores and pimps bound for the fires of Hell. In the end, the street kids chased his rattling bones over the Tiber and we drank to his departure. Good riddance; he was a disaster for business. He gave holy relics a bad name just when I've managed to acquire a splinter of the True Cross from a dealer in Smyrna.

The Night (unprompted)

When the bite had healed, he found he could only go out at night. He liked the rain slanting across the wavering street lamps, the traffic lights commanding empty roads, the clouds scudding across the moon. He preferred suburban streets, drawn to where it was dark and still. He began to linger in half alleys, crouching by shadowed walls and garden fences. When people strode past unaware it added a sharp joy to his concealment. He took a late bus beyond the last estate and spent the night amidst the whispering trees.

He discovered parks. He could wander the bland paths, and if anyone was there to note his aimless pace they assumed there was a dog rooting in the bushes. Before long he delved into the bushes himself, and here he found the closest match of his desires. He would penetrate the deepest shrubbery and squat, tasting the night air, smelling the bushes, hearing the blind worms nosing through the black earth.

Once he was shocked by a terrier who barked and scurried at him and he had to flee, trotting fast from a burly shout of, "Hey you!"

The next night he brought a spade. In the furthest corner of the bushes he dug a deep slanting hole that he could fit his whole body in. Then, scrabbling earth to cover himself, he lay, enveloped in soft darkness.

Snow

Prompted by a final sentence: "Everything is very quiet and it has begun to snow"

The night Elmore Jones dies is the coldest night of the year. The plumbers and secretaries and bank workers have returned to their homes, drawn their curtains and gathered round the TV, hands paused between tray and mouth as a goal is or isn't scored, a boyfriend betrayed, a house made over and re-valued.

Elmore sits in silence though, curtain and window open to the night. He is old and has seen enough of what this world has to offer, its pairings and partings, its recycled entertainments. His eye is waiting for one last different sight, his ear alert for a call he has not heard before. He puts on his coat, his hat and scarf, his fleece-lined boots, and ventures into the night. He walks past the few houses, some already lit with Christmas decorations, past the dark church, out to where the field begins and slopes down to stream and woodland. He finds a fallen log and watches the glints of light on the rippling water, watches as though there is a puzzle there that will be solved if he looks long enough.

Then he lies down and closes his eyes. In rustling and creaking, chirp and whisper, the life of the wood buzzes around him until in the deepest watch of the night, even that ceases. And still Elmore lies.

Everything is very quiet and it has begun to snow.

The Window

Prompted by a sentence to end with, "And then she closed the window."

Annabel was watching her husband George, who had been drinking all afternoon. It was George who had insisted on inviting Jimmy and Tessa and their daughters to stay with them for the week. He was circling the table now, pouring wine, resting a hand casually, almost caressingly, on each shoulder in turn, his face reddening and sweating in the afternoon sun. How everyone turned towards him as he leant close to pour the wine, responding like puppies to the heat of his hand.

It was the kind of day everyone imagines on cold, wet London weekends. Two tables laid end to end under the tree, white table cloths strewn with bottles of wine and baguette crumbs, friends sprawled around the table, children running off to the pool and back again to pluck peaches and grapes from the wicker fruit basket. Everyone laughing, glowing with wine and sun.

Lisette was clearing plates and asking if madame wanted her to make coffee. It was George too who had insisted, "so that you can have a holiday as well." Annabel was torn between the need to get up and help - embarrassed to actually have a servant, even for these few days - and the compulsion to sit here watching Tessa, dressed in a bikini top and cotton skirt, almost touching foreheads with her husband as he whispered something that had her laughing with delight.

Tessa's husband Jimmy was watching the children – in transition between childhood and puberty - squealing and wrestling in the pool.

After lunch they played boules; all of them except George and Tessa who stayed at the table, drinking. And then - when Annabel turned to look some time later - they had disappeared.

Annabel excused herself, asked her son William to take her turn though he groaned and said they only needed two points to win and why was she going off now, and headed down the lavender-bordered path to the house.

Inside it was suddenly cool. She stood quite still and as her ears attuned to the silence she heard giggling, then a sound like something heavy being bumped along a stone floor. She followed the sound down the hallway into the courtyard at the side of the house and looked through the dusty window of the stone hut that must once have stored olives or wine and now served as a utility room.

It took her a moment to understand what she was seeing - George's buttocks bucking and thrusting against Tessa whose flowered skirt was up round her waist, each thrust driving the washing machine a few centimetres across the old flagged floor.

She could have turned away; pretended she hadn't seen what she had so often imagined, but instead pushed open the door and went in. It was Tessa who saw her first, her face and body freezing in shock, and then George's drunken, lust-slack face turned towards her as Annabel - speaking quite calmly - asked if he would be good enough to come to their room as she needed to speak to him.

Upstairs in the bedroom she stood at the window for a moment, looking down at the tables under the trees where Jimmy, William and the girls were now sitting again, and as she opened the window they looked up and she gave a little wave.

She heard George come in and turned, and before he could say anything, before she could even make out exactly which expression he had composed his face into, she leaned back a little over the window ledge and, half to him and half to the audience below, in a voice that once upon a time had reached the back stalls from the proscenium arch, shouted,

"What do you think her husband and her daughters, and your own son William would feel if they knew you were fucking Tessa less than two minutes ago." And then she closed the window.

Chance Encounters
Unprompted

The Atlanta Clarion, September 9th, 1881
THE EYES OF A KILLER
by William D. Peabody

He had a flat belly for a man with silver hair. Long black jeans, black boots heeled with silver spurs. His waist was cinched with a black silver studded holster belt holding his two famous guns, mother of pearl handled solid silver pistols. Above, a slim black shirt, shoelace tie with a silver clasp, a fox beard and burnished eyes. Yes sir your intrepid reporter was looking into the eyes of the Duke, the most famous killer in the West, and he survived to tell you the tale.

"Yup, I got these from a dead man", and he laughed long and loud. "But don't get me wrong, the gentleman did not die by my hand. We were passengers thrown together by chance on the Denver train. In the afternoon we conversed a bit and in the night, as we swayed in our dark seats, he cried out and keeled over. Dead as a doornail. Being at that time financially inconvenienced, I decided that before I called the guard, I might move my friend's interesting looking wooden case from his luggage to my own. Only much later, after I'd left the train in Denver, where I had a little business to attend to, did I have the opportunity to open the case and find this pair of beauties inside.

"Before that I dressed decent but plain. Blue jeans, suede leather jacket, cowpoke hat, that was my style. But life has the darnedest way of picking you up and pointing you some place new, don't it? Those guns were the changing of me. I knew I had to dress up fine to take them two out walking. And it was after a while, when I'd got to look pretty much like I do now, that I started to be known as the Duke. But I ain't no European royalty whatever they may say and I'm happy to put the record straight. Here you can hold one if you like".

I put down my notebook and took the gun.

"Heavy, ain't it? Half as heavy again as an iron gun. Needs a different technique but it's just as fast".

Just then the conductor came by and looked a little surprised to see me holding the gun. I suppose I don't look like a fighting man, being perhaps rather short and round of face and belly, but none of us can help our appearance. Nevertheless I had long been fascinated with brave tales of the West and it was a dream of mine to travel that way when circumstances permitted and to collate some of the best tales into a book or two. I had grown tired of five hundred worders on pumpkin pie competitions, diphtheria outbreaks and Wednesday night presentations on 'A Tour of Europe's Lesser Known Museums'. Now, returning to New York on the overnight train, fate had thrown me together with something quite different and the Duke seemed more than happy to submit to my questioning. It would form one of an occasional series I wrote under the strapline 'Chance Encounters'. Not only would it pay ten dollars and make my name better known but it would serve well as the first chapter of my book.

"These guns have killed a lot of men. But I never did shoot anyone that didn't need killing real bad. Well except one time in a poker game when a gentleman had the poor judgement to call me a faggot on account of the way I dress. And I only winged him, just to teach him some manners. No, I don't regret any of them".

Then he went pensive for a minute and passed his hand across his eyes. "Except one", he said in a different voice, low and sad. "You see as my reputation grew, people thought they had to take the Duke, just to prove something to themselves. This one was just a kid. Good looking but farm fresh, wet behind the ears and dumb as a cocky little rooster. Figured killing me was the quickest route to fame and fortune. He was waiting for me as I came out of Ray's barber shop in Bakersfield".

" 'Hey Duke' he called out as I stepped off the sidewalk to cross to the saloon. 'People say you're the best, but I think you're old and slow and I aim to prove it.' "

"I got no quarrel with you, kid" I said. "Go home to your ma. All you'll get from me is pain and darkness. But the boy wouldn't listen and he told me that whether I liked it or not he was going to draw on me and I'd better defend myself. Well I shot him in the stomach before he'd even got his daddy's old gun out of its holster. He was writhing and scrabbling and bleeding into the dirt a long time and calling on his ma before we got him up on a table in the saloon, but Doc Holliday" (my eyes widened) "whispered to me that not even a French surgeon could save this boy. He died clutching my hand, staring into the bowels of death. I ain't never got that look out of my mind", and he sighed.

Soon afterwards the train pulled into Baltimore and The Duke gathered his bags, shook my hand most sincerely and we said our goodbyes. He'd come all this way, he said, to pay his regards to the widow of an old partner of his and he winked.

I was writing up my observations of the Duke when the conductor returned down the carriage. "Quite a rare experience that", I said. "Meeting a famous gunslinger on a train ride to New York".

The conductor laughed showing the whitest teeth. "The Duke, sir? Why he's never been further West than Virginia. He's a well known character down in the Southern states. Works the small circuses with a tame Cherokee and a girl who shoots apples blindfolded. Yes sir, a real character".

Bowlby

Unprompted

It was the name that caught my eye. I was idly flicking through a paper I'd picked up as we boarded; the Express or Mail, certainly not one I'd normally read. There was a photo and a name, Anthony Bowlby, and a story about some kind of scientific fraud to do with animal cloning. Even after twenty years I recognised him.

When I was fourteen, my father moved us to Paris. He'd been assigned to the Embassy and I was enrolled in an international school in the Marais. Our apartment was on the outskirts, and as pupils were not normally expected to take the bus or the metro, and my parents were unable to chauffeur me, I was to be picked up by the school bus.

The first morning, I waited on the street with some anxiety. Whenever I have to make a journey, especially one that I've not made before, I always expect it to be more complicated or more difficult than it turns out to be. But that day the bus soon appeared, easily identifiable in its school colours of mauve and cream, and drew up outside our apartment.

As I scanned for a place, I had a quick impression of faces turned towards me with friendly, even amused expressions. I took the only seat left, next to a fat and dishevelled boy. When I turned to look at him, I realised he'd fallen asleep, and within moments his head had slumped onto my shoulder. I tried to jerk him awake but he remained glued to me for the rest of the journey which I passed mortified with embarrassment, heightened by laughter from behind me.

I elbowed him sharply when the bus drew up at the school, and when he opened his eyes and sat up he looked at my shoulder, which I discovered was soaked by drool.

"I always do that" he said.

He was in the same class as me and I watched him through the day. He sat on his own, next to the wall, and seemed to occupy a different world than the rest of us. He never spoke unless a teacher addressed him directly, and then he seemed to slowly rise up from somewhere deep and hidden, with little idea of what had been said. Only in one session did something different happen. There was a question about the periodic table that no-one was able to answer.

"Bowlby, you know this surely," the teacher said rather irritatedly.

Bowlby surfaced slowly from wherever he had been. "Know what?" he said.

"The periodic table".

And, as though utterly indifferent, Bowlby recited the periodic table from Hydrogen to Ununoctium. When he finished there was silence until Dench, a pinch-faced boy, shouted out "Bowlby, you're so weird", and everyone laughed.

At the end of the day, I was already on the bus when Bowlby got on. The space next to me was occupied, but those who had empty seats beside them rushed to fill them with coats and bags, and the boys, as if by habit, pushed him away so that he was funnelled down to the back of the bus. I heard a girl say, "Bowlby, don't even think about it, you're disgusting" and then he must have found a seat as I heard no more.

A couple of days later, I walked into the boys' washroom at the end of morning break. Bowlby was lying half out of one of the cubicles, whilst Dench, with an air of furious concentration, was kicking him in the ribs. Two other boys that I didn't know looked on in fascination. Bowlby was making no attempt to protect himself and even appeared to be giggling. There became something frenzied, almost desperate in the way Dench was attacking him, and the harder he did so, the more Bowlby laughed. Without much thinking about it I grabbed Dench from behind, wrestled him to the floor and held him there with a neck hold. When he found he couldn't move, despite his struggles, he gasped to the others to help him, but luckily they held back. I kept hold of him until he stopped wriggling, then I let him go, and without looking me in the eye he and the others walked out.Bowlby slowly got up with his back to me and made an effort to tuck in his shirt. Then he turned and, rather red in the face, held out his hand. "Bowlby", he said.

"I'm Watson" I replied.

"Yes, I know. Eric Watson. Thank you for that. One day he'll really hurt me. Would you help me again, Eric, if I needed you?"

"Of course" I said, sealing my fate.

Some people are born friends, some achieve friendship and some have friendship thrust upon them. Rescuing, and then promising to protect, Bowlby placed me under a kind of obligation, and the next morning, although there were other seats on the bus to choose from, I felt compelled to sit next to him and suffer him to dribble all over me once more. As we got off the bus I did ask him whether he couldn't control himself and he said no. He had always fallen asleep as soon as he got into a moving vehicle and there was nothing that he could do to change it. His father had taken him to a number of doctors, none of whom could even offer an explanation, let alone a cure.

Being seen with Bowlby seemed to act like an inoculation against any other friendships, and so when he invited me to visit him at his house one Saturday, I accepted out of loneliness as much as anything else. Besides, I was curious.

He lived quite nearby. It was a hot day and I walked there along still, tree-lined streets, carefully checking my map. It felt more like rural France than Paris. The villa was set behind green iron gates that opened onto a gravel drive. I pressed a bell in the wall by the door and after a long wait, Bowlby answered. "Hello Eric" he said, "I didn't think you'd come."

He showed me around the house. "This is my father's study" he said, "and this is my father's bedroom," and "this is where my father and I eat breakfast together".

I wanted to ask about his mother but I couldn't. We went up to his room. All but one of the curtains were drawn and it was hot and stuffy. Apart from a messy bed, most of the room was taken up by bookshelves and a desk full of narrow drawers that ran along the whole of one wall. On the desk were a microscope and several jars of what looked like plants.

"Have a look" said Bowlby, picking one up. It took me a moment but then I saw a mantis, almost indiscernible against the leaves. Bowlby started pulling out drawer after drawer filled with trays of butterflies and moths, neatly pinned onto card, each labelled with name and species.

"My father and I did these ourselves" he said. "We caught some of them in the garden here and some on holiday. But we have to buy the rare ones."

Bowlby noticed me looking at two glistening skeletons in glass cases on a shelf above the desk.

"Cats" he said.

Suddenly it felt stifling in the close room and I asked if we could go outside. The gardens that surrounded the villa on all sides were overgrown and wild. We wandered around rather aimlessly, then sat on a slatted bench in the sun.

"What do you want to do?" asked Bowlby.

I said I didn't mind.

"I wonder if you've ever seen this" he said. "I'll be back in a minute".

The garden was completely still, though I could hear the buzzing of insects, waxing and waning, and the repetitive call of a single bird.

Bowlby came back with a bottle of purple liquid. "Come and watch" he said.

We went over to one of the small patches of grass left between the encroaching bushes. Bowlby poured the liquid onto a section of the grass.

"What is it?" I asked.

"It's potassium permanganate. You have to be patient but it's worth it".

We squatted facing each other for several minutes, looking down at the grass. Then there was a movement and a worm burrowed out of the soil, followed by another, until the whole section of grass was covered with dead and dying worms.

"You can't do it too often" said Bowlby. "You have to wait for the worm population to build up again. But we can do it again in a couple of weeks if you like."

After that day Bowlby and I must have drifted apart and I don't think I ever went back to his house. I started to make new friends at school; one of them my first girlfriend. Not long after that, Bowlby and his father moved away. I have no memory of saying goodbye.

My Saturday

Prompted by a class assignment "Describe your Saturday as if you had been asked by your teacher in school"

"The bard himself trod these streets" my Dad says, as usual, as we set off for the High Street.

The bard is William Shakespeare of course. I know what's coming next.

"And Jack the Ripper" he adds.

We're in our brown suits and brown shoes and white shirts. "Like peas in a pod" they say though he's about ten times bigger than me.

A few steps behind, Uncle Billy clunks along. He's not my uncle really but he's been around as long as I can remember. He does some kind of work for my Dad.

"A bit simple" aunt Elsie calls him.

She's my real aunt, my Dad's eldest sister. When I was smaller Uncle Billy used to pick me up and hold me upside down by my feet till my head filled up and my eyes swelled out. I never minded much because I liked him better than my real uncles. He was the only one I could tell about what happened at school.

I don't know what he did, but the day after I told him, Joe Wilson and his dad came up to me outside the school and his dad said "tell him" and Joe scuffed the ground and mumbled about being sorry and I'm pretty sure he was crying though he didn't look up so I couldn't really see.

"And you tell your Dad and Billy that he's sorry, and I'm sorry too, and it won't happen again" Joe's dad said, looking at me, and he gave Joe a smack round the head and then he definitely did start crying. And not far away, by the railings, I saw Joe's friends watching, and I started to think I might be safe now from all of them.

We do this every Saturday afternoon and it's definitely the best bit of the week. This morning I was allowed to lie in and then Mum made us a fry up. I took my bike out for a bit, just up and down the road, and then I hung around and played with Rex in the garden. He's supposed to be my dog but he doesn't take any notice of what I tell him, and won't ever bring the ball back properly like other dogs do and I have to chase him and try and wrestle the slimy thing out of his mouth. Then Mum made cheese sandwiches for me and Dad and Billy and Eloise, and afterwards Dad said to me "fancy a stroll?" and when I laughed, because he always says that on Saturdays when he's here, he said, "well go and get your togs on". Eloise is my little sister and she's named after someone in a film my Mum and Dad once saw.

Going out with my Dad makes me feel ten feet tall. Everyone knows him and everyone wants to say hello and is always very polite. "Afternoon Mr. Fraser", they say, and then they look at me and say "and afternoon to you too son". Harry Fraser is my Dad and he's the most important person around here.

It's a hot day and when we get to the High Street it's bursting because the football's finished for the summer, and the heat brings out all the smells of the fruit and veg from the market, and the melting tar, and then we go in the Queen Vic and it's cooler and smells of beer and Panatellas. People my age aren't really allowed in pubs but I'm with my Dad. He and Billy have pints and I get a bitter lemon and some crisps with the salt in the screwed up blue paper you have to hunt for. People were coming up to my Dad all the time at the bar and saying, "Nice to see you out and about Harry" and I knew that meant that they were glad to see him back because he'd had to go away for a while.

Then something happened. A long-haired man in a tee-shirt whom I'd never seen before came up and started saying how he really had to have a word with my Dad.

"You owe me Harry" he kept saying.

And Dad laughed and said "Can't you see I'm out with my boy".

And then the man got up really close to my Dad and started whispering something and my Dad just looked over and said "Billy" once and Billy moved faster than I'd ever seen him and grabbed the man by his hair and dragged him out the back of the pub and he was squealing all the way. And my Dad said "Let's go son" and I didn't see Billy again till after we got back home.

We went home the long way, right along the High Street, past the Crown and Shuttle and the Town Hall.

"I saw Maurice Hope fight here" my Dad said. "All of Shoreditch and Hackney came to support him, even though he was a blackie. He was a local boy you see. Knocked out Len Gibbs in three rounds".

And then we went by the Rainbow and when my Dad stopped to chat with the doorman I looked inside and saw photos of women without their tops on. I thought one of them might be my friend Gary's sister because he says she comes here and takes her clothes off and dances but none of them looked like her.

When we got home I had to change out of my suit and I watched Doctor Who and then Billy came back and my Mum had got winkles and prawns for tea. Rex kept making bad smells during the meal and my Mum told me to put him out and then she said "He's as bad as your Dad", and Billy laughed so much he started choking and spitting bits of prawn all over the table and my Dad had to slap him on the back. Then my Dad and Billie went out and I played with Eloise a bit and went to bed.

Printed in Great Britain
by Amazon

32470690R00169